Practical Bookkeeping for the Small Business

Practical Bookkeeping for the Small Business

Complete information on how to keep accurate financial records with this easily learned system that can be adapted to any small business

Mary Lee Dyer

Contemporary Books, Inc.
Chicago

Published by Contemporary Books, Inc.
180 North Michigan Avenue, Chicago, Illinois 60601
Manufactured in the United States of America
Library of Congress Catalog Card Number: 77-92438
International Standard Book Number: 0-8092-8207-0 (cloth)
0-8092-8206-2 (paper)

Published simultaneously in Canada by
Beaverbooks, Ltd.
150 Lesmill Road
Don Mills, Ontario M3B 2T5
Canada

With special thanks to
Owensboro Business College
and to John

Contents

INTRODUCTION

This book is designed to meet the needs of the small business owner or manager for keeping accurate financial records, through a system which can be learned quickly and which can be adapted easily to any kind of business.

Why a Good Bookkeeping System Is Necessary

The lack of a good bookkeeping system is one of the principle causes of business failure, and also prevents many firms from growing. Sound bookkeeping is essential to the proper management of any business, and without it the owner can never see just how his business is doing. Good records can quickly point out any problem areas, such as excessive payroll expenses or high inventories. Accurate payroll, income, and expense records are required by the government. Overpayment of creditors or incorrect billing of customers are eliminated by a good bookkeeping system.

Everyone who wants to own or manage a business must learn basic bookkeeping in order to manage a business profitably. The housewife should understand how to balance a checking account and how to run her home on a budget. Individuals who are elected treasurer of social and civic clubs, of church organizations, of bowling leagues, and of PTA groups, will find their positions to be much more fun—and they will be of much greater service to their organizations—when they have a knowledge of proper bookkeeping practises.

What This Book Can Do for You

Many people wish to learn bookkeeping but are unable to take the time to attend lengthy formal courses in the subject, o they are hesitant to take courses because of a fear that they may not have the proper educational background.

Although some businesses employ a bookkeeping service, the cost is relatively high; and many businessmen and women would prefer to learn proper bookkeeping themselves, thus avoiding this additional expense.

This book provides the small businessman with all of the information he needs to keep a simple and accurate bookkeeping system. The material can be studied at home and learned in a relatively short time. Each of the five chapters contains only four to eight pages of reading material. The entire method of presentation used is designed to promote fast learning and sound reasoning. The language is simple and the concepts are explained logically.

In the book, the correct uses of a checking account and of petty cash are learned and practiced. Making out payrolls, providing for deductions, and maintaining necessary payroll records are all studied and illustrated. Basic accounting reasoning and terms are taught. The entire bookkeeping cycle, from the initial entry through closing the books, is explained.

There are two methods used in bookkeeping, both acceptable to the Internal Revenue Service: the Cash Basis, employed by most service-type firms; and the Accrual Basis, used primarily in merchandising companies. Both methods are covered in this book. The Cash Basis is taught in chapters three and four, and its use is illustrated in many different service-type firms, from an insurance company to a barber shop. The Accrual Basis is explained and its methods are practised in chapter five.

How to Use This Book

This book is a combined textbook and workbook. First, a paragraph or section is read. Next, an example is studied, and then a similar problem is worked. The solution is then immediately checked in the answer key at the back of the book. The in-chapter problems are easy to understand and work; they're not at all difficult, nor are they time-consuming. The reader will learn the material much more quickly by working out each problem in order as he or she comes to it in the book.

There are summary problems at the end of each chapter, which help one understand terms included in the chapter. They also coordinate the information learned in the chapter, and develop the ability to apply this information to practical situations and individual needs. The solutions for the summary problems are included in the Answer Key at the back of this book.

The entire book should be read. A retailer must understand the knowledge presented earlier, before the chapter on retailing is meaningful. A person interested solely in bookkeeping for a service-type firm will find helpful information in the retailing chapter, such as allowing for cash shortages, keeping books for a partnership, and receiving cash discounts on purchases. A businessman can decide to use the Cash Basis of Accounting even though he has accounts owed to him and by him. Then he must keep accurate records in an Accounts Receivable Book and an Accounts Payable Book, as discussed in chapter five.

The method for paying state sales tax described in chapter three is generally acceptable for a service-type firm, if income from the sale of merchandise is small. Most states require that retailers use the method of figuring sales tax explained in chapter five.

Accounting reports can be written on ruled forms or typed on plain paper. Both kinds are shown in this book. In setting up the bookkeeping system in the way this book has illustrated, pads of three-column journal paper can be purchased inexpensively at any office supply store, and then be put into loose-leaf notebooks; or, if desired, special accounting notebooks and paper can be utilized.

Where Do We Go From Here?

By following the principles outlined in this book, bookkeeping can be both enjoyable and profitable.

1 THE CHECKING ACCOUNT

Almost all companies keep their money in the bank; therefore, knowing how to use a checking account is essential to a bookkeeper.

Getting Your Signature Authorized

If the company has not had a checking account before, or if someone new has been authorized by the firm to sign company checks, bank signature cards must be filled out. These cards are obtained at the bank, completed and signed by the authorized individual, and returned to the bank. There they are kept on file to be compared with the signatures on the checks to make certain that they are not forged. Thus, it is important that the bookkeeper sign the card with the same name, initials, and style of writing that he or she will be using to sign the checks.

Signature Card

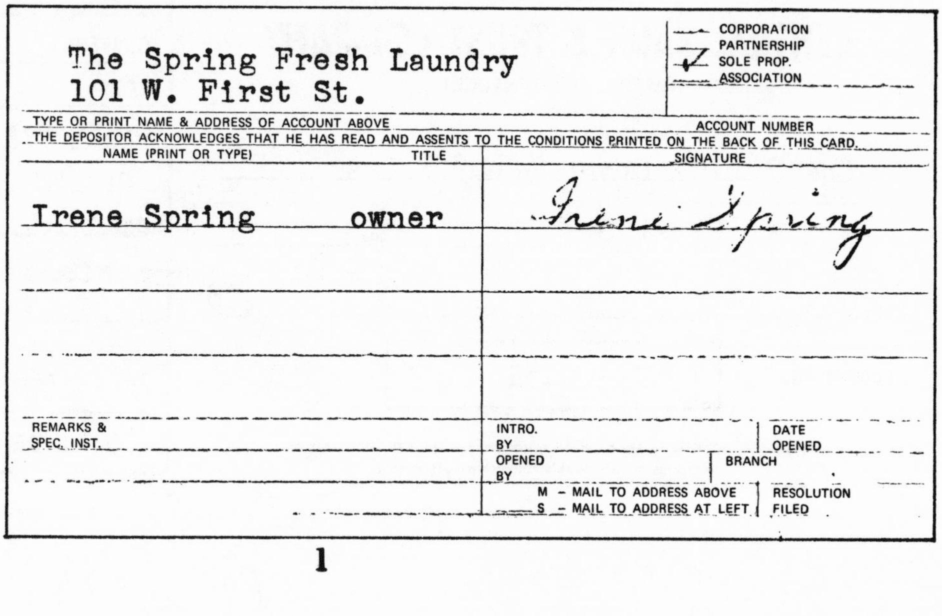
The Spring Fresh Laundry
101 W. First St.

CORPORATION
✓ PARTNERSHIP
SOLE PROP.
ASSOCIATION

TYPE OR PRINT NAME & ADDRESS OF ACCOUNT ABOVE — ACCOUNT NUMBER

THE DEPOSITOR ACKNOWLEDGES THAT HE HAS READ AND ASSENTS TO THE CONDITIONS PRINTED ON THE BACK OF THIS CARD.

NAME (PRINT OR TYPE)	TITLE	SIGNATURE
Irene Spring	owner	Irene Spring

REMARKS & SPEC. INST.

INTRO. BY — DATE OPENED

OPENED BY — BRANCH

M - MAIL TO ADDRESS ABOVE
S - MAIL TO ADDRESS AT LEFT

RESOLUTION FILED

1A. Please fill out this signature card, assuming that you are the new bookkeeper for the Nelson O. Fault Insurance Company, a sole proprietorship (owned by one person).

JOINT ACCOUNT-3

Nelson O. Fault Insurance Company

The undersigned hereby agree to the rules, regulations and by-laws of the NATIONAL BOULEVARD BANK OF CHICAGO, to the Co-Depositor Clause below and to the clauses on the reverse hereof relating to collections and to examination of returned statements and cancelled checks.

Sign Here Nelson O. Fault

CO-DEPOSITOR CLAUSE

All moneys now on deposit, or at any time deposited by us or either of us, with said Bank to the credit of this account, or in accounts in continuation hereof, are and shall be so deposited by us and received by said Bank upon the following terms and conditions of repayment, viz:

That the amount thereof, or any part, and any interest thereon shall be paid by said Bank to us, or either of us, whether the other or others be living or not, or to the heirs, executors, administrators, or assigns of the survivor of us, or upon the written order of any person or persons so entitled to payment. Payment of funds to survivor contingent upon release from Inheritance Tax Office.

We further agree that any of us, may deposit and endorse for deposit in this account and in accounts in continuation hereof, checks, drafts, notes and orders belonging or payable to any of us, and may cash and endorse for negotiation any of the same. Said Bank shall have the right to charge against this account and accounts in continuation hereof any liabilities, at any time existing, of any of the undersigned to you. Our intention is to create a joint tenancy in this account, and in accounts in continuation hereof, with the right of survivorship

DATE ____________ ACCEPTED ____________

FORM 368 10M 4-73 BANK OFFICIAL

Making a Bank Deposit

The bank provides each commercial checking account customer with a pad of deposit slips imprinted with the individual account number and a bag in which to carry the deposit to the bank. The bank will also provide a supply of envelopes that can be used to make a deposit after the bank is closed. The money and original of the deposit slip are placed in the envelope and inserted in the slot located on the outside of the bank for night deposits.

In order to get the bank deposit ready, total all paper money and show this amount on the deposit slip after "currency." Show the total of the change after "coin." List each check that is to be deposited in the bank by the name of the individual or company who made out the check, and show its amount. Total the deposit, and date the deposit slip.

Deposit Slip

DEPOSITED WITH

CENTRAL BANK & TRUST COMPANY

OWENSBORO, KENTUCKY

For The Spring Fresh Laundry

101 W. First St.

Date July 19 1976

ACCOUNT NO. 10839-00431

Checks and other items are received for deposit subject to the terms and conditions of this bank's collection agreement.

	DOLLARS	CENTS
CURRENCY	218	00
COIN	9	26
CHECKS (List Separately)		
John Doe	11	07
Sam Smith	9	95
Bessie Jones	23	00
TOTAL OF CHECKS LISTED ON BACK	271	28
TOTAL DEPOSIT		

1B. *Please make out today's deposit slip. You have counted $5.40 in change, $78.00 in bills, and you have received the following checks: Beula V. Deeds $98.00, Oscar U. Kidd $47.90, and P.G. Clean $54.20.*

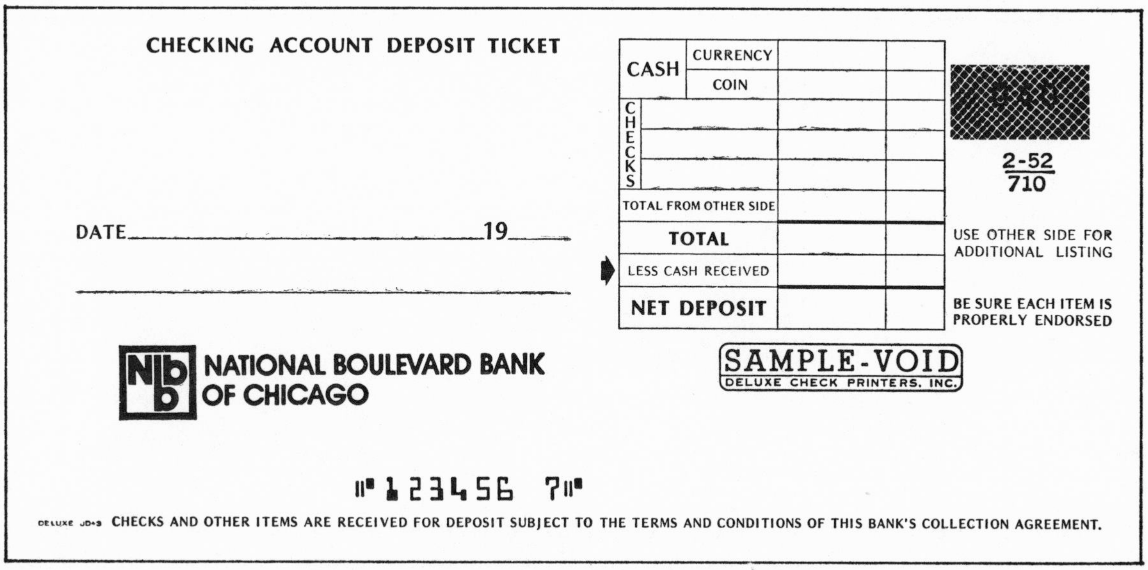
CHECKING ACCOUNT DEPOSIT TICKET

DATE ____________________ 19____

CASH	CURRENCY		
	COIN		
CHECKS			
TOTAL FROM OTHER SIDE			
TOTAL			
LESS CASH RECEIVED			
NET DEPOSIT			

2-52/710

USE OTHER SIDE FOR ADDITIONAL LISTING

BE SURE EACH ITEM IS PROPERLY ENDORSED

NATIONAL BOULEVARD BANK OF CHICAGO

SAMPLE-VOID
DELUXE CHECK PRINTERS, INC.

⑈123456 7⑈

DELUXE JD-3 CHECKS AND OTHER ITEMS ARE RECEIVED FOR DEPOSIT SUBJECT TO THE TERMS AND CONDITIONS OF THIS BANK'S COLLECTION AGREEMENT.

All checks that are to be deposited must be endorsed either in writing or by stamping them with a stamp, which can be purchased from the bank for a small charge. The endorsement goes on the back left side of the check. If the endorsement is handwritten, both the company name plus the bookkeeper's authorized signature are signed. Just above the signatures it is important to write, "Pay to the order of (name of your bank)." Then if the check is lost before it has been deposited no one can cash it. This kind of full endorsement can also be used to make the check payable to a person.

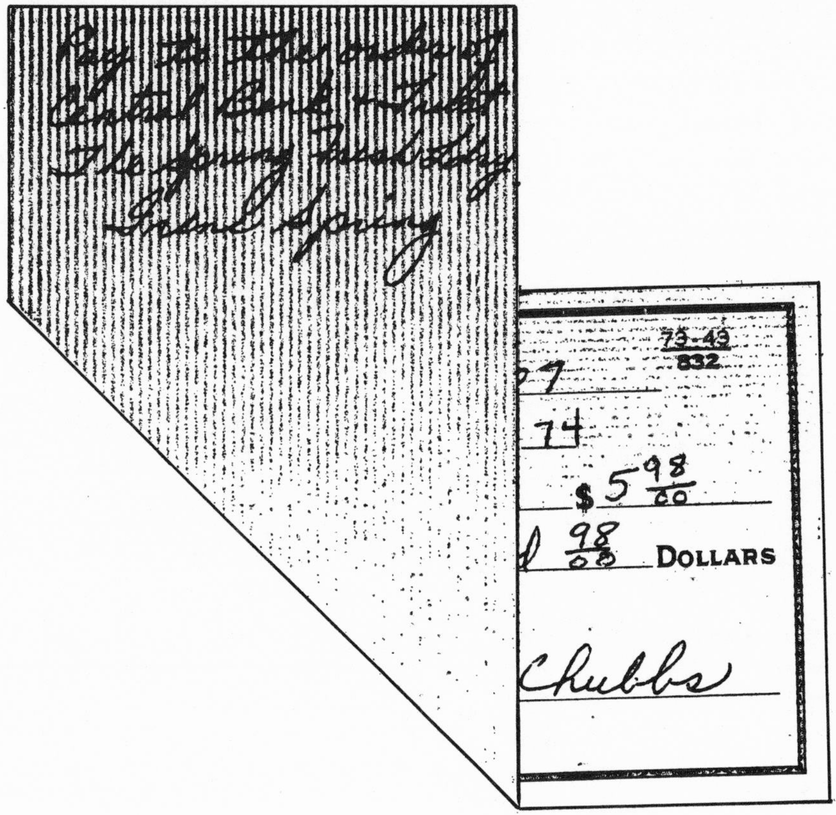

Endorsed Check

1C. As bookkeeper, please endorse the three checks made out to N.O. Fault Insurance Company so they can be deposited in the National Boulevard Bank.

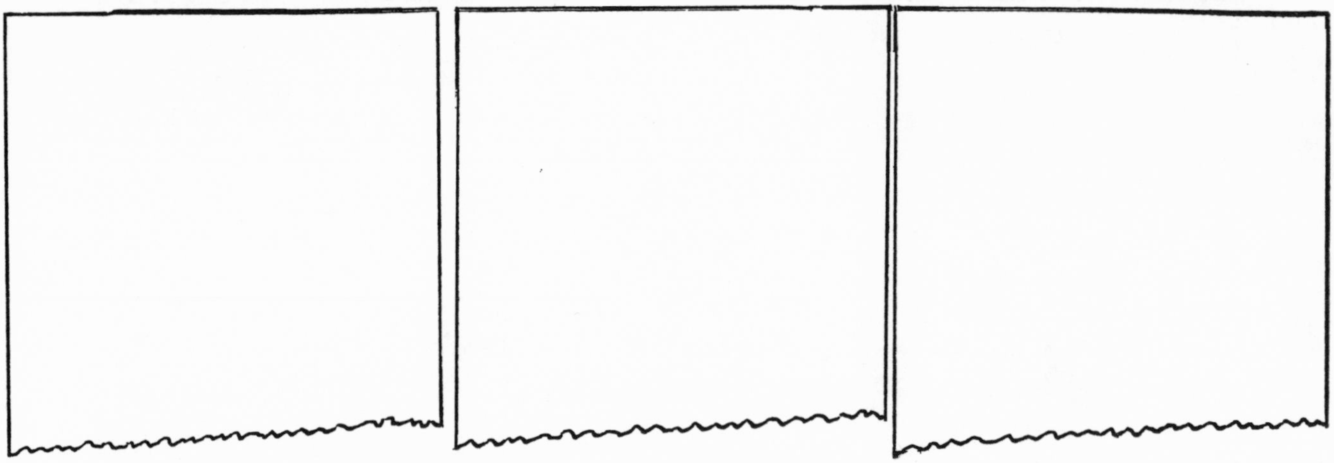

The original of the deposit slip and the cash plus the endorsed checks are then taken to the bank, where a receipt for the deposit is given. This receipt and the carbon copy of the deposit slip are then stapled to the back of the check stub in the checkbook. The total amount of this deposit is added to the bank balance on the check stub so you will have an accurate record of how much money is in your checking account.

Writing Checks

Checks can be made out to withdraw money from a checking account or to pay a bill. When a check is made out to a person or to a company, a receipt is not needed. The person receiving the check must endorse it before it can be cashed; and the bank then mails the check, which is stamped "canceled," along with the bank statement to the bookkeeper. These canceled checks should be kept for a five-year period to serve as a receipt and in case of income tax audit.

Example of a Check

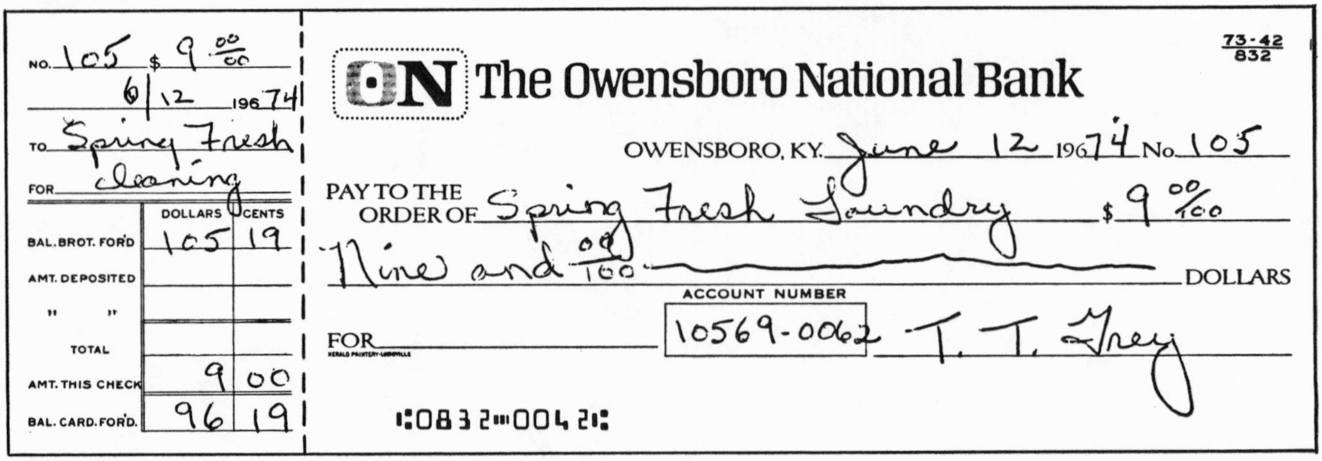

DATE

In writing the check, the date should be today's date. Dating a check for some time in the future (when one plans to have enough money in the bank to cover the check) should never be done and is illegal in certain circumstances.

PAY TO THE ORDER OF

A check made out to cash will not serve as a receipt and can be cashed by anyone if it is lost. Therefore, the bookkeeper should always make out the check to "Pay to the order of" the individual or company she is paying.

AMOUNT

The amount of the check is written in figures immediately next to the dollar sign. Any part less than a dollar is put over 100. The same amount is then written in words on the line below, starting at the far left. A straight or wavy line is used to fill in the unused part of the line. In this way the amount of money cannot be altered.

SIGNATURE

The signature is the same name, same initials, and same style of writing that were used on the signature card.

CHECK STUB

It is very important to fill out the check stub and refigure the bank balance immediately after making out the check. For commercial accounts the stub is usually attached directly to the check, and the stub remains at that place in the checkbook when the check is torn out.

1D. Please make out a check for $95.62 to the Linus Blanket Company. The checking account has a balance of $855.00 before this check is made out.

If an error is made on the check, the word "void" should be written across the check and on the check stub. The voided check is then torn out and filed in case it is needed for an income tax audit.

At times a supplier will not accept a company check but will require a cashier's check. This is purchased at the bank.

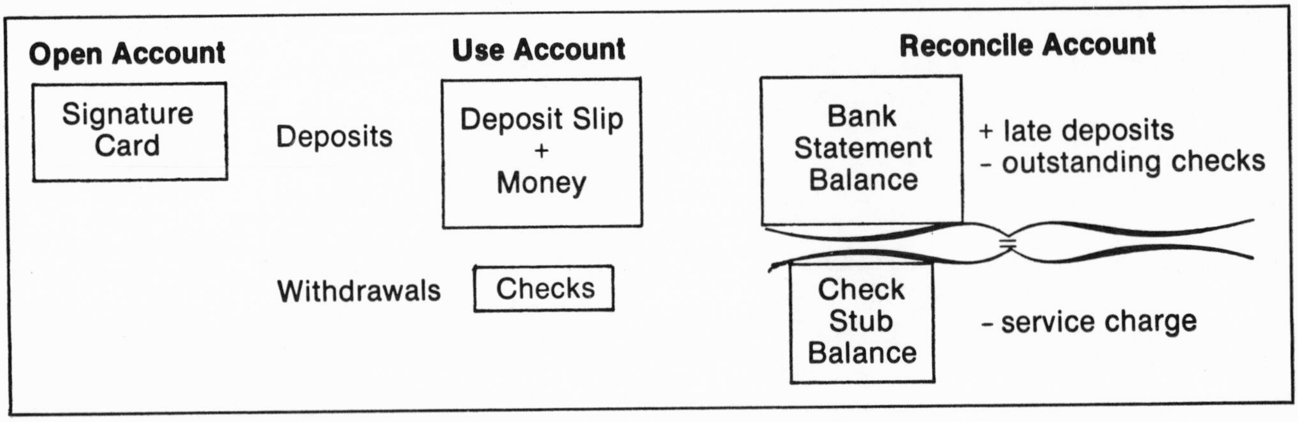

Checking the Bank Statement

Banks usually send statements to their checking account customers once a month. Bank statements list the deposits made during the month and the checks that have been deducted from the company's account. These canceled checks are included in the envelope with the bank statement. The bank statement then shows the amount of money left in the checking account.

However, this is not necessarily the amount of money that is left unspent in the account. There is no way that the bank can know about the checks made out by the bookkeeper that have not been cashed as yet. Consequently, they have not been deducted from the bank's account balance. These are known as "outstanding checks." There is a delay of several days between the time that the bank prepares its statement and the time it is received in the mail by the account customer. Therefore, the statement will not include any deposits made during that time. Thus, the bank statement balance is correct except for two things that the bank could not know about: (1) any outstanding checks and (2) any late deposits. To learn whether there are outstanding checks, compare each of the canceled checks with the check stubs. As the correct stub is found, put a check mark on it. When finished, all stubs without a check mark are outstanding. Also compare the deposits listed on the bank statement with those shown on the check stub, and place a check mark next to each of these on the check stub. If any deposits do not have a check mark, they are late deposits and have not been included in the bank's balance.

On the bank's statement, under the "check" column, are one or more amounts of money followed by the letters "s.c." These are the bank's service charges and have already been deducted from the checking account. They should be recorded on the check stub and subtracted from its total. Your check stub total should now be correct, and it is ready to be compared with the bank statement. This comparison of check stub record with the bank statement record is called "reconciling the bank statement."

Most bank statements have a place to reconcile on the back of the statement. There, all outstanding checks are listed and totaled. This total represents all of the money that has been spent without the bank's knowledge. It is subtracted from the bank's final balance shown on the bank statement. Any late deposits are then added. This reconciled bank statement total should agree exactly with the check stub total after the service charge was deducted. If they do not agree, check the arithmetic on the check stub, make certain that there are no outstanding checks or late deposits that were not included; and, if all else fails to reconcile, check with the bank.

ON **The Owensboro National Bank**

OWENSBORO, KENTUCKY 42302 • DDD CODE 502: 683-3571

MEMBER: Federal Deposit Insurance Corporation • Federal Reserve System

ACCOUNT NUMBER	DATE
10839-00431	6-30-74

The Spring Fresh Laundry
101 W. First St.
Owensboro, Kentucky 42301

BALANCE AS SHOWN ON PREVIOUS STATEMENT	NO. OF DEPOSITS	TOTAL AMOUNT OF DEPOSITS THIS MONTH	NO. OF CHECKS	TOTAL AMOUNT OF CHECKS THIS MONTH	SERVICE CHARGE	BALANCE AS OF THIS STATEMENT DATE
589.91	3	700.39	10	633.65	2.15	654.50

CHECKS	CHECKS	CHECKS	DEPOSITS	MO.	DAY	BALANCE
19.00	5.00			6	10	565.91
			185.00	6	11	750.91
55.18				6	15	695.73
150.12	1.10			6	18	544.51
			325.26	6	20	869.77
229.00				6	23	640.77
13.50	22.46			6	25	604.81
93.00			190.13	6	26	701.94
45.29	2.15 sc			6	28	654.50

Bank Statement

1E. *Upon receiving your bank statement in the mail today, and on checking the canceled checks against the check stub, you found the following checks were outstanding: No. 174— $16.35, No. 177— $8.19, No. 178— $20.42, No. 179— $83.00. One deposit for $322.24 shown on your check stub does not appear on the bank statement. On the statement there is a $2.89 amount followed by an s.c. Your check stub total (as of the last check written) is $985.53. The bank statement total is $788.36. Please reconcile the bank statement.*

MONTH ____________________ 19 ______

THIS FORM IS PROVIDED TO HELP YOU BALANCE YOUR BANK STATEMENT

CHECKS OUTSTANDING - NOT CHARGED TO ACCOUNT

NO.	$	
TOTAL	$	

BANK BALANCE SHOWN ON THIS STATEMENT $____________

ADD +

DEPOSITS NOT CREDITED IN THIS STATEMENT (IF ANY) $____________

____

____

SUB-TOTAL $____________

SUBTRACT —

CHECKS OUTSTANDING $____________

BALANCE $____________

SHOULD AGREE WITH CHECK BOOK BALANCE AFTER DEDUCTING SERVICE CHARGE (IF ANY) SHOWN ON THIS STATEMENT FOR PRESENT MONTH.

Each depositor insured to $40,000

FDIC

FEDERAL DEPOSIT INSURANCE CORPORATION

If any of the deposited checks turn out to be a bad check, the bank deducts it from the checking account and returns it to the company that made the deposit. It is included with the bank statement and should be deducted from the check stub balance. This is known as a "dishonored check."

Keeping Petty Cash

If a customer needs a dime for the parking meter, writing out a check won't help him. It is convenient and often necessary to have some money in the office. Therefore, most businessmen keep what is known as a petty cash fund. It is usually an amount under $100 and is used to pay for small items or services. Only one or two persons should be allowed to take money from the petty cash box or drawer.

NO. 5 $ 10¢

RECEIVED OF PETTY CASH

DATE 1/18 19 74

FOR Parking Meter

CHARGE TO Miscellaneous Expense
ACCOUNT

APPROVED BY RECEIVED BY
IRS

TOPS FORM 3008

Petty Cash Voucher

A pad of "petty cash vouchers" is kept in the same drawer with the money. Whenever money is taken out of petty cash, a voucher for that amount is made out immediately. It should show the date, what the money was used for, what account should be charged, and the initials of the person making out the voucher.

1F. *The accounts for which your company usually spends petty cash are: Auto Expense, Stationery and Office Supplies Expense, and Miscellaneous Expense. Please make out petty cash vouchers for these expenditures. (1) Spent $2.00 on car washing to get rid of the "Do Not Wash! Dirt Test!" that someone wrote with their finger on the side of the company car. (2) Paid the paper boy $2.50 for the office subscription to the* Pickeyune Tribune. *(3) Bought $30.00 worth of typewriter erasers. (4) The boss got $10.00 to take Miss Trixie LaMoore (a customer) to lunch. Use your own dates in the month of January, 1976.*

PETTY CASH

$

For

Charge to Account

Signed

Date

Rediform 9G 009

PETTY CASH

________________________ $________

For________________________

____

____

____

Charge to Account________________________

Signed________________________

Date________________

Rediform 9G 009

PETTY CASH

________________________ $________

For________________________

____

____

____

Charge to Account________________________

Signed________________________

Date________________

Rediform 9G 009

PETTY CASH

________________________ $________

For________________________

____

____

____

Charge to Account________________________

Signed________________________

Date________________

Rediform 9G 009

PETTY CASH STATEMENT

At the end of the month the money in the petty cash drawer will be getting low. It is time to make out a statement showing the amount and use of the petty cash spent during the month. The title of this statement is "Petty Cash Statement for the Month of (month), (year)."

The petty cash vouchers should be taken out of the drawer and sorted in stacks according to the account to be charged on each voucher. All vouchers to be charged to the same account are then totaled. Each of these accounts is then listed on the petty cash statement and the total amount to be charged to each account is shown. The amounts spent are then totaled.

Petty Cash Statement
March 31, 1974

Auto Expense	$ 8.00
Stationery Expense	5.00
Miscellaneous Expense	18.50
Total Spent	$31.50
Amount Left	18.50
March 1 Total	$50.00

Next, the money in the petty cash drawer should be counted and shown on the statement. When the amount of petty cash spent during the month is added to the amount left in the drawer, this should total what was in the petty cash drawer at the beginning of the month. If it does not, there was probably an error in making change. The difference should be added to the Miscellaneous Expense account if the total is less than the amount in the drawer at the beginning of the month. The difference should be subtracted from that charged to Miscellaneous Expense if the total is greater than it was at the beginning of the month.

1G. Please make out a petty cash statement for this month. $50.00 was in the drawer on the first of the month. The only petty cash vouchers used are those listed in Problem 1F.

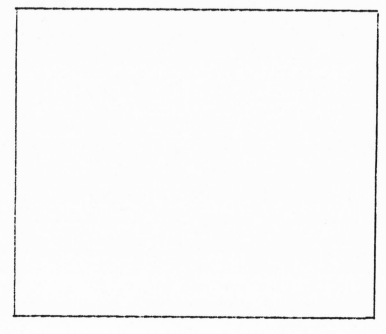

PUTTING BACK THE MONEY USED

More money will be needed for petty cash next month. Therefore, a check for the amount of petty cash used should be made out and cashed so the money can be put back in the drawer to start next month. The check is made out to pay to the order of Petty Cash.

1H. Please make out the check that you would need to cash after completing the petty cash statement in 1G. Your bank balance is the last amount shown in problem 1D.

102 $________

________ 19____

TO________

	DOLLARS	CENTS
BAL. FOR'D		
DEPOSITS		
"		
TOTAL		
THIS CHECK		
OTHER DEDUCTIONS		
BAL. FOR'D		

102

2-52
710

________ 19____

PAY TO THE ORDER OF________ $________

________ DOLLARS

NATIONAL BOULEVARD BANK OF CHICAGO

SAMPLE-VOID
DELUXE CHECK PRINTERS, INC.

MEMO________

⑆0710⑉0052⑆ ⑈123456 7⑈ 0102

DELUXE CHECK PRINTERS • RJ-1

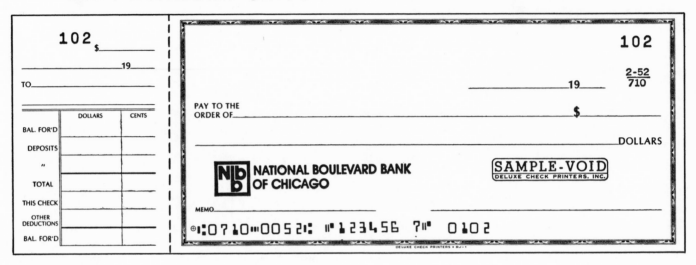

PUTTING IT ALL TOGETHER

Chapter Summary Problems

A. WHAT IS IT?

Please fill in the blanks with the correct words from those listed below:

voucher	canceled check
reconciling	outstanding check
service charge	late deposit
voided	currency
cashier's check	endorsed
dishonored check	check stub
signature card	bank statement
deposit slip	petty cash fund
night deposit	

1. If you wish to put money in the bank after the bank is closed, slide the envelope into the slot marked ________________.
2. A ________________ is a bad check.
3. A ________________ is a check that has cleared the bank and has been deducted from your checking account.
4. When money is removed from petty cash, a ________________ is filled out.
5. A ________________ is added to the bank statement balance when reconciling the bank statement.

6. If there is an error in making out a check, the check should be ________________.
7. Each month the bank sends a ________________ to notify the checking account customer of the amount of money that he has in the account.
8. If a supplier does not want to take your check, he may request that you pay him with a ________________, which you can get at the bank.
9. The bank deducts a fee, known as a ________________, for handling your checking account.
10. Before cashing a check made out to you, it must be ________________.
11. Each time money is put in the checking account, a ________________ must be included with the cash.
12. Payments are made either by check or out of the ________________.
13. Making the bank statement balance agree with the check stub balance is known as ________________.
14. ________________ is a term for paper bills.
15. After writing a check, you should write the amount of the check on the ________________ and refigure your bank balance.
16. The first thing to do when opening a checking account is fill out the ________________.
17. Each ________________ is subtracted from the bank statement balance when reconciling the bank statement.

B. USING WHAT YOU KNOW

You have just been hired by the Nelson O. Fault Insurance Company to take care of cash receipts and disbursements. Please fill out the appropriate form correctly for each of the following:

1. Sept. 1—Sign the bank's signature card authorizing you to make out checks for the Nelson O. Fault Insurance Co.
2. Sept. 5—Make out a check to George Winstead for $135.04 to pay a bill owed to him. The previous check stub balance had been $1,519.40.
3. Sept. 6—Take $8.50 out of the petty cash drawer to pay for window washing. Accounts that are normally charged for petty cash expenditures are: Auto Expense, Postage Expense, Stationery and Office Supplies Expense, and Miscellaneous Expense.
4. Sept. 6—Make out a check for $91.95 to Smith Furniture Store for a new chair for the office.
5. Sept. 6—Write a $57.30 check to Office Supplies, Inc., for office stationery.
6. Sept. 10—Deposit $3.25 in change, $519.00 in bills, and the two checks shown (those written by F. Balfour and F. W. Falls). Prepare the checks for deposit.
7. Sept. 11—Take $24 out of petty cash to pay the paper boy for four months.
8. Sept. 15—Pay $19.88 to the Taylor Garage for car repairs. (Pay by check.)
9. Sept. 18—Make out a check for $100 to Mr. Fault for money he wishes to withdraw for his personal use.
10. Sept. 23—Take $2.20 out of petty cash to buy a supply of paper clips.
11. Sept. 23—Deposit $5.90 in change, $455 in bills, and the check from Robert F. Lowe.
12. Sept. 27—Make out a $56 check to Janitorial Services, Inc. for cleaning the carpet.
13. Sept. 29—Take $3.60 out of petty cash for money to buy stamps.
14. Sept. 30—Deposit $2.25 in change and $98 in bills.
15. Sept. 30—Make out a petty cash statement for the month of September. $50 was in the drawer at the beginning of the month. $12.70 is left in the drawer now.
16. Sept. 30—Make out a check to bring petty cash back up to $50.
17. Oct. 1—Received the bank statement. All canceled checks that are included are listed on the bank statement. Please check them off on the check stubs, check deposits, and reconcile the statement.

JOINT ACCOUNT-3

Nelson O. Fault Insurance Company

The undersigned hereby agree to the rules, regulations and by-laws of the NATIONAL BOULEVARD BANK OF CHICAGO, to the Co-Depositor Clause below and to the clauses on the reverse hereof relating to collections and to examination of returned statements and cancelled checks.

Sign Here: Nelson O. Fault

CO-DEPOSITOR CLAUSE

All moneys now on deposit, or at any time deposited by us or either of us, with said Bank to the credit of this account, or in accounts in continuation hereof, are and shall be so deposited by us and received by said Bank upon the following terms and conditions of repayment, viz:

That the amount thereof, or any part, and any interest thereon shall be paid by said Bank to us, or either of us, whether the other or others be living or not, or to the heirs, executors, administrators, or assigns of the survivor of us, or upon the written order of any person or persons so entitled to payment. Payment of funds to survivor contingent upon release from Inheritance Tax Office.

We further agree that any of us, may deposit and endorse for deposit in this account and in accounts in continuation hereof, checks, drafts, notes and orders belonging or payable to any of us, and may cash and endorse for negotiation any of the same. Said Bank shall have the right to charge against this account and accounts in continuation hereof any liabilities, at any time existing, of any of the undersigned to you. Our intention is to create a joint tenancy in this account, and in accounts in continuation hereof, with the right of survivorship

DATE ____________ ACCEPTED ____________

FORM 368 10M 4-73 BANK OFFICIAL

---

103 $______

______ 19___

TO ______

	DOLLARS	CENTS
BAL. FOR'D		
DEPOSITS		
"		
TOTAL		
THIS CHECK		
OTHER DEDUCTIONS		
BAL. FOR'D		

103

______ 19___ 2-52/710

PAY TO THE ORDER OF ______ $______

______ DOLLARS

NATIONAL BOULEVARD BANK OF CHICAGO

SAMPLE-VOID
DELUXE CHECK PRINTERS, INC.

MEMO ______

⑆0710⑈0052⑆ ⑈123456 7⑈ 0153

DELUXE CHECK PRINTERS • RJ-1

PETTY CASH

______ $______

For ______

Charge to Account ______

Signed ______

Date ______

Rediform 9G 009

104 $______

______ 19___

TO______

	DOLLARS	CENTS
BAL. FOR'D		
DEPOSITS		
"		
TOTAL		
THIS CHECK		
OTHER DEDUCTIONS		
BAL. FOR'D		

104

2-52/710

______ 19___

PAY TO THE ORDER OF______ $______

______ DOLLARS

NATIONAL BOULEVARD BANK OF CHICAGO

SAMPLE-VOID
DELUXE CHECK PRINTERS, INC.

MEMO______

⑆0710⑈0052⑆ ⑈123456 7⑈ 0154

DELUXE CHECK PRINTERS • RJ-1

105 $______

______ 19___

TO______

	DOLLARS	CENTS
BAL. FOR'D		
DEPOSITS		
"		
TOTAL		
THIS CHECK		
OTHER DEDUCTIONS		
BAL. FOR'D		

105

2-52/710

______ 19___

PAY TO THE ORDER OF______ $______

______ DOLLARS

NATIONAL BOULEVARD BANK OF CHICAGO

SAMPLE-VOID
DELUXE CHECK PRINTERS, INC.

MEMO______

⑆0710⑈0052⑆ ⑈123456 7⑈ 0155

DELUXE CHECK PRINTERS • RJ-1

DATE______ 19___

Checks and other items are received for deposit subject to the terms and conditions of this bank's collection agreement.

CURRENCY, COUPONS AND BONDS SHOULD BE SENT BY REGISTERED MAIL INSURED.
PLEASE PRINT MAILING ADDRESS IF NOT SHOWN BELOW

NATIONAL BOULEVARD BANK
OF CHICAGO
WRIGLEY BUILDING
410 N. MICHIGAN AVE • CHICAGO, ILLINOIS 60611

CHECKS		CHECKS		CHECKS	

TOTAL FROM ABOVE		
CURRENCY		
COIN		
TOTAL		
LESS CASH		
TOTAL DEPOSIT		

SPACE FOR ADDITIONAL LISTINGS ON REVERSE SIDE

ENDORSE ALL CHECKS (YOUR NAME)
PAY TO THE ORDER OF NATIONAL BOULEVARD BANK
1. SEND BOTH COPIES TO BANK WITH YOUR DEPOSIT
2. RECEIPT WILL BE RETURNED TO YOU
3. REVERSE CARBON BEFORE USING REVERSE SIDE

NO. 103

DATE Sept. 7 1976

56-308
441

PAY TO THE ORDER OF Nelson O. Fault Insurance Company $ 59.20

Fifty-nine and 20/00---------------------------------- DOLLARS

THE DELAWARE COUNTY BANK
DELAWARE, OHIO

MEMO

F. Balfour

⑆0441⑈0308⑆

DELUXE CHECK PRINTERS LCH (1)

NO. 567

DATE Sept. 19 1976

56-308
441

PAY TO THE ORDER OF Nelson O. Fault Insurance Company $ 119.00

One hundred nineteen and no---------------------- DOLLARS

THE DELAWARE COUNTY BANK
DELAWARE, OHIO

MEMO

F. W. Falls

⑆0441⑈0308⑆

DELUXE CHECK PRINTERS LCH (1)

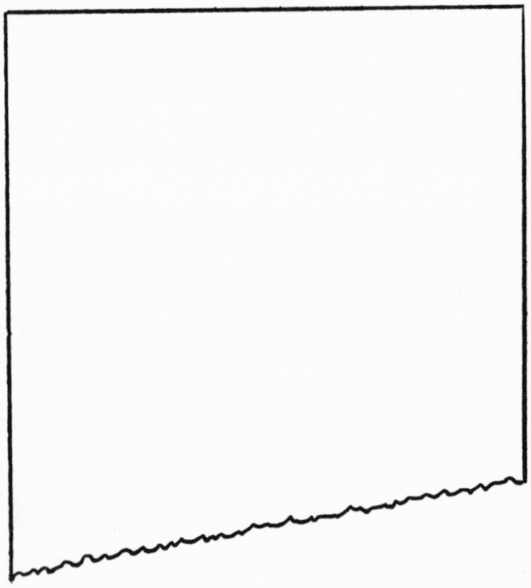

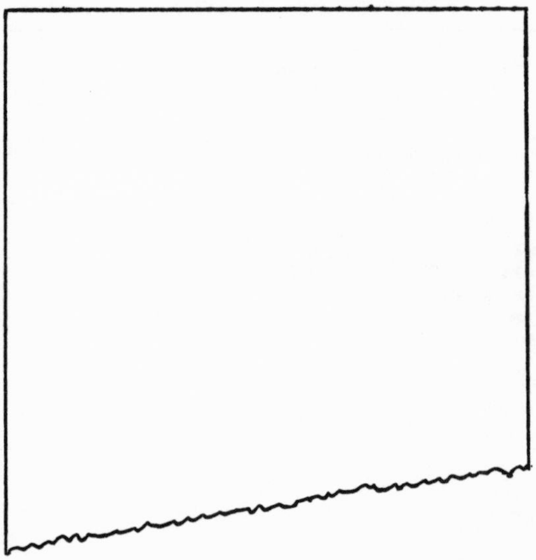

PETTY CASH

______________________________ $ __________

For ______________________________

____

____

____

Charge to Account ______________________________

Signed ______________________________

Date ______________

Rediform 9G 009

---

107 $ __________

__________ 19 ____

TO __________

	DOLLARS	CENTS
BAL. FOR'D		
DEPOSITS		
"		
TOTAL		
THIS CHECK		
OTHER DEDUCTIONS		
BAL. FOR'D		

107

2-52
710

__________ 19 ____

PAY TO THE ORDER OF ______________________________ $ __________

______________________________ DOLLARS

NATIONAL BOULEVARD BANK OF CHICAGO

SAMPLE-VOID
DELUXE CHECK PRINTERS, INC.

MEMO __________

⑆0710⑉0052⑆ ⑈123456 7⑈ 0157

DELUXE CHECK PRINTERS • RJ-1

---

106 $ __________

__________ 19 ____

TO __________

	DOLLARS	CENTS
BAL. FOR'D		
DEPOSITS		
"		
TOTAL		
THIS CHECK		
OTHER DEDUCTIONS		
BAL. FOR'D		

106

2-52
710

__________ 19 ____

PAY TO THE ORDER OF ______________________________ $ __________

______________________________ DOLLARS

NATIONAL BOULEVARD BANK OF CHICAGO

SAMPLE-VOID
DELUXE CHECK PRINTERS, INC.

MEMO __________

⑆0710⑉0052⑆ ⑈123456 7⑈ 0156

DELUXE CHECK PRINTERS • RJ-1

PETTY CASH

____________________ $________

For____________________

Charge to Account____________________

Signed____________________

Date____________________

Rediform 9G 009

DATE____________________ 19____

Checks and other items are received for deposit subject to the terms and conditions of this bank's collection agreement.

CURRENCY, COUPONS AND BONDS SHOULD BE SENT BY REGISTERED MAIL INSURED.
PLEASE PRINT MAILING ADDRESS IF NOT SHOWN BELOW

NATIONAL BOULEVARD BANK
OF CHICAGO
WRIGLEY BUILDING
410 N. MICHIGAN AVE • CHICAGO, ILLINOIS 60611

CHECKS		CHECKS		CHECKS	
		TOTAL FROM ABOVE			
		CURRENCY			
		COIN			
		TOTAL			
		LESS CASH			
		TOTAL DEPOSIT			

SPACE FOR ADDITIONAL LISTINGS ON REVERSE SIDE

ENDORSE ALL CHECKS (YOUR NAME)
PAY TO THE ORDER OF NATIONAL BOULEVARD BANK
1: SEND BOTH COPIES TO BANK WITH YOUR DEPOSIT
2: RECEIPT WILL BE RETURNED TO YOU
3: REVERSE CARBON BEFORE USING REVERSE SIDE

NO. 201

DATE Sept. 20 19 76

56-308
441

PAY TO THE ORDER OF Nelson O. Fault Insurance Company $17.80

Seventeen and 80/00---------------------------------- DOLLARS

THE DELAWARE COUNTY BANK
DELAWARE, OHIO

MEMO

Robert F. Lowe

⑆0441⑈0308⑆

DELUXE CHECK PRINTERS LCH (1)

108 $

19

TO

	DOLLARS	CENTS
BAL. FOR'D		
DEPOSITS		
"		
TOTAL		
THIS CHECK		
OTHER DEDUCTIONS		
BAL. FOR'D		

108

19

2-52
710

PAY TO THE ORDER OF $

DOLLARS

NATIONAL BOULEVARD BANK OF CHICAGO

SAMPLE-VOID
DELUXE CHECK PRINTERS, INC.

MEMO

⑆0710⑈0052⑆ ⑈123456 7⑈ 0158

DELUXE CHECK PRINTERS • RJ-1

PETTY CASH

______________________________ $__________

For______________________________

____

____

____

Charge to Account______________________________

Signed______________________________

Date____________________

Rediform 9G 009

DATE______________________19____

Checks and other items are received for deposit subject to the terms and conditions of this bank's collection agreement.

CURRENCY, COUPONS AND BONDS SHOULD BE SENT BY REGISTERED MAIL INSURED.

PLEASE PRINT MAILING ADDRESS IF NOT SHOWN BELOW

NATIONAL BOULEVARD BANK
OF CHICAGO
WRIGLEY BUILDING
410 N. MICHIGAN AVE • CHICAGO, ILLINOIS 60611

CHECKS		CHECKS		CHECKS	
		TOTAL FROM ABOVE			
		CURRENCY			
		COIN			
		TOTAL			
		LESS CASH			
		TOTAL DEPOSIT			

SPACE FOR ADDITIONAL LISTINGS ON REVERSE SIDE

ENDORSE ALL CHECKS (YOUR NAME)
PAY TO THE ORDER OF NATIONAL BOULEVARD BANK
1: SEND BOTH COPIES TO BANK WITH YOUR DEPOSIT,
2: RECEIPT WILL BE RETURNED TO YOU
3: REVERSE CARBON BEFORE USING REVERSE SIDE

Petty Cash Statement
for the Month of ________, 1976

109 $________

________ 19____

TO________

	DOLLARS	CENTS
BAL. FOR'D		
DEPOSITS		
"		
TOTAL		
THIS CHECK		
OTHER DEDUCTIONS		
BAL. FOR'D		

109

2-52
710

________ 19____

PAY TO THE
ORDER OF________ $________

________ DOLLARS

NATIONAL BOULEVARD BANK
OF CHICAGO

SAMPLE-VOID
DELUXE CHECK PRINTERS, INC.

MEMO________

⑆0710⑉0052⑆ ⑈123456 7⑈ 0159

DELUXE CHECK PRINTERS • RJ-1

NATIONAL BOULEVARD BANK OF CHICAGO
400-410 N. MICHIGAN AVE., 237 E. GRAND AVE.,
PHONE (312) 467-4100 • MEMBER FDIC

Nelson O. Fault Insurance Company
707 N. 9th Street
Chicago, Illinois

ACCOUNT NUMBER
123456-7
DATE OF STATEMENT
9/30/76

BEGINNING BALANCE	NUMBER	TOTAL CHECKS & DEBITS	NUMBER	TOTAL DEPOSITS & CREDITS	SERVICE CHARGE	ENDING BALANCE
1519.40	5	368.22	2	1179.15	2.00	2328.33

DATE	CHECKS AND DEBITS		DEPOSITS & CREDITS	BALANCE
9-8	57.30			1462.10
9-10			700.45	2162.55
9-12	135.04			2027.51
9-20	100.00	19.88		1907.63
9-23			478.70	2386.33
9-29	56.00	2.00SC		2328.33

LP - LIST OF CHECKS
OD - OVERDRAWN
RT - RETURNED ITEM
SC - SERVICE CHARGE

CC - CERTIFIED CHECK
CM - CREDIT MEMO
DM - DEBIT MEMO
MC - MISC. CHARGE

PLEASE EXAMINE AT ONCE
REPORT ALL EXCEPTIONS TO OUR AUDIT DEPT.
WITHIN 10 DAYS.

MONTH ______________________ 19 ________

THIS FORM IS PROVIDED TO HELP YOU BALANCE YOUR BANK STATEMENT

CHECKS OUTSTANDING - NOT CHARGED TO ACCOUNT

NO.	$	
TOTAL	$	

BANK BALANCE SHOWN ON THIS STATEMENT $________

ADD +

DEPOSITS NOT CREDITED IN THIS STATEMENT (IF ANY) $________

____

____

SUB-TOTAL $________

SUBTRACT —

CHECKS OUTSTANDING $________

BALANCE $________

SHOULD AGREE WITH CHECK BOOK BALANCE AFTER DEDUCTING SERVICE CHARGE (IF ANY) SHOWN ON THIS STATEMENT FOR PRESENT MONTH.

Each depositor insured to $40,000

FDIC

FEDERAL DEPOSIT INSURANCE CORPORATION

2 PAYROLL

When figuring the total amount to be paid to company employees, it is very important to be exactly correct because few employees have the information to know whether their pay is accurate. A new firm receives an employer's number from the Federal Internal Revenue Service and is then supplied with all of the federal payroll tax forms and tables that are needed.

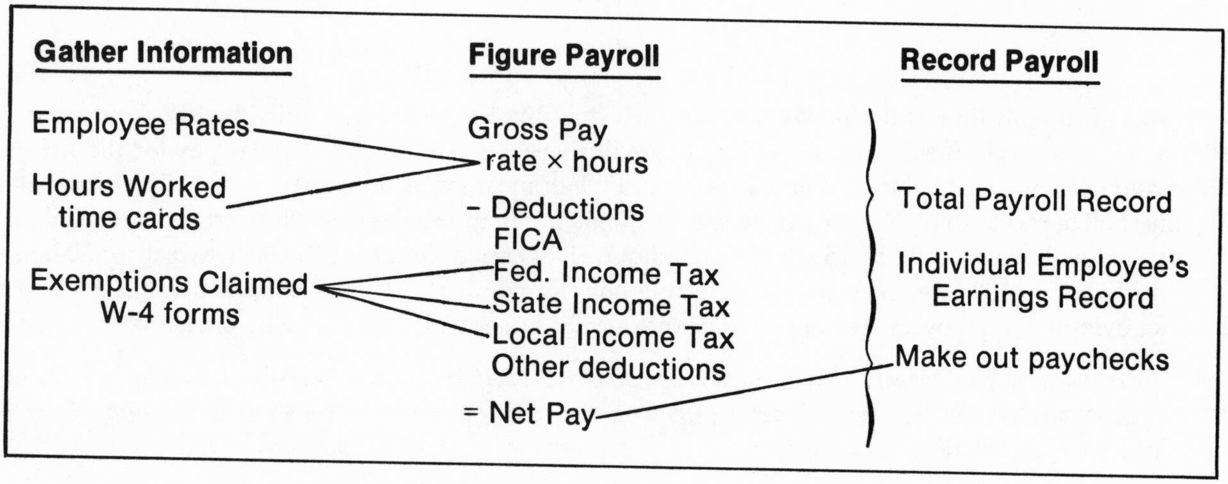

Information on New Employees

As soon as an employee is hired, he should fill out an Employee Withholding Exemption Certificate (called a W-4 form). This shows how many exemptions the employee is claiming, and is used in figuring his federal income tax to be withheld. The employee's Social Security number and how much he is to be paid are also recorded and kept on file.

Form **W-4**
(Rev. Aug. 1972)
Department of the Treasury
Internal Revenue Service

Employee's Withholding Allowance Certificate
(This certificate is for income tax withholding purposes only; it will remain in effect until you change it.)

Type or print your full name: Darnabee Smith
Your social security number: 555-33-1115
Home address (Number and street or rural route): 100 Snoop Street
Marital status: ☒ Single ☐ Married
(If married but legally separated, or wife (husband) is a nonresident alien, check the single block.)
City or town, State and ZIP code: Los Angeles, California 89012

1 Total number of allowances you are claiming 3
2 Additional amount, if any, you want deducted from each pay (if your employer agrees) . . . . $

I certify that to the best of my knowledge and belief, the number of withholding allowances claimed on this certificate does not exceed the number to which I am entitled.

Signature ▶ Darnabee Smith Date ▶ Jan 1, 1976

Pay Rates

Most employees are paid a certain amount per hour, per week, or per month. Those on an hourly or weekly pay rate generally receive their paychecks each week. Someone earning $4.20 per hour, working 35 hours, would receive $147 total (or gross) pay.

2A. *What would be the gross pay for an employee who earned $3.50 per hour if he worked 40 hours this week?*

Many firms pay time and a half for overtime, which is usually any time an individual works more than 40 hours in one week. If someone worked 42 hours this week, he would earn regular pay for the first 40 hours and overtime for the last two hours. Time and a half means that the overtime rate of pay is regular pay plus half of regular pay. For the person earning $3.50 per hour regular pay, the overtime rate would be $3.50 plus one-half of $3.50 ($1.75), or $5.25 per hour. If an employee earns $100.00 per week for 40 hours of work, dividing $100 by 40 hours equals $2.50 per hour for regular time; and time and a half is $3.75 per hour for overtime. Employees are not paid for overtime if it has not been approved by the manager.

2B. *Your company, Jane's Pond Detective Agency, pays time and a half for any time worked over 40 hours a week. An employee named Columbone regularly earns $180 for a 40-hour week, and he worked 45 hours this week. His overtime was approved. What is his gross pay?*

In most offices an employee can be a few minutes late reporting to work and still receive full pay. Find out the rules of your company regarding how late an individual can be before you deduct this from his pay.

In most cases, a person must be employed by the firm for several months before he is paid for time off due to illness. Find out the company's policies concerning payment for sick days.

How to Figure the Payroll

DETERMINE THE GROSS PAY OF EACH EMPLOYEE

First find out the amount of time each employee worked this week (or this month, for monthly payrolls.) For hourly employees, collect the time cards or sign-in sheets, and total the number of hours worked each day. On the time card example shown below, Columbone was three minutes late on Monday.

Columbone #007

week ending 1/28/76

M	T	W	T	F
8:03	8:00	7:59	8:04	7:57
11:58	12:03	12:00	12:01	11:58
1:01	12:59	1:01	1:00	1:00
5:00	4:58	5:04	5:00	5:02
7:00				
10:02				

McClown #001

week ending 1/28/76

M	T	W	T	F
8:01	7:59	8:03	8:00	7:36
11:56	12:01	12:02	11:59	12:03
12:56	1:04	1:02	1:00	1:04
5:00	5:04	5:00	5:02	4:58
			6:30	
			8:31	

but his company doesn't take anything out of an employee's pay unless he is more than five minutes late. He rang out for lunch two minutes early. He came back from lunch one minute late, rang out at 5:00 p.m., and then returned to work three more hours that night. This overtime was approved. He worked a total of 11 hours on Monday and eight hours each of the other four days. This totals 43 hours worked for the week.

2C. *Decide from the time card how many hours McClown worked this week. What would be the gross pay for each man if Columbone earns $180 per week and McClown earns $200 per week, for a 40-hour week? (Overtime was approved.)*

WITHHOLDING MONEY FOR DEDUCTIONS

Employees do not receive their total gross pay in their paychecks. Employers hold out the amount each employee owes to the government for income tax and Social Security tax, and later pay it to the government for the employees. The employer is responsible (or liable) for all money withheld for taxes until the time he pays it to the government.

The Federal Internal Revenue Service will supply you with tables showing how much tax an employee owes out of each paycheck. A person with many dependents to support does not pay as much income tax as one with fewer dependents. Therefore, in order to know how much to deduct from a paycheck for income tax, find out how many dependents (called withholding allowances or exemptions) the employee claimed on his W-4 form (Employee Withholding Exemption Certificate.) Follow the numbers across the top of the Federal Income Tax Withholding Table until you have found the number he claimed, and then find this week's gross pay at the left of the table. The point where these two columns meet shows how much of the paycheck the employee owes in federal income tax.

2D. *Based on the gross earnings shown in problem 2C, how much should be deducted from the Columbone and McClown paychecks for federal income taxes? Both men are single and claim only themselves as exemptions.*

Most states and cities have income taxes also, and will give you tables showing the amounts to be withheld from paychecks for their taxes (see tables on following pages).

Employees also owe money from their paychecks to FICA (Federal Insurance Contributions Act), which is commonly called Social Security. Currently 5.85% of the employee's gross pay is owed and withheld to be paid to the federal government for FICA. The Federal Internal Revenue Service supplies tables to be used, which simplify figuring the amount owed.

A person does not pay Social Security tax on any earnings over $15,300 during the year 1976. Therefore, if today were December 6, 1976, and an employee had already earned $15,200 between January 1, 1976, and his most recent paycheck, you would withhold 5.85% of only the next $100, no matter how much more he earned during the rest of 1976. This maximum pay for FICA(or Social Security) deductions has been increased each year. The maximum pay for FICA deductions during 1981 is $29,700 at a rate of 6.65%. During 1982 the maximum pay is $32,400 at a rate of 6.7%.

2E. *For the week ending 1/28/76, how much should you deduct from the paychecks of Columbone and McClown for Social Security, using the gross pay shown in problem 2C?*

There are other deductions that can be withheld from paychecks: pension fund, credit union, insurance, and the like. In each case, these deductions reduce the amount paid to the employees but increase the amount that the employer owes and will later pay to someone else for his employees.

SINGLE Persons—WEEKLY Payroll Period

And the wages are—		And the number of withholding allowances claimed is—										
At least	But less than	0	1	2	3	4	5	6	7	8	9	10 or more
		The amount of income tax to be withheld shall be—										
$80	$82	$12.00	$9.10	$6.50	$3.90	$1.80	$0	$0	$0	$0	$0	$0
82	84	12.40	9.50	6.90	4.30	2.10	0	0	0	0	0	0
84	86	12.80	9.80	7.20	4.60	2.30	.30	0	0	0	0	0
86	88	13.20	10.20	7.60	5.00	2.60	.60	0	0	0	0	0
88	90	13.60	10.60	8.00	5.40	2.90	.90	0	0	0	0	0
90	92	14.10	11.00	8.30	5.70	3.20	1.20	0	0	0	0	0
92	94	14.50	11.40	8.70	6.10	3.50	1.40	0	0	0	0	0
94	96	14.90	11.90	9.00	6.40	3.90	1.70	0	0	0	0	0
96	98	15.30	12.30	9.40	6.80	4.20	2.00	0	0	0	0	0
98	100	15.70	12.70	9.80	7.20	4.60	2.30	.30	0	0	0	0
100	105	16.50	13.40	10.40	7.80	5.20	2.80	.80	0	0	0	0
105	110	17.50	14.50	11.50	8.70	6.10	3.50	1.50	0	0	0	0
110	115	18.60	15.50	12.50	9.60	7.00	4.40	2.20	.10	0	0	0
115	120	19.60	16.60	13.60	10.50	7.90	5.30	2.90	.80	0	0	0
120	125	20.70	17.60	14.60	11.60	8.80	6.20	3.60	1.50	0	0	0
125	130	21.70	18.70	15.70	12.60	9.70	7.10	4.50	2.20	.20	0	0
130	135	22.80	19.70	16.70	13.70	10.70	8.00	5.40	2.90	.90	0	0
135	140	23.80	20.80	17.80	14.70	11.70	8.90	6.30	3.70	1.60	0	0
140	145	24.90	21.80	18.80	15.80	12.80	9.80	7.20	4.60	2.30	.30	0
145	150	25.90	22.90	19.90	16.80	13.80	10.80	8.10	5.50	3.00	1.00	0
150	160	27.50	24.50	21.40	18.40	15.40	12.30	9.50	6.90	4.30	2.00	0
160	170	29.60	26.60	23.50	20.50	17.50	14.40	11.40	8.70	6.10	3.50	1.40
170	180	31.70	28.70	25.60	22.60	19.60	16.50	13.50	10.50	7.90	5.30	2.80
180	190	33.80	30.80	27.70	24.70	21.70	18.60	15.60	12.60	9.70	7.10	4.50
190	200	35.90	32.90	29.80	26.80	23.80	20.70	17.70	14.70	11.70	8.90	6.30
200	210	38.10	35.00	31.90	28.90	25.90	22.80	19.80	16.80	13.80	10.70	8.10
210	220	40.40	37.10	34.00	31.00	28.00	24.90	21.90	18.90	15.90	12.80	9.90
220	230	42.70	39.30	36.10	33.10	30.10	27.00	24.00	21.00	18.00	14.90	11.90
230	240	45.10	41.60	38.30	35.20	32.20	29.10	26.10	23.10	20.10	17.00	14.00
240	250	47.80	43.90	40.60	37.30	34.30	31.20	28.20	25.20	22.20	19.10	16.10
250	260	50.50	46.60	42.90	39.60	36.40	33.30	30.30	27.30	24.30	21.20	18.20
260	270	53.20	49.30	45.40	41.90	38.60	35.40	32.40	29.40	26.40	23.30	20.30
270	280	56.20	52.00	48.10	44.20	40.90	37.60	34.50	31.50	28.50	25.40	22.40
280	290	59.30	54.80	50.80	46.90	43.20	39.90	36.60	33.60	30.60	27.50	24.50
290	300	62.40	57.90	53.50	49.60	45.70	42.20	38.90	35.70	32.70	29.60	26.60
300	310	65.50	61.00	56.50	52.30	48.40	44.60	41.20	37.80	34.80	31.70	28.70
310	320	68.60	64.10	59.60	55.10	51.10	47.30	43.50	40.10	36.90	33.80	30.80
320	330	71.70	67.20	62.70	58.20	53.80	50.00	46.10	42.40	39.10	35.90	32.90
330	340	74.80	70.30	65.80	61.30	56.90	52.70	48.80	44.90	41.40	38.10	35.00
340	350	78.30	73.40	68.90	64.40	60.00	55.50	51.50	47.60	43.70	40.40	37.10
350	360	81.80	76.80	72.00	67.50	63.10	58.60	54.20	50.30	46.40	42.70	39.40
360	370	85.30	80.30	75.30	70.60	66.20	61.70	57.20	53.00	49.10	45.20	41.70
370	380	88.80	83.80	78.80	73.70	69.30	64.80	60.30	55.90	51.80	47.90	44.00
380	390	92.30	87.30	82.30	77.20	72.40	67.90	63.40	59.00	54.50	50.60	46.70
390	400	95.80	90.80	85.80	80.70	75.70	71.00	66.50	62.10	57.60	53.30	49.40
400	410	99.30	94.30	89.30	84.20	79.20	74.10	69.60	65.20	60.70	56.20	52.10
410	420	102.80	97.80	92.80	87.70	82.70	77.60	72.70	68.30	63.80	59.30	54.80
420	430	106.30	101.30	96.30	91.20	86.20	81.10	76.10	71.40	66.90	62.40	57.90
430	440	109.80	104.80	99.80	94.70	89.70	84.60	79.60	74.50	70.00	65.50	61.00
440	450	113.30	108.30	103.30	98.20	93.20	88.10	83.10	78.00	73.10	68.60	64.10
450	460	116.80	111.80	106.80	101.70	96.70	91.60	86.60	81.50	76.50	71.70	67.20
460	470	120.30	115.30	110.30	105.20	100.20	95.10	90.10	85.00	80.00	74.90	70.30
470	480	123.80	118.80	113.80	108.70	103.70	98.60	93.60	88.50	83.50	78.40	73.40
480	490	127.30	122.30	117.30	112.20	107.20	102.10	97.10	92.00	87.00	81.90	76.90
		35 percent of the excess over $490 plus—										
$490 and over		129.10	124.00	119.00	114.00	108.90	103.90	98.80	93.80	88.70	83.70	78.60

Social Security Employee Tax Table—Continued

5.85 percent employee tax deductions

Wages		Tax to be withheld	Wages		Tax to be withheld	Wages		Tax to be withheld	Wages		Tax to be withheld
At least	But less than		At least	But less than		At least	But less than		At least	But less than	
$177.70	$177.87	$10.40	$188.81	$188.98	$11.05	$199.92	$200.09	$11.70	$211.03	$211.20	$12.35
177.87	178.04	10.41	188.98	189.15	11.06	200.09	200.26	11.71	211.20	211.37	12.36
178.04	178.21	10.42	189.15	189.32	11.07	200.26	200.43	11.72	211.37	211.54	12.37
178.21	178.38	10.43	189.32	189.49	11.08	200.43	200.60	11.73	211.54	211.71	12.38
178.38	178.55	10.44	189.49	189.66	11.09	200.60	200.77	11.74	211.71	211.89	12.39
178.55	178.72	10.45	189.66	189.83	11.10	200.77	200.95	11.75	211.89	212.06	12.40
178.72	178.89	10.46	189.83	190.00	11.11	200.95	201.12	11.76	212.06	212.23	12.41
178.89	179.06	10.47	190.00	190.18	11.12	201.12	201.29	11.77	212.23	212.40	12.42
179.06	179.24	10.48	190.18	190.35	11.13	201.29	201.46	11.78	212.40	212.57	12.43
179.24	179.41	10.49	190.35	190.52	11.14	201.46	201.63	11.79	212.57	212.74	12.44
179.41	179.58	10.50	190.52	190.69	11.15	201.63	201.80	11.80	212.74	212.91	12.45
179.58	179.75	10.51	190.69	190.86	11.16	201.80	201.97	11.81	212.91	213.08	12.46
179.75	179.92	10.52	190.86	191.03	11.17	201.97	202.14	11.82	213.08	213.25	12.47
179.92	180.09	10.53	191.03	191.20	11.18	202.14	202.31	11.83	213.25	213.42	12.48
180.09	180.26	10.54	191.20	191.37	11.19	202.31	202.48	11.84	213.42	213.59	12.49
180.26	180.43	10.55	191.37	191.54	11.20	202.48	202.65	11.85	213.59	213.77	12.50
180.43	180.60	10.56	191.54	191.71	11.21	202.65	202.83	11.86	213.77	213.94	12.51
180.60	180.77	10.57	191.71	191.89	11.22	202.83	203.00	11.87	213.94	214.11	12.52
180.77	180.95	10.58	191.89	192.06	11.23	203.00	203.17	11.88	214.11	214.28	12.53
180.95	181.12	10.59	192.06	192.23	11.24	203.17	203.34	11.89	214.28	214.45	12.54
181.12	181.29	10.60	192.23	192.40	11.25	203.34	203.51	11.90	214.45	214.62	12.55
181.29	181.46	10.61	192.40	192.57	11.26	203.51	203.68	11.91	214.62	214.79	12.56
181.46	181.63	10.62	192.57	192.74	11.27	203.68	203.85	11.92	214.79	214.96	12.57
181.63	181.80	10.63	192.74	192.91	11.28	203.85	204.02	11.93	214.96	215.13	12.58
181.80	181.97	10.64	192.91	193.08	11.29	204.02	204.19	11.94	215.13	215.30	12.59
181.97	182.14	10.65	193.08	193.25	11.30	204.19	204.36	11.95	215.30	215.48	12.60
182.14	182.31	10.66	193.25	193.42	11.31	204.36	204.53	11.96	215.48	215.65	12.61
182.31	182.48	10.67	193.42	193.59	11.32	204.53	204.71	11.97	215.65	215.82	12.62
182.48	182.65	10.68	193.59	193.77	11.33	204.71	204.88	11.98	215.82	215.99	12.63
182.65	182.83	10.69	193.77	193.94	11.34	204.88	205.05	11.99	215.99	216.16	12.64
182.83	183.00	10.70	193.94	194.11	11.35	205.05	205.22	12.00	216.16	216.33	12.65
183.00	183.17	10.71	194.11	194.28	11.36	205.22	205.39	12.01	216.33	216.50	12.66
183.17	183.34	10.72	194.28	194.45	11.37	205.39	205.56	12.02	216.50	216.67	12.67
183.34	183.51	10.73	194.45	194.62	11.38	205.56	205.73	12.03	216.67	216.84	12.68
183.51	183.68	10.74	194.62	194.79	11.39	205.73	205.90	12.04	216.84	217.01	12.69
183.68	183.85	10.75	194.79	194.96	11.40	205.90	206.07	12.05	217.01	217.18	12.70
183.85	184.02	10.76	194.96	195.13	11.41	206.07	206.24	12.06	217.18	217.36	12.71
184.02	184.19	10.77	195.13	195.30	11.42	206.24	206.42	12.07	217.36	217.53	12.72
184.19	184.36	10.78	195.30	195.48	11.43	206.42	206.59	12.08	217.53	217.70	12.73
184.36	184.53	10.79	195.48	195.65	11.44	206.59	206.76	12.09	217.70	217.87	12.74
184.53	184.71	10.80	195.65	195.82	11.45	206.76	206.93	12.10	217.87	218.04	12.75
184.71	184.88	10.81	195.82	195.99	11.46	206.93	207.10	12.11	218.04	218.21	12.76
184.88	185.05	10.82	195.99	196.16	11.47	207.10	207.27	12.12	218.21	218.38	12.77
185.05	185.22	10.83	196.16	196.33	11.48	207.27	207.44	12.13	218.38	218.55	12.78
185.22	185.39	10.84	196.33	196.50	11.49	207.44	207.61	12.14	218.55	218.72	12.79
185.39	185.56	10.85	196.50	196.67	11.50	207.61	207.78	12.15	218.72	218.89	12.80
185.56	185.73	10.86	196.67	196.84	11.51	207.78	207.95	12.16	218.89	219.06	12.81
185.73	185.90	10.87	196.84	197.01	11.52	207.95	208.12	12.17	219.06	219.24	12.82
185.90	186.07	10.88	197.01	197.18	11.53	208.12	208.30	12.18	219.24	219.41	12.83
186.07	186.24	10.89	197.18	197.36	11.54	208.30	208.47	12.19	219.41	219.58	12.84
186.24	186.42	10.90	197.36	197.53	11.55	208.47	208.64	12.20	219.58	219.75	12.85
186.42	186.59	10.91	197.53	197.70	11.56	208.64	208.81	12.21	219.75	219.92	12.86
186.59	186.76	10.92	197.70	197.87	11.57	208.81	208.98	12.22	219.92	220.09	12.87
186.76	186.93	10.93	197.87	198.04	11.58	208.98	209.15	12.23	220.09	220.26	12.88
186.93	187.10	10.94	198.04	198.21	11.59	209.15	209.32	12.24	220.26	220.43	12.89
187.10	187.27	10.95	198.21	198.38	11.60	209.32	209.49	12.25	220.43	220.60	12.90
187.27	187.44	10.96	198.38	198.55	11.61	209.49	209.66	12.26	220.60	220.77	12.91
187.44	187.61	10.97	198.55	198.72	11.62	209.66	209.83	12.27	220.77	220.95	12.92
187.61	187.78	10.98	198.72	198.89	11.63	209.83	210.00	12.28	220.95	221.12	12.93
187.78	187.95	10.99	198.89	199.06	11.64	210.00	210.18	12.29	221.12	221.29	12.94
187.95	188.12	11.00	199.06	199.24	11.65	210.18	210.35	12.30	221.29	221.46	12.95
188.12	188.30	11.01	199.24	199.41	11.66	210.35	210.52	12.31	221.46	221.63	12.96
188.30	188.47	11.02	199.41	199.58	11.67	210.52	210.69	12.32	221.63	221.80	12.97
188.47	188.64	11.03	199.58	199.75	11.68	210.69	210.86	12.33	221.80	221.97	12.98
188.64	188.81	11.04	199.75	199.92	11.69	210.86	211.03	12.34	221.97	222.14	12.99

MAKING OUT THE PAYCHECKS

Checks used for payroll usually have a double stub so one stub can be left in the checkbook and one can be given to the employee with his paycheck. The stubs show the hours worked, gross pay, the amount of each deduction, and the balance paid to the employee, which is called his net pay. After the stub is complete, the check is made out to the employee for his net pay.

2F. *Write out checks to Columbone and McClown using the information you have gathered in problems 2C through 2E. Make out the third check to Darnabee Smith, who has three exemptions, earns $172 for a regular 40-hour week, and worked 45 hours this week. Use tax tables provided.*

293

DATE ________ 19 ____

TO ________

FOR ________

BAL. FOR'D	105	00	TOTAL WAGES		
DEP.			SOCIAL SEC. TAX		
			U. S. INC. TAX		
			STATE INC. TAX		
TOTAL					
THIS CHECK			TOTAL DED.		
BALANCE			CHECK		

DETACH BEFORE CASHING CHECK

STATEMENT OF EARNINGS AND DEDUCTIONS FOR EMPLOYEE'S RECORD COVERING PAY PERIOD TO AND INCLUDING DATE SHOWN BELOW

DATE ________ 19 ____

TO ________

TOTAL WAGES		
SOCIAL SECURITY TAX		
WITHHOLDING U. S. INCOME TAX		
STATE INCOME TAX		
TOTAL DEDUCTIONS		
AMOUNT THIS CHECK		

293

________ 19 ____ 2-52/710

PAY TO THE ORDER OF ________ $ ________

________ DOLLARS

NATIONAL BOULEVARD BANK OF CHICAGO

SAMPLE-VOID
DELUXE CHECK PRINTERS, INC.

⑈000293⑈ ⑆0710⑉0052⑆ ⑈123456 7⑈

294

DATE ________ 19 ____

TO ________

FOR ________

BAL. FOR'D			TOTAL WAGES		
DEP.			SOCIAL SEC. TAX		
			U. S. INC. TAX		
			STATE INC. TAX		
TOTAL					
THIS CHECK			TOTAL DED.		
BALANCE			CHECK		

DETACH BEFORE CASHING CHECK

STATEMENT OF EARNINGS AND DEDUCTIONS FOR EMPLOYEE'S RECORD COVERING PAY PERIOD TO AND INCLUDING DATE SHOWN BELOW

DATE ________ 19 ____

TO ________

TOTAL WAGES		
SOCIAL SECURITY TAX		
WITHHOLDING U. S. INCOME TAX		
STATE INCOME TAX		
TOTAL DEDUCTIONS		
AMOUNT THIS CHECK		

294

________ 19 ____ 2-52/710

PAY TO THE ORDER OF ________ $ ________

________ DOLLARS

NATIONAL BOULEVARD BANK OF CHICAGO

SAMPLE-VOID
DELUXE CHECK PRINTERS, INC.

⑈000294⑈ ⑆0710⑉0052⑆ ⑈123456 7⑈

295

DATE ________ 19 ____

TO ________

FOR ________

BAL. FOR'D			TOTAL WAGES		
DEP.			SOCIAL SEC. TAX		
			U. S. INC. TAX		
			STATE INC. TAX		
TOTAL					
THIS CHECK			TOTAL DED.		
BALANCE			CHECK		

DETACH BEFORE CASHING CHECK

STATEMENT OF EARNINGS AND DEDUCTIONS FOR EMPLOYEE'S RECORD COVERING PAY PERIOD TO AND INCLUDING DATE SHOWN BELOW

DATE ________ 19 ____

TO ________

TOTAL WAGES		
SOCIAL SECURITY TAX		
WITHHOLDING U. S. INCOME TAX		
STATE INCOME TAX		
TOTAL DEDUCTIONS		
AMOUNT THIS CHECK		

295

________ 19 ____ 2-52/710

PAY TO THE ORDER OF ________ $ ________

________ DOLLARS

NATIONAL BOULEVARD BANK OF CHICAGO

SAMPLE-VOID
DELUXE CHECK PRINTERS, INC.

⑈000295⑈ ⑆0710⑉0052⑆ ⑈123456 7⑈

Payroll Records

There are two kinds of payroll records that are made out, or added to, at the same time the employee paychecks are being figured. One is the Total Payroll Record; the other is the Individual Employee's Earnings Record.

The Total Payroll Record shows the names, hours worked, gross pay, deductions, and net pay for all persons receiving checks on this payroll date. Thus, each Total Payroll Record sheet contains all of the information concerning one particular payroll. These sheets are kept in a payroll book, and a new page is usually started each time employees are paid.

The Individual Employee's Earnings Record sheets can be kept at the back of the same payroll book. Each employee has a separate sheet, showing his gross pay, deductions, and net pay for each payday during the year. The sheet also should show his total gross income from January first of this year through each payday. This is his yearly cumulative income, and it is necessary in order to know when to stop deducting from his wages for Social Security. When figuring employees' deductions, always check the Individual Employee's Earnings Record sheets to know whether an employee has already earned the maximum pay for Social Security deductions and therefore owes no more money for FICA until the first of next year.

2G. *If Columbone, McClown, and Smith are the only employees receiving checks on this payday, make out a Total Payroll Record sheet for this payroll of 1/28/76; and add data to the Individual Employee's Earnings Record sheets for each man.*

Total Payroll Record
Jane's Pond Detective Agency
Payroll for week ending 1/21/76

Name	Reg. Hours	O.T. Hours	Reg. Pay	O.T. Pay	Gross Pay	Fed. Inc. Tax	FICA	Net Pay
Columbone	40	1	180	6.75	186.75	30.80	10.92	145.03
McClown	40	2	200	10.00	210.00	37.10	12.29	160.61
Smith	40	0	172	0	172.00	22.60	10.06	139.34
Total			552	16.75	568.75	90.50	33.27	444.98

Total Payroll Record
Jane's Pond Detective Agency
Payroll for ______ ending __________

Name	Reg. Hours	O.T. Hours	Reg. Pay	O.T. Pay	Gross Pay	Fed. Inc. Tax	FICA	Net Pay

Individual Employee's Earnings Record

employee Columbone
number 007

Week Ending	Reg. Pay	O.T. Pay	Gross Pay	Cumulative Pay	Fed. Inc. Tax	FICA Tax	Net Pay
1-7-76	180	0	180.00	180.00	30.80	10.53	138.67
1-14-76	180	6.75	186.75	366.75	30.80	10.92	145.03
1-21-76	180	6.75	186.75	553.50	30.80	10.92	145.03

Individual Employee's Earnings Record

employee McClown
number 001

Week Ending	Reg. Pay	O.T. Pay	Gross Pay	Cumulative Pay	Fed. Inc. Tax	FICA Tax	Net Pay
1-7-76	200	0	200.00	200.00	35.00	11.70	153.30
1-14-76	200	0	200.00	400.00	35.00	11.70	153.30
1-21-76	200	10.00	210.00	610.00	37.10	12.29	160.61

Individual Employee's Earnings Record

employee Darnabee Smith
number 0013

Week Ending	Reg. Pay	O.T. Pay	Gross Pay	Cumulative Pay	Fed. Inc. Tax	FICA Tax	Net Pay
1-7-76	172	12.90	184.90	184.90	24.70	10.82	149.38
1-14-76	172	12.90	184.90	369.80	24.70	10.82	149.38
1-21-76	172	12.90	184.90	554.70	24.70	10.82	149.38

Paying Withheld Taxes to the Government

The city, state, and federal governments send forms to the employer to be used when paying the taxes withheld from the employee's paychecks. These forms show whether payment is to be made at the end of the month, at the end of each three-month period, or at the end of the year. The total amount that has been held out of each employee's paycheck and is now owed to the government by the employer can be found by checking the Individual Employee's Earnings Records. Add up the amount that has been deducted since payment was last made to the government. This is the amount owed.

If deductions had been made throughout the year for a city income (or payroll) tax, payable at the end of the year, the City Income Tax Deductions column of each employee's Individual Employee's Earnings Record would be totaled for the year. In early January of the following year, a check would be made out to the city for the total amount deducted from all of the company's employees for city income tax. When this check was mailed, the employer would no longer be liable (no longer owes) for city income tax because it would be paid.

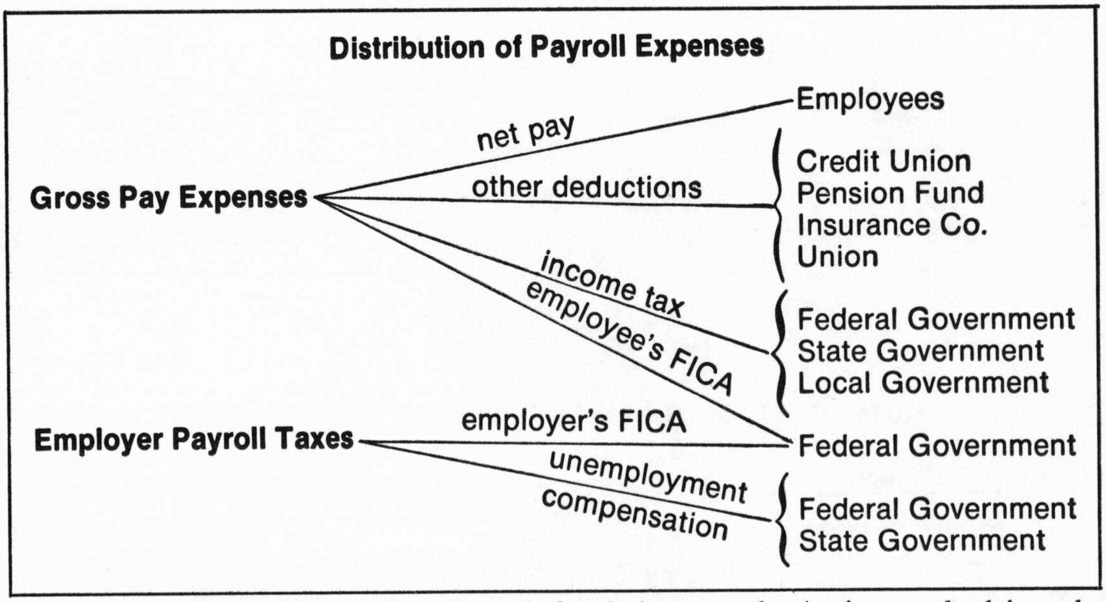

State income taxes usually are paid at the end of each three months. Again, one check is made out for the total withheld from all of the employees' paychecks during that quarter of the year. Then the employer is no longer liable for state income tax.

Federal income taxes are paid in the same check with the Social Security tax. Since Social Security is supported equally by both the employer and the employee, the employer must match the amount deducted from the employee's paycheck with his own funds. This is another expense to the employer, the expense of the employer's payroll taxes. Every time he hires another person, the employer has the expense of paying his salary plus the expense of matching his Social Security taxes. Using the Individual Employee's Earnings Record, the ferderal income tax deductions from all employee paychecks during the month are added. Then the amounts deducted for Social Security payments (or FICA) during the month are added and doubled. (The first half is the payment made by the employees out of their paychecks. The second half is the amount the employer is contributing to match the employees' payments.) The grand total of both the federal income tax deductions and double the FICA tax deductions for all employees is the amount owed to the government this month.

If this total amount owed for the month is over $100, it must be paid early each month for the past month's payrolls. A form called a Federal Tax Deposit form is filled out, showing the amount to be paid. It is mailed, along with a check, to a bank in your area which is qualified to receive these payments. If you have not been notified which bank to send your payments to, call the Internal Revenue Service.

2H. Please figure the amount owed to the Federal Internal Revenue Service for the Jane's Pond Detective Agency payrolls for the month of January. (Use the Individual Employee's Earnings Records from 2G.) Then make out the check and the Federal Tax Deposit form.

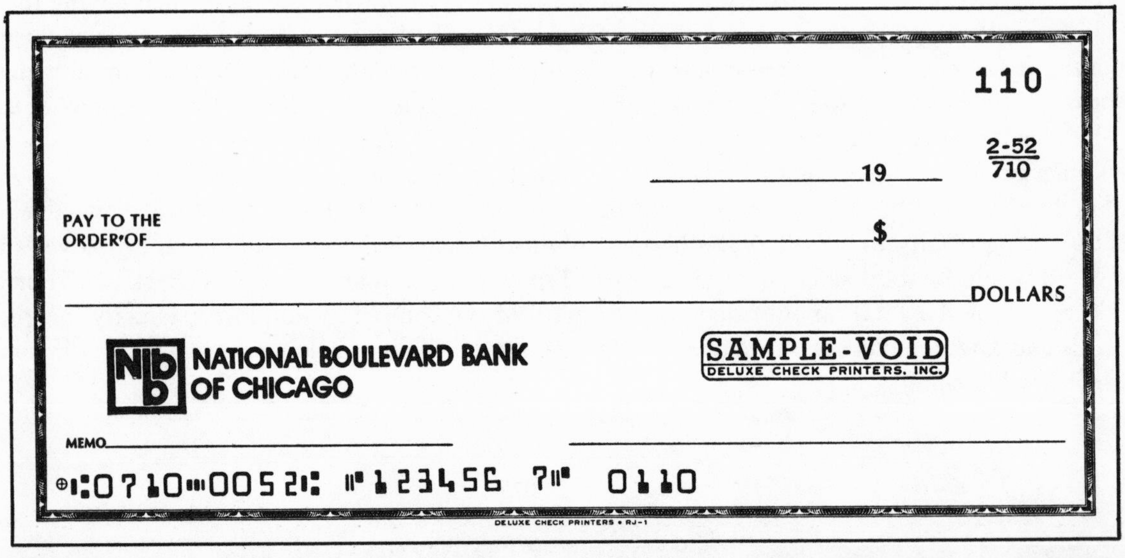

FEDERA . TAX DEPOSIT

NAME OF BANK: *National Boulevard*

AMOUNT OF DEPOSIT — DOLLARS | CENTS

FORM AND TAX CLASS
- 501 WITHHELD INCOME AND FICA TAXES
- 503 CORPO: ` ON INCO. E TAXES
- 504 EXCISE TAXES
- 507 RAII OAD RETIREMENT TAXES
- 508 UNE. PLOYMENT TAXES
- 511 AGRICULTURAL WORKERS 'ICA TAXES AND VOLUNTARILY .ITHHELD INCOME TAX
- 512 TAX WITHHELD AT SOURCE ON NONRESIDEN ALIENS, FOR-EIGN CORPO: ATIONS, TAX-FREE COVENANT BONDS

DO NOT USE T I S FORM TO DEPOSIT TO A TAX C.ASS OT IER THAN II DICATED.

IRS Return

Employer Identification Number: *23-027123*

March 1976
Tax Period Ending

Bank Name/Date Stamp

Verify preprinted data; if incorrect, see instructions on reverse.
Enter amount of deposit and name of bank where deposited in space above.

Do Not Write In Space Below

DEPARTMENT OF THE TREASURY . FISCAL SERVICE
Bureau of Government Financial Operations . FTD Form Rev. Jan. 1976

If the total amount owed for the month's federal income tax plus FICA is less than $100 it is paid at the end of every three months, instead of monthly; and the Federal Tax Deposit form is not needed.

Whether payment is made monthly or quarterly, an Employer's Quarterly Federal Tax Return is filled out at the end of every three months, showing the amounts deducted for each individual employee's income tax, plus the total Social Security withheld and doubled (for the employer's share). If payment is made quarterly, this return shows the amount owed, and a check is sent in with the return. If payment was sent in monthly, the total tax figured on this report should be the same as the amount of the three monthly Federal Tax Deposit forms added together, and this Employer's Quarterly Federal Tax Return (shown below and following) is just to show the federal government how the amounts paid were figured.

SCHEDULE B—RECORD OF FEDERAL TAX DEPOSITS

Deposit period ending:		A. Tax liability for period	B. Amount deposited	C. Date of deposit
Overpayment from previous quarter				
First month of quarter	1st through 7th day	$ 276.50		
	8th through 15th day	274.56		
	16th through 22d day	285.86		
	23d through last day	558.64	$1395.56	7-14-76
1 First month total	1	1395.56		
Second month of quarter	1st through 7th day	275.60		
	8th through 15th day	260.54		
	16th through 22d day	242.88		
	23d through last day	257.26	1036.28	8-14-76
2 Second month total	2	1036.28		
Third month of quarter	1st through 7th day	302.08		
	8th through 15th day	264.82		
	16th through 22d day	261.74		
	23d through last day	525.15	1353.79	9-15-76
3 Third month total	3	1353.79		
4 Total for quarter (total of items 1, 2, and 3)		$ 3785.63	$3785.63	
5 Final deposit made for quarter. (Enter zero if the final deposit made for the quarter is included in item 4.)			-0-	
6 Total deposits for quarter (total of items 4 and 5)—enter here and in item 20, page 1			$3785.63	

☆ U.S. GOVERNMENT PRINTING OFFICE : 1975—O-591-482

Form 941 (Rev. Oct. 1975) Department of the Treasury Internal Revenue Service

Employer's Quarterly Federal Tax Return

SSA Use Only

F ☐ 2 ☐ U ☐ E ☐
S ☐ 1 ☐ L ☐ T ☐
X ☐ 0 ☐ V ☐ A ☐

Schedule A—Quarterly Report of Wages Taxable under the Federal Insurance Contributions Act—FOR SOCIAL SECURITY

List for each nonagricultural employee the WAGES taxable under the FICA which were paid during the quarter. If you pay an employee more than $14,100 in a calendar year, report only the first $14,100 of such wages. In the case of "Tip Income," see Instructions on page 4. IF WAGES WERE NOT TAXABLE UNDER THE FICA, MAKE NO ENTRIES IN ITEMS 1 THROUGH 9 AND 14 THROUGH 18.

1. Total pages of this return including this page and any pages of Form 941a ▶ 1

2. Total number of employees listed ▶ 10

3. (First quarter only) Number of employees (except household) employed in the pay period including March 12th ▶

4. EMPLOYEE'S SOCIAL SECURITY NUMBER (000 00 0000)	5. NAME OF EMPLOYEE (Please type or print)	6. TAXABLE FICA WAGES Paid to Employee in Quarter (Before deductions) Dollars Cents	7. TAXABLE TIPS REPORTED (See page 4) Dollars Cents
495-33-9056	Tom Katz	$ 2137.00	
376-42-2459	Jim Lee	1440.00	
352-12-3496	Fred C. Dohr	1350.00	
273-66-4225	John Marshall	2806.03	
255-59-1239	June White	211.25	
266-54-9696	S.B. Brown	652.50	
413-31-8671	Joyce Ross	70.00	
230-10-6817	Christy Kein	2548.05	
239-52-8619	Carol Dwyer	2800.00	
387-80-5009	R.A. Kuhn	2100.00	

If you need more space for listing employees, use Schedule A continuation sheets, Form 941a.

Totals for this page—Wage total in column 6 and tip total in column 7 ⟶ $16114.83

8. TOTAL WAGES TAXABLE UNDER FICA PAID DURING QUARTER. $ $16114.83

(Total of column 6 on this page and continuation sheets.) Enter here and in item 14 below.

9. TOTAL TAXABLE TIPS REPORTED UNDER FICA DURING QUARTER. $ -0-

(Total of column 7 on this page and continuation sheets.) Enter here and in item 15 below. (If no tips reported, write "None.")

Employer's name, address, employer identification number, and calendar quarter. (If not correct, please change)

Name (as distinguished from trade name) | Date quarter ended

Trade name, if any: Recordland Corp. | Employer Identification No.: 35-100598

Address and ZIP code: 45 Stereo St., Chicago, IL 53601

Entries must be made both above and below this line; if address different from previous return check here ☐

Name (as distinguished from trade name) | Date quarter ended

Trade name, if any: Recordland Corp | Employer Identification No.: 35-100598

Address and ZIP code: 45 Stereo St., Chicago, IL 53601

T | FP
FF | I
FD | TOT

10. Total Wages And Tips Subject To Withholding Plus Other Compensation →	$16114	83
11. Amount Of Income Tax Withheld From Wages, Tips, Annuities, etc. (See instructions)	1900	20
12. Adjustment For Preceding Quarters Of Calendar Year	-0-	
13. Adjusted Total Of Income Tax Withheld →	1900	20
14. Taxable FICA Wages Paid (Item 8) . . $ 16,114.83 multiplied by 11.7% = TAX	1885	43
15. Taxable Tips Reported (Item 9) . . $ .... multiplied by 5.85% = TAX	-0-	
16. Total FICA Taxes (Item 14 plus Item 15) →	1885	43
17. Adjustment (See instructions)	-0-	
18. Adjusted Total Of FICA Taxes →	1885	43
19. Total Taxes (Item 13 plus Item 18)	3785	63
20. TOTAL DEPOSITS FOR QUARTER (INCLUDING FINAL DEPOSIT MADE FOR QUARTER) AND OVERPAYMENT FROM PREVIOUS QUARTER LISTED IN SCHEDULE B (See instructions on page 4)	3785	63
Note: If undeposited taxes at the end of the quarter are $200 or more, the full amount must be deposited with an authorized commercial bank or a Federal Reserve bank. This deposit must be entered in Schedule B and included in item 20.		
21. Undeposited Taxes Due (Item 19 Less Item 20—This Should Be Less Than $200). Pay To Internal Revenue Service And Enter Here →	-0-	

22. If Item 20 Is More Than Item 19, Enter Excess Here ▶ $ And Check If You Want It ☐ Applied To Next Return, Or ☐ Refunded.

23. If not liable for returns in the future write **"FINAL"** (See instructions) ▶ Date final wages paid ▶

Under penalties of perjury, I declare that I have examined this return, including accompanying schedules and statements, and to the best of my knowledge and belief it is true, correct and complete.

Date Jan. 2, 1977 Signature John Marshall Title (Owner, etc) Owner

Form 941 (10-75)

Making out the W-2 Forms

Soon after the end of the year (before January 31) the employer must make out a Wage and Tax Statement called a W-2 form for each person who was employed by his firm at any time during the year. This shows the employee's gross salary for the year and his total deductions for FICA (or Social Security) and for income tax. One copy of the form is kept on file by the employer. One copy is sent to the District Director of Internal Revenue, another copy goes to the state tax department, and the remaining copies are mailed to the employees or former employees.

For Official Use Only

Wage and Tax Statement 1975

23-021123
Jane's Pond Detective Agency
101 Theive's Alley
Los Angeles, California 90812

Type or print EMPLOYER'S name, address, ZIP code and Federal identifying number.

Copy A For Internal Revenue Service Center

Employer's State identifying number: 23-021123-001

21 ☐

Employee's social security number	1 Federal income tax withheld	2 Wages, tips, and other compensation	3 FICA employee tax withheld	4 Total FICA wages
555-33-1115	1510.00	9880.00	577.98	9880.00

Type or print Employee's name, address, and ZIP code below. (Name must aline with arrow)			
Name ▶ Darnabee Smith, 100 Snoop Street, Los Angeles, California 90812	5 Was employee covered by a qualified pension plan, etc.? no	6 *	7 *
	8 State or local tax withheld 301.00	9 State or local wages 9880.00	10 State or locality state
	11 State or local tax withheld 98.80	12 State or local wages 9880.00	13 State or locality city

* See instructions on back of Copy D

Form W–2 See instructions on Form W–3 and back of Copy D Department of the Treasury—Internal Revenue Service ☆ GPO: 1975 — 0-575-022 EI-36-2441915

Unemployment Compensation

Unemployment compensation is a fund paid into by employers only (in most states), which is used by workers who have been laid off due to lack of work and who are seeking other employment.

The federal government requires employers in all states of the nation to pay not less than 3.2% of the total gross earnings that have been paid to all of their employees to either the state or federal governments for the unemployment compensation fund. These payments are another employer's payroll tax expense.

Unemployment compensation is administered by the state governments, but the percentages that they charge vary among the states. The state government will send you a form showing the percentage charged by your state. Each three months one of these forms is to be filled out and mailed with a check. The total gross payroll for the three months is multiplied by the percent used in your state in order to determine the amount of the check.

If your state charges less than 3.2% for unemployment compensation, the remainder is paid to the federal government at the end of the year.

In the same way that all payments to Social Security for the year stop when an employee has earned $15,300 in 1976, the employer's payments to state and federal unemployment compensation for a particular employee stop when that employee has earned $4,200 since January first of this year; and the payments don't begin again until the next year. The Individual Employee's Earnings Record provides this information on total gross earnings to date.

21. *Your state charges 2.7% for unemployment compensation. If Columbone earned $2,340 each quarter of this year and McClown earned $2,600, how much unemployment compensation would you have paid to the state government at the end of the first three months? How much would you have to pay to the federal government for unemployment compensation at the end of the year?*

Payroll Time Schedule

Employee Hired

Fill out W-4

Prior to Payday

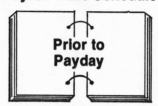

Gather Payroll Information
Figure Payroll Information

Payday

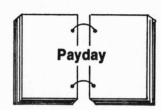

Make Out Paychecks
Record Payroll

Payroll Tax Due Dates

3rd or 15th of Month

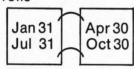

Federal Tax Deposit tickets paid at bank for previous month's payrolls*

Jan 31 / Jul 31 — Apr 30 / Oct 30

1) 941 forms mailed to Fed. govt.
2) State withholding income tax paid for previous quarter (in most states)
3) State unemployment compensation paid for previous quarter
4) Fed. unemployment compensation paid if owe $100 or more

Jan 31

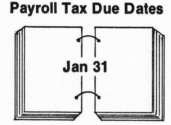

1) W-2 forms sent to employees
2) Fed. 940 form reconciling previous year's Fed. unemployment compensation payments sent with check for balance due
3) Forms sent to state reconciling state unemployment compensation payments for previous year
4) Some states require that their copy of W-2s + form reconciling state income tax paid last year be sent by this date

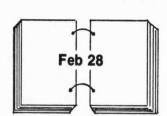

Feb 28

1) W-3 form sent to Fed. government along with their copy of W-2s
2) Some states require that their copy of W-2s + form reconciling state income tax paid last year be sent by this date

*If amount owed exceeds $2,000, see instructions on back of Employer's Federal Quarterly Tax Return.

PUTTING IT ALL TOGETHER

Chapter Summary Problems

A. WHAT IS IT?

Please fill in the blanks with the correct words from those listed below:

time card	W-2 form
Total Payroll Record	W-4 form
gross pay	deductions
net pay	overtime
FICA	unemployment compensation
employer's payroll tax expense	
Individual Employee's Earnings Record	
Federal Tax Deposit form	
federal unemployment compensation	
Employer's Quarterly Federal Tax Return	

1. Generally time and a half is the pay rate for ______________.
2. The total pay, including any deduction, is called the ______________.
3. At the end of the year, each person who was employed during the past year is sent a ______________, which shows total earnings and taxes withheld during the year.
4. A ______________ is sent to the bank with a check for the total amount owed for FICA and federal income tax; however, this form is not needed if the amount is less than $100.
5. ______________ is a tax paid into by both the employer and employee.
6. ______________ is collected from the employer by the state in order to set up a fund paid to employees who have been laid off and are seeking other employment.
7. Hourly workers usually show how many hours they have worked by using a sign-in sheet or a ______________.
8. The ______________ shows how many exemptions an employee claims and is used to figure his federal income tax deductions.
9. An employee's gross pay, deductions, and net pay for each payday, plus his total earnings from the beginning of the year through each payday, are shown on the ______________.
10. ______________ is a tax paid to the federal government by employers whenever the percentage their state collects for this tax is less than 3.2% of the employee's paychecks.
11. A new ______________ sheet is started for each payroll date and shows a complete record of that payroll.
12. All amounts withheld from the employee's paychecks are called ______________.
13. The employee receives his ______________ in his paycheck.
14. The ______________ is sent in every three months so the government can make certain that the Federal Tax Deposit forms were figured correctly.
15. Paying his part of the FICA plus all of the unemployment compensation is the ______________.

B. USING WHAT YOU KNOW

You have been asked to take care of the payroll for the newly formed Holiday Party Service. The employer number that has been assigned is 362436. Miss Val N. Tyne, Social Security number 395–25–1195, is being paid $4.70 per hour for a 40-hour week; she claims one exemption. Mr. Hal O. Whean, Social Security number 457–22–7515, is being paid $4.00 per hour for a 40-hour week; he claims one exemption. The policy of the company is to deduct from an employee's pay if he is over five minutes late coming to work or five minutes early leaving work. Time and a half is paid for all hours worked over 40. All overtime for both employees has been approved. Your city collects a payroll tax of 1% of the total gross income, so this should be deducted from the paychecks in addition to the federal income tax and FICA. Use the tables shown in the chapter.

Fill out the correct forms and checks for each of the following:

1. Dec. 10—Make out the weekly paychecks and the payroll records, using the sign-in sheets.
2. Dec. 17—Do the necessary work to take care of this week's payroll.
3. Dec. 24—Take care of this payroll.
4. Dec. 31—Make out the checks and records for this week's payroll.
5. Dec. 31—Make out the W-2 forms.
6. Jan. 3—Write a check to your city for the payment of the city payroll tax for last year.
7. Jan. 3—Take care of the payment of the Federal Tax Deposit form.
8. Jan. 3—Make out the Employer's Quarterly Tax Return.

Sign-In Sheet for December, 1976

Week		Miss Tyne						Mr. Whean					
Ending		In	Out	In	Out	In	Out	In	Out	In	Out	In	Out
12-10	M	8	12	1	5			8	12	1	5		
	T	8:30	12	1	5			8	12	1	5		
	W	8	12	1	5			8	12	1	5:30	7	9
	T	8	12	1	5			8	12	1	5		
	F	8	12	1	4			8	12	1	6		
12-17	M	8	12	1	5:30			8	12	1	5		
	T	8	12	1	5			8	12	1	5	7	8
	W	8	12	1	5	7	8	8	12	1	5	7	9
	T	8	12	1	5:30			8	12	1	5	7	8
	F	8	12	1	5:30			8	12	1	6	8	10
12-24	M	8	12	1	5	7	8	8	12	1	5	7	8
	T	8	12	1	5			8	1	2	6	8	10
	W	8	12	1	6:30			8	12	1	5	7	8
	T	8	12	1	6			8	12	1	5	8	9
	F	8	12	1	5	7	8	8	12	1	5	7	8
12-31	M	8	1	2	6			8	12	1	5:30		
	T	8	12	1	5			8	12:30	1	5		
	W	8	12	1	5	7	8	8	12	1	5	8	9
	T	8	12	1	5	7	9	8	12	1	5	7	9
	F	8	12	got afternoon off with pay				8	12	got afternoon off with pay			

Individual Employee's Earnings Record

Name ______________________

week ending	reg. pay	o.t. pay	gross pay	cumulative pay	Fed. inc. tax	FICA tax	city tax	net pay
Total								

296

DATE ______________________ 19____

TO ______________________

FOR ______________________

BAL. FOR'D	2298	33
DEP.		
DEP.		
TOTAL		
THIS CHECK		
BALANCE		

TOTAL WAGES		
SOCIAL SEC. TAX		
U. S. INC. TAX		
STATE INC. TAX		
TOTAL DED.		
CHECK		

DETACH BEFORE CASHING CHECK

STATEMENT OF EARNINGS AND DEDUCTIONS FOR EMPLOYEE'S RECORD COVERING PAY PERIOD TO AND INCLUDING DATE SHOWN BELOW

DATE ______________________ 19____

TO ______________________

TOTAL WAGES		
SOCIAL SECURITY TAX		
WITHHOLDING U. S. INCOME TAX		
STATE INCOME TAX		
TOTAL DEDUCTIONS		
AMOUNT THIS CHECK		

297

DATE ______________________ 19____

TO ______________________

FOR ______________________

BAL. FOR'D		
DEP.		
DEP.		
TOTAL		
THIS CHECK		
BALANCE		

TOTAL WAGES		
SOCIAL SEC. TAX		
U. S. INC. TAX		
STATE INC. TAX		
TOTAL DED.		
CHECK		

DETACH BEFORE CASHING CHECK

STATEMENT OF EARNINGS AND DEDUCTIONS FOR EMPLOYEE'S RECORD COVERING PAY PERIOD TO AND INCLUDING DATE SHOWN BELOW

DATE ______________________ 19____

TO ______________________

TOTAL WAGES		
SOCIAL SECURITY TAX		
WITHHOLDING U. S. INCOME TAX		
STATE INCOME TAX		
TOTAL DEDUCTIONS		
AMOUNT THIS CHECK		

Individual Employee's Earnings Record

Name ______________________

week ending	reg. pay	o.t. pay	gross pay	cumulative pay	Fed. inc. tax	FICA tax	city tax	net pay
Total								

296

________________ 19____ 2-52/710

PAY TO THE ORDER OF ____________________________ $________

PAYROLL ____________________________ DOLLARS

NATIONAL BOULEVARD BANK OF CHICAGO

SAMPLE-VOID
DELUXE CHECK PRINTERS, INC.

⑈000296⑈ ⑆0710⑉0052⑆ ⑈123456 7⑈

DELUXE CHECK PRINTERS PS-3

297

________________ 19____ 2-52/710

PAY TO THE ORDER OF ____________________________ $________

PAYROLL ____________________________ DOLLARS

NATIONAL BOULEVARD BANK OF CHICAGO

SAMPLE-VOID
DELUXE CHECK PRINTERS, INC.

⑈000297⑈ ⑆0710⑉0052⑆ ⑈123456 7⑈

DELUXE CHECK PRINTERS PS-3

298

DATE ____________________ 19____

TO ____________________

FOR ____________________

BAL. FOR'D		
DEP.		
TOTAL		
THIS CHECK		
BALANCE		

TOTAL WAGES		
SOCIAL SEC. TAX		
U. S. INC. TAX		
STATE INC. TAX		
TOTAL DED.		
CHECK		

DETACH BEFORE CASHING CHECK

STATEMENT OF EARNINGS AND DEDUCTIONS FOR EMPLOYEE'S RECORD COVERING PAY PERIOD TO AND INCLUDING DATE SHOWN BELOW

DATE ____________________ 19____

TO ____________________

TOTAL WAGES		
SOCIAL SECURITY TAX		
WITHHOLDING U. S. INCOME TAX		
STATE INCOME TAX		
TOTAL DEDUCTIONS		
AMOUNT THIS CHECK		

299

DATE ____________________ 19____

TO ____________________

FOR ____________________

BAL. FOR'D		
DEP.		
TOTAL		
THIS CHECK		
BALANCE		

TOTAL WAGES		
SOCIAL SEC. TAX		
U. S. INC. TAX		
STATE INC. TAX		
TOTAL DED.		
CHECK		

DETACH BEFORE CASHING CHECK

STATEMENT OF EARNINGS AND DEDUCTIONS FOR EMPLOYEE'S RECORD COVERING PAY PERIOD TO AND INCLUDING DATE SHOWN BELOW

DATE ____________________ 19____

TO ____________________

TOTAL WAGES		
SOCIAL SECURITY TAX		
WITHHOLDING U. S. INCOME TAX		
STATE INCOME TAX		
TOTAL DEDUCTIONS		
AMOUNT THIS CHECK		

298

19___ 2-52/710

PAY TO THE ORDER OF ______________________ $______

PAYROLL

______________________ DOLLARS

NATIONAL BOULEVARD BANK OF CHICAGO

SAMPLE-VOID
DELUXE CHECK PRINTERS, INC.

⑈000298⑈ ⑆0710⑉0052⑆ ⑈123456 7⑈

DELUXE CHECK PRINTERS PS-3

299

19___ 2-52/710

PAY TO THE ORDER OF ______________________ $______

PAYROLL

______________________ DOLLARS

NATIONAL BOULEVARD BANK OF CHICAGO

SAMPLE-VOID
DELUXE CHECK PRINTERS, INC.

⑈000299⑈ ⑆0710⑉0052⑆ ⑈123456 7⑈

DELUXE CHECK PRINTERS PS-3

300

DATE ____________ 19____

TO ____________

FOR ____________

BAL. FOR'D		
DEP.		
TOTAL		
THIS CHECK		
BALANCE		

TOTAL WAGES		
SOCIAL SEC. TAX		
U. S. INC. TAX		
STATE INC. TAX		
TOTAL DED.		
CHECK		

DETACH BEFORE CASHING CHECK

STATEMENT OF EARNINGS AND DEDUCTIONS FOR EMPLOYEE'S RECORD COVERING PAY PERIOD TO AND INCLUDING DATE SHOWN BELOW

DATE ____________ 19____

TO ____________

TOTAL WAGES		
SOCIAL SECURITY TAX		
WITHHOLDING U. S. INCOME TAX		
STATE INCOME TAX		
TOTAL DEDUCTIONS		
AMOUNT THIS CHECK		

301

DATE ____________ 19____

TO ____________

FOR ____________

BAL. FOR'D		
DEP.		
TOTAL		
THIS CHECK		
BALANCE		

TOTAL WAGES		
SOCIAL SEC. TAX		
U. S. INC. TAX		
STATE INC. TAX		
TOTAL DED.		
CHECK		

DETACH BEFORE CASHING CHECK

STATEMENT OF EARNINGS AND DEDUCTIONS FOR EMPLOYEE'S RECORD COVERING PAY PERIOD TO AND INCLUDING DATE SHOWN BELOW

DATE ____________ 19____

TO ____________

TOTAL WAGES		
SOCIAL SECURITY TAX		
WITHHOLDING U. S. INCOME TAX		
STATE INCOME TAX		
TOTAL DEDUCTIONS		
AMOUNT THIS CHECK		

300

________________19____ 2-52/710

PAY TO THE ORDER OF____ $__________

PAYROLL

____ DOLLARS

NATIONAL BOULEVARD BANK
OF CHICAGO

SAMPLE-VOID
DELUXE CHECK PRINTERS, INC.

000300 07100052 123456 7

DELUXE CHECK PRINTERS PS-3

301

________________19____ 2-52/710

PAY TO THE ORDER OF____ $__________

PAYROLL

____ DOLLARS

NATIONAL BOULEVARD BANK
OF CHICAGO

SAMPLE-VOID
DELUXE CHECK PRINTERS, INC.

000301 07100052 123456 7

DELUXE CHECK PRINTERS PS-3

302

DATE ________________ 19____

TO ________________

FOR ________________

BAL. FOR'D		
DEP.		
TOTAL		
THIS CHECK		
BALANCE		

TOTAL WAGES		
SOCIAL SEC. TAX		
U. S. INC. TAX		
STATE INC. TAX		
TOTAL DED.		
CHECK		

DETACH BEFORE CASHING CHECK

STATEMENT OF EARNINGS AND DEDUCTIONS FOR EMPLOYEE'S RECORD COVERING PAY PERIOD TO AND INCLUDING DATE SHOWN BELOW

DATE ________________ 19____

TO ________________

TOTAL WAGES		
SOCIAL SECURITY TAX		
WITHHOLDING U. S. INCOME TAX		
STATE INCOME TAX		
TOTAL DEDUCTIONS		
AMOUNT THIS CHECK		

303

DATE ________________ 19____

TO ________________

FOR ________________

BAL. FOR'D		
DEP.		
TOTAL		
THIS CHECK		
BALANCE		

TOTAL WAGES		
SOCIAL SEC. TAX		
U. S. INC. TAX		
STATE INC. TAX		
TOTAL DED.		
CHECK		

DETACH BEFORE CASHING CHECK

STATEMENT OF EARNINGS AND DEDUCTIONS FOR EMPLOYEE'S RECORD COVERING PAY PERIOD TO AND INCLUDING DATE SHOWN BELOW

DATE ________________ 19____

TO ________________

TOTAL WAGES		
SOCIAL SECURITY TAX		
WITHHOLDING U. S. INCOME TAX		
STATE INCOME TAX		
TOTAL DEDUCTIONS		
AMOUNT THIS CHECK		

302

19____ 2-52/710

PAY TO THE ORDER OF ____________________ $________

PAYROLL

____________________ DOLLARS

NATIONAL BOULEVARD BANK OF CHICAGO

SAMPLE-VOID
DELUXE CHECK PRINTERS, INC.

⑈000302⑈ ⑆0710⑉0052⑆ ⑈123456 7⑈

DELUXE CHECK PRINTERS PS-3

303

19____ 2-52/710

PAY TO THE ORDER OF ____________________ $________

PAYROLL

____________________ DOLLARS

NATIONAL BOULEVARD BANK OF CHICAGO

SAMPLE-VOID
DELUXE CHECK PRINTERS, INC.

⑈000303⑈ ⑆0710⑉0052⑆ ⑈123456 7⑈

DELUXE CHECK PRINTERS PS-3

Total Payroll Record
Holiday Party Service
Payroll for week ending ________

Name	Reg. Hours	O.T. Hours	Reg. Pay	O.T. Pay	Gross Pay	Fed. Inc. Tax	FICA Tax	City Tax	Net Pay
Total									

Total Payroll Record
Holiday Party Service
Payroll for week ending ________

Name	Reg. Hours	O.T. Hours	Reg. Pay	O.T. Pay	Gross Pay	Fed. Inc. Tax	FICA Tax	City Tax	Net Pay
Total									

Total Payroll Record
Holiday Party Service
Payroll for week ending ________

Name	Reg. Hours	O.T. Hours	Reg. Pay	O.T. Pay	Gross Pay	Fed. Inc. Tax	FICA Tax	City Tax	Net Pay
Total									

Total Payroll Record
Holiday Party Service
Payroll for week ending ________

Name	Reg. Hours	O.T. Hours	Reg. Pay	O.T. Pay	Gross Pay	Fed. Inc. Tax	FICA Tax	City Tax	Net Pay
Total									

For Official Use Only

Wage and Tax Statement 1975

Type or print EMPLOYER'S name, address, ZIP code and Federal identifying number.

Copy A For Internal Revenue Service Center

Employer's State identifying number

21 ☐

Employee's social security number	1 Federal income tax withheld	2 Wages, tips, and other compensation	3 FICA employee tax withheld	4 Total FICA wages

Type or print Employee's name, address, and ZIP code below. (Name must aline with arrow)			
Name ▶	5 Was employee covered by a qualified pension plan, etc.?	6 *	7 *
	8 State or local tax withheld	9 State or local wages	10 State or locality
	11 State or local tax withheld	12 State or local wages	13 State or locality

* See instructions on back of Copy D

Form W–2 See instructions on Form W–3 and back of Copy D

Department of the Treasury—Internal Revenue Service
☆ GPO: 1975 — O-575-022 EI-36-2441915

For Official Use Only

Wage and Tax Statement 1975

Type or print EMPLOYER'S name, address, ZIP code and Federal identifying number.

Copy A For Internal Revenue Service Center

Employer's State identifying number

21 ☐

Employee's social security number | 1 Federal income tax withheld | 2 Wages, tips, and other compensation | 3 FICA employee tax withheld | 4 Total FICA wages

Type or print Employee's name, address, and ZIP code below. (Name must aline with arrow)

Name ▶ | 5 Was employee covered by a qualified pension plan, etc.? | 6 * | 7 *

8 State or local tax withheld | 9 State or local wages | 10 State or locality

11 State or local tax withheld | 12 State or local wages | 13 State or locality

* See instructions on back of Copy D

Form W–2 See instructions on Form W–3 and back of Copy D

Department of the Treasury—Internal Revenue Service
☆ GPO: 1975 — O-575-022 EI-36-2441915

111

2-52
710

19____

PAY TO THE
ORDER OF________________________________ $________

____ DOLLARS

NATIONAL BOULEVARD BANK
OF CHICAGO

SAMPLE-VOID
DELUXE CHECK PRINTERS, INC.

MEMO________________ ____________________

⑆0710⑉0052⑆ ⑈123456 7⑈ 0111

DELUXE CHECK PRINTERS • RJ-1

FEDERA . TAX
DEPOSIT

DEPARTMENT OF THE TREASURY - FISCAL SERVICE
Bureau of Government Financial Operations - FTD Form Rev. Jan. 1976

FORM AND TAX CLASS
501 WITHHELD INCOME AND FICA TAXES
503 CORPO. \ ON INCO. E TAXES
504 EXCISE TAXES
507 RAII OAD RETIREMENT TAXES
508 UNE. PLOYMENT TAXES
511 AGRICULTURAL WORKERS' TCA TAXES AND VOLUNTARILY .ITHHELD INCOME TAX
512 TAX WITHHELD AT SOURCE ON NONRESIDEI ALIENS, FOREIGN CORPO. ATIONS, TAX-FREE COVENANT BONDS

DO NOT USE T I S FORM TO DEPOSIT TO A TAX C .ASS OT IER THAN I! - DICATED.

NAME OF BANK

AMOUNT OF DEPOSIT
DOLLARS | CENTS

IRS Return

Employer Identification Number

Tax Period Ending

verify preprinted data; if incorrect, see instructions on reverse.
amount of deposit and name of bank where deposited in space above.

Bank Name/Date Stamp

Do Not Write In Space Below

112

2-52
710

19____

PAY TO THE
ORDER OF________________________________ $________

____ DOLLARS

NATIONAL BOULEVARD BANK
OF CHICAGO

SAMPLE-VOID
DELUXE CHECK PRINTERS, INC.

MEMO________________ ____________________

⑆0710⑉0052⑆ ⑈123456 7⑈ 0112

DELUXE CHECK PRINTERS • RJ-1

Form 941 (Rev. Oct. 1975) Department of the Treasury Internal Revenue Service

Employer's Quarterly Federal Tax Return

Schedule A—Quarterly Report of Wages Taxable under the Federal Insurance Contributions Act—FOR SOCIAL SECURITY

List for each nonagricultural employee the WAGES taxable under the FICA which were paid during the quarter. If you pay an employee more than $14,100 in a calendar year, report only the first $14,100 of such wages. In the case of "Tip Income," see Instructions on page 4. IF WAGES WERE NOT TAXABLE UNDER THE FICA, MAKE NO ENTRIES IN ITEMS 1 THROUGH 9 AND 14 THROUGH 18.

SSA Use Only

F ☐	2 ☐	U ☐	E ☐
S ☐	1 ☐	L ☐	T ☐
X ☐	0 ☐	V ☐	A ☐

1. Total pages of this return including this page and any pages of Form 941a ▶
2. Total number of employees listed ▶
3. (First quarter only) Number of employees (except household) employed in the pay period including March 12th ▶

4. EMPLOYEE'S SOCIAL SECURITY NUMBER 000 00 0000	5. NAME OF EMPLOYEE (Please type or print)	6. TAXABLE FICA WAGES Paid to Employee in Quarter (Before deductions) Dollars Cents	7. TAXABLE TIPS REPORTED (See page 4) Dollars Cents

If you need more space for listing employees, use Schedule A continuation sheets, Form 941a.

Totals for this page—Wage total in column 6 and tip total in column 7 ⟶

8. TOTAL WAGES TAXABLE UNDER FICA PAID DURING QUARTER. $ ◁
(Total of column 6 on this page and continuation sheets.) Enter here and in item 14 below.

9. TOTAL TAXABLE TIPS REPORTED UNDER FICA DURING QUARTER. $ ◁
(Total of column 7 on this page and continuation sheets.) Enter here and in item 15 below. (If no tips reported, write "None.")

Employer's name, address, employer identification number, and calendar quarter. (If not correct, please change)

Name (as distinguished from trade name) — Date quarter ended

Trade name, if any — Employer Identification No.

Address and ZIP code

Entries must be made both above and below this line; if address different from previous return check here ☐

Name (as distinguished from trade name) — Date quarter ended

Trade name, if any — Employer Identification No.

Address and ZIP code

T	FP
FF	I
FD	TOT

10. Total Wages And Tips Subject To Withholding Plus Other Compensation . . . . . ⟶
11. Amount Of Income Tax Withheld From Wages, Tips, Annuities, etc. (See instructions) . . .
12. Adjustment For Preceding Quarters Of Calendar Year . . . .
13. Adjusted Total Of Income Tax Withheld . . . . ⟶
14. Taxable FICA Wages Paid (Item 8) . . $.................... multiplied by 11.7% = TAX
15. Taxable Tips Reported (Item 9) . . . $.................... multiplied by 5.85% = TAX
16. Total FICA Taxes (Item 14 plus Item 15) . . . . ⟶
17. Adjustment (See instructions) . . . .
18. Adjusted Total Of FICA Taxes . . . . ⟶
19. Total Taxes (Item 13 plus Item 18) . . . .
20. TOTAL DEPOSITS FOR QUARTER (INCLUDING FINAL DEPOSIT MADE FOR QUARTER) AND OVERPAYMENT FROM PREVIOUS QUARTER LISTED IN SCHEDULE B (See instructions on page 4) . . . .
Note: If undeposited taxes at the end of the quarter are $200 or more, the full amount must be deposited with an authorized commercial bank or a Federal Reserve bank. This deposit must be entered in Schedule B and included in item 20.
21. Undeposited Taxes Due (Item 19 Less Item 20—This Should Be Less Than $200). Pay To Internal Revenue Service And Enter Here . . . . ⟶
22. If Item 20 Is More Than Item 19, Enter Excess Here ▶ $ And Check If You Want It ☐ Applied To Next Return, Or ☐ Refunded.
23. If not liable for returns in the future write "FINAL" (See instructions) ▶ Date final wages paid ▶

Under penalties of perjury, I declare that I have examined this return, including accompanying schedules and statements, and to the best of my knowledge and belief it is true, correct and complete.

Date .... Signature .... Title (Owner, etc) ....

Form 941 (10-75)

SCHEDULE B—RECORD OF FEDERAL TAX DEPOSITS

Deposit period ending:		A. Tax liability for period	B. Amount deposited	C. Date of deposit
Overpayment from previous quarter				
First month of quarter	1st through 7th day			
	8th through 15th day			
	16th through 22d day			
	23d through last day			
1 First month total	1			
Second month of quarter	1st through 7th day			
	8th through 15th day			
	16th through 22d day			
	23d through last day			
2 Second month total	2			
Third month of quarter	1st through 7th day			
	8th through 15th day			
	16th through 22d day			
	23d through last day			
3 Third month total	3			
4 Total for quarter (total of items 1, 2, and 3)				
5 Final deposit made for quarter. (Enter zero if the final deposit made for the quarter is included in item 4.)				
6 Total deposits for quarter (total of items 4 and 5)—enter here and in item 20, page 1				

☆ U.S. GOVERNMENT PRINTING OFFICE : 1975—O-591-482

3
THE BASIS OF BOOKKEEPING

The Bookkeeping Equation

Assets	=	**Liabilities**	+	**Owner's Equity**
(owned)		(owed)		(owned clear of debt)

Assets		=	**Liabilities**		+	**Owner's Equity**	
+	-		-	+		-	+

Debit	**Credit**
(left)	(right)

The purpose of bookkeeping is to keep track of the dollar value of everything affecting a company so that, at any time, the owner can tell the total amount he owns, plus how much of that value is owed to someone else and how much of it is his free and clear of debt. All that a company or a person owns is either owed to someone or is owned clear of debt.

The accounting term for the dollar value of everything owned is assets. This includes things (like cars) and rights (like stocks and patents)—all that you legally own, whether it is in your possession or not. The term for the amount that is owed to any other person or firm is liabilities. All value that is not owed to anyone else but is owned free and clear of debt is known as owner's equity.

Bookkeeping Equation

The basis of all bookkeeping is the equation:

Assets	=	Liabilities	+	Owner's Equity
(all that is owned)		(what is owed)		(what is clear of debt)

3A. Fill in the blanks for the four companies listed below and write which one you would rather own and why.

	Assets	*Liabilities*	*Owner's Equity*
1)	*$ 1,000*	*$ 800*	______
2)	______	*2,000*	*$3,000*
3)	*3,000*	______	*2,000*
4)	*10,000*	*9,000*	______

3B. Identify each of the following with an A for asset, an L for liability, or OE for owner's equity:

____*Automobile*
____*Owed to Adams Company*
____*Unpaid meat bill*
____*Office furniture*
____*Owed to grocery store*
____*Typewriter*
____*Government bonds*
____*Any item we owe*
____*Any item we own*
____*The amount of the difference between total assets and total liabilities*

The bookkeeping equation is changing all of the time, and its parts are being increased or decreased whenever something happens to change the values. If new things of value are added, the assets increase; when they are lost, assets decrease. If more money is owed, liabilities increase; when it is repaid, liabilities decrease. If more of value is owned (assets) without any more being owed (liabilities), owner's equity increases; or if the same amount is owned (assets) but less of it is owed (liabilities), there is more of value free of debt—so again owner's equity increases. When the amount owned (assets) goes down without a similar reduction in the amount owed (liabilities), there isn't as much to own free and clear, so owner's equity decreases; and when the same amount is owned (assets) but more of it is owed to someone else (liabilities), owner's equity decreases.

Accounts

In bookkeeping, each of the assets, of the liabilities, and the owner's equity are listed separately and are called accounts. Each account has an increase side and a decrease side, but these are not the same for all of the kinds of accounts. All asset accounts are increased on the left side of the account and decreased on the right side. The other side of the bookkeeping equation is just the opposite. Liabilities and owner's equity accounts are increased on the right side and decreased on the left. Please memorize this because it will be used in everything you do in bookkeeping.

Assets		=	**Liabilities**		+	**Owner's Equity**	
+	−		−	+		−	+

Instead of saying left and right, accountants use the terms debit and credit. Debit means left. Credit means right.

(left)	**(right)**
Debit	**Credit**

The following example explains how accounts are recorded.

1/5/76 I started a business giving driving lessons. I had a car worth $2,000, and I had $200 cash in the bank. I owed $1,500 to the bank through a mortgage on the car. (The total value of all that my new company owned is $2,200, that is, the $2,000 car and the $200 cash in the bank. Asset accounts are set up for each of these; and their value is put on the increase side, which is the left or debit side for all asset accounts. If I owe $1,500 to the bank, this is a liability and is added to what I owe by entering it on the right or credit side of the Car Mortgage account. If I own $2,200 worth and owe on $1,500 of it, this means that $700 is mine free and clear, so owner's equity is added to on the right or credit side of the account.)

1/8/76 Bought $20 worth of driving instruction manuals from the Nova Operators' Outlet and charged them. (1. One thing that has happened is that I now have driving manuals. 2. This is something of value and is, therefore, an asset. 3. I will want to increase my assets. 4. The way to increase an asset is on the left or debit side. 1. Another thing affected is that the manuals were charged. 2. I owe this so it is a liability. 3. Since I owed nothing before, this is an increase in liabilities. 4. The way to increase a liability is on the right or credit side.)

1/10/76 I paid the bill to Nova Operators' Outlet. (1. One thing affected is my cash. 2. Cash is an asset, something of value. 3. I have less than before paying the bill. 4. Decrease an asset account on the credit or right side. 1. Another thing affected is what I owe to the Outlet. 2. This is a liability. 3. I owe less, since it is paid. 4. Decrease a liability on the debit or left side.)

1/12/76 I bought new seat covers for the car and paid $50 for them. (1. One thing affected is cash. 2. It is an asset. 3. Cash decreased. 4. Decrease an asset on the credit or right side. 1. The other thing affected is that I now have seat covers. 2. They are an asset, something of value. 3. I have more than I did have. 4. Increase an asset on the debit or left side. In this case, I have the same total value. All that has happened is that the assets have changed form from cash to seat covers.)

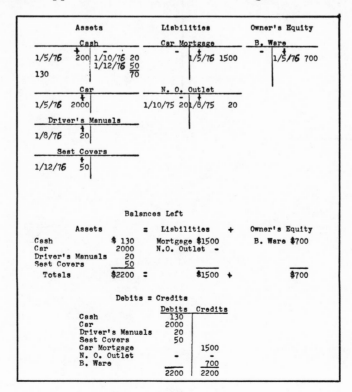

Assets

Cash

+		−	
1/5/76	200	1/10/76	20
		1/12/76	50
130			70

Car

+			
1/5/76	2000		

Driver's Manuals

+			
1/8/76	20		

Seat Covers

+			
1/12/76	50		

Liabilities

Car Mortgage

−		+	
		1/5/76	1500

N. O. Outlet

−		+	
1/10/75	20	1/8/75	20

Owner's Equity

B. Ware

−		+	
		1/5/76	700

Balances Left

Assets		=	Liabilities	+	Owner's Equity
Cash	$ 130		Mortgage $1500		B. Ware $700
Car	2000		N.O. Outlet -		
Driver's Manuals	20				
Seat Covers	50				
Totals	$2200	=	$1500	+	$700

Debits = Credits

	Debits	Credits
Cash	130	
Car	2000	
Driver's Manuals	20	
Seat Covers	50	
Car Mortgage		1500
N. O. Outlet	-	-
B. Ware		700
	2200	2200

Please notice the reasoning in each case: 1. What is one thing affected? 2. What kind of account is it? 3. Did it increase or decrease? 4. On which side do you increase or decrease that kind of account? Then these steps are repeated for the other account that is affected.

Always, at least two accounts are affected by anything you record. If your reasoning is correct, one account will be debited (put on the left side) and the other account will be credited (put on the right side) for the same amount. If you find that you are debiting both accounts (or crediting both), review your reasoning.

3C. A friend, Mr. Stein, has asked you to keep the accounts for his new costume rental business. Please use the account forms below, and go through each of the four steps before recording. Remember that you are keeping the records for the business, not for Mr. Stein personally.

6/19/76 Mr. Stein invested $3,000 cash in the business, Frank N. Stein Costumes.
6/21/76 Mr. Stein bought $1,000 worth of costumes and paid for them.
6/25/76 He bought another $500 worth of costumes and charged them at Costume Suppliers.
6/27/76 Mr. Stein invested another $200 cash.
6/28/76 He felt that $100 worth of the first costumes purchased were of a poor quality and returned them. He got his money back.
6/30/76 He paid Costume Suppliers what he owed them.

Frank N. Stein Costumes

Assets		Liabilities		Owner's Equity	
Cash		Costume Suppliers		Mr. Stein	
+	-	-	+	-	+

Costumes	
+	-

Owner's Equity Accounts

What is owned free and clear of debt can be increased in two different ways: either by investing more in the business or by earning an income. The owner's equity can be decreased by withdrawing money from the business or by having an expense which the owner has nothing to show for (like paying the rent or having equipment repaired.)

In the same way that separate accounts are set up for the assets and liabilities, so the owner's equity accounts are kept separate. The owner's account (sometimes called Capital) is used for investments in the business; and, since an investment increases the owner's equity in the business, it is credited (entered on the right side of the owner's account.) Income accounts, since they add to what is owned free and clear, are also credited.

Withdrawals take away from what the owner has clear of debt in his company. Therefore, every time he takes more money out of the company this is debited (shown on the left) to the Withdrawals account, since owner's equity is decreased on the debit side. If more is owed without adding an asset or if cash is spent without adding an asset (as in the case of salaries or taxes), this is a normal business expense which leaves less for the owner to have free and clear. Thus, expenses take from owner's equity and each additional expense is debited to an expense account.

There are four kinds of owner's equity accounts: the owner's account (or Capital) and income accounts, which add to owner's equity; and the Withdrawals and expense accounts, in which each additional entry takes from owner's equity.

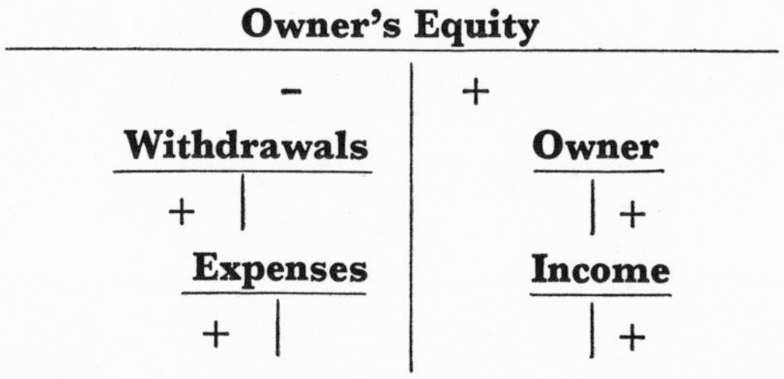

Although it is easy to reason how the various accounts are added to, it is important to memorize this now.

3D. *All of the titles of your accounts are listed below. Please show the letter of the account to be debited in each case and also the letter of the account to be credited in each case. Remember to reason: 1. What is one thing affected? 2. What kind of account is it? 3. Did it increase or decrease? 4. How do I increase or decrease this kind of account? Then reason in the same manner for the other account affected.*

Holme's Sweet Homes

A.	Cash	H.	Withdrawals
B.	Automobile	I.	Commission Income
C.	Office Furniture	J.	Electricity Expense
D.	Office Machines	K.	Rent Expense
E.	Owed to Adams Company	L.	Telephone Expense
F.	Owed to Thompson Garage	M.	Advertising Expense
G.	Holmes, Realtor	N.	Automobile Expense

	Debit	Credit
Received cash for sale of old office desk.	______	______
Paid cash to Adams Company in part payment of the cash owed.	______	______
Received cash as commission for the sale of a house.	______	______
Paid cash for rent of office.	______	______
Paid cash for a new automobile.	______	______
Paid cash for gas and oil for auto.	______	______
Owner withdrew money from the business.	______	______
Paid cash for new office machine.	______	______
Received cash from sale of old office machine.	______	______
Paid cash for advertisement in newspaper.	______	______
Paid cash for telephone bill.	______	______
Paid cash for electricity bill.	______	______
Owner invested more money in the business.	______	______

Trial Balance

Since one account is always debited for the same amount that is credited to another account, this provides the bookkeeper with a way of checking his or her accuracy. Debits should always equal credits.

Before checking this, each account is balanced. All of the amounts on the same side of an account are added. If there are also amounts on the other side of the account, they are added. After subtracting the smaller side from the larger, this balance is placed in small figures on the larger side.

Cash in Bank

	+	-
	1,000	50
	100	150
	10	80
	1,500	900
	10	
1,440	2,620	1,180

In this case $1,440 is the debit balance for Cash in Bank.

When all of the accounts are totaled and balanced, they are listed on a form called a Trial Balance. The debit or credit balance of each account is shown. Then all the debit balances are added, and this must agree with the total of all the credit balances. Both are double underlined to show that they balance. A Trial Balance is for the bookkeeper's use and is always made out at the end of the month so that errors will not be carried over to next month.

After the accounts in problem 3C had been totaled and balanced, they would look like those in the example for 3C.

Frank N. Stein Costumes

Cash in Bank

	+		-
6/19	3000	6/21	1000
6/27	200	6/30	500
6/28	100		
1800	3300		1500

Owed Suppliers

	-		+
6/30	500	6/25	500

Mr. Stein

-		+
	6/19	3000
	6/27	200
		3200

Costumes

	+		-
6/21	1000	6/28	100
6/25	500		
1400	1500		

Frank N. Stein Costumes
Trial Balance
June 30, 1976

	Debit	Credit
Cash in Bank	1800	
Costumes	1400	
Owed Suppliers	—	—
Mr. Stein		3200
	3200	3200

The bookkeeping equation is another way to check accuracy. Here, Cash in Bank and Costumes are assets, totaling $3,200. Liabilities are zero, and owner's equity is $3,200. Thus Assets = Liabilities plus Owner's Equity. When the account balances are shown in the form of the bookkeeping equation, this is called the Balance Sheet.

3E. *George has asked you to keep his financial books for him. Record each of the following. Then total and balance all of the accounts and make out a Trial Balance.*

5/8 *George decided to make some extra money this summer cutting lawns, since he had a lawn mower worth $50. George had nothing else of value.*
5/9 *George mowed Mr. Brown's yard and received $8 in cash.*
5/11 *He got $10 from cutting Mrs. Fall's yard and $5 from raking it.*
5/13 *A good movie was on so George spent $3 of his money on the movie.*
5/15 *He decided a grass catcher would help, so he bought one for $16 and charged it.*
5/16 *The lawn mower wasn't working well, so he had it fixed for $7 and paid the repair bill.*
5/20 *He mowed Mrs. Smith's yard for $8.*
5/21 *He bought lawn mower gas for $1 cash.*
5/25 *He paid the bill for the cost of the grass catcher.*

George's Lawn Care

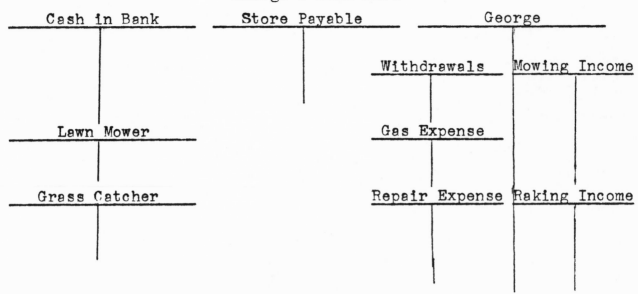

Cash in Bank

Store Payable

George

Withdrawals

Mowing Income

Lawn Mower

Gas Expense

Grass Catcher

Repair Expense

Raking Income

George's Lawn Care
Trial Balance
May 30, 1976

3F. *You began a business giving music lessons. Please record the following in their accounts; total and balance the accounts; and prepare a Trial Balance. Remember that you are keeping books for the business, not your own personal accounts.*

3/5 *You began a business giving music lessons. You had $20 cash in the bank and a piano worth $300.*
3/6 *You bought a music book for $5.50 and charged it.*
3/10 *You gave six lessons at $5 a piece.*
3/13 *You bought a metronome for $20 and paid for it.*
3/14 *You gave a $5 lesson and got cash.*
3/15 *The metronome was defective, so you returned it and got your money back.*

3/20 You bought another metronome for $18 and charged it.
3/25 You paid the music store for the book.
3/26 Gave Billy a $6 lesson and he paid you.
3/26 Billy kicked the piano and caused $50 damage. You had it fixed and charged the repair bill.
3/30 Withdrew $10 from the business to buy a set of leg irons.

Beginner's Piano Lessons

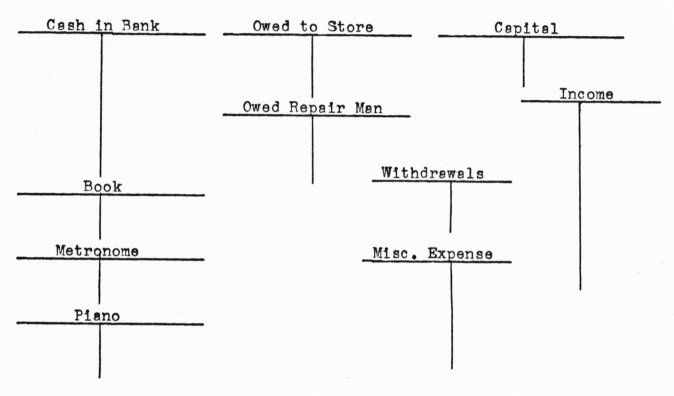

Cash in Bank

Owed to Store

Capital

Income

Owed Repair Man

Withdrawals

Book

Metronome

Misc. Expense

Piano

Make out Trial Balance below.

If debits don't equal credits on the Trial Balance, check your math in each account and make certain that on each date the same amount was debited that was credited. Also make sure that the balances were written correctly on the Trial Balance.

Accounting for Petty Cash

It was mentioned in Chapter 1 that often a company needs to keep some cash in the office, in addition to that kept in the bank, and that this is known as Petty Cash. Both cash accounts, being something of value, are asset accounts.

When the Petty Cash account is first set up, a check is written taking money out of the bank, so the account Cash in Bank is credited. Since the asset Petty Cash is being added to, it is debited and now shows the amount that is to be in the petty cash drawer at the beginning of each month. Unless this amount is to be changed, the Petty Cash account is never debited or credited again.

The petty cash spent during the month is not recorded in the accounts until the end of the month. Whenever petty cash is spent a voucher is made out, showing the account to be charged for each expenditure. These amounts are then recorded in the accounts at the end of the month when the amount that is used is put back in the petty cash drawer.

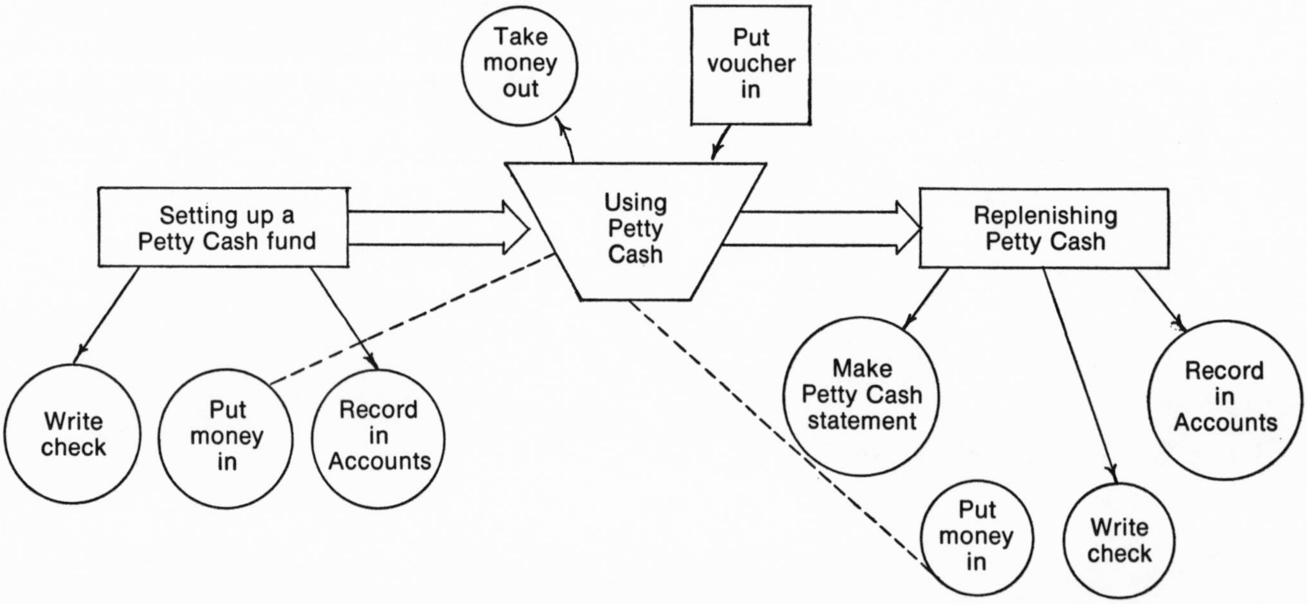

You will recall that at the end of the month a Petty Cash Statement is made out. This shows the total amount of petty cash spent, and it lists each account for which petty cash was used. Also, a check is made out to put the used-up money back in the petty cash drawer. When recording this check in the accounts, Cash in Bank is reduced and, therefore, credited; and each account that used petty cash during the past month (according to the Petty Cash Statement) is charged now and is, therefore, debited. Please look back to problem 1G. The Petty Cash Statement showed the following accounts: Auto Expense—$2, Stationery and Office Supplies—$30, Miscellaneous Expense—$12.50. A check was made out (in 1H) and the $44.50 was put back in the drawer. When this is recorded in the accounts, each of the three expense accounts will be debited (since they are the result of money spent without getting an asset to show for it; and thus, they decrease owner's equity.) Cash in Bank will be credited for the amount of the check.

Cash in Bank (Dr.)	Cash in Bank (Cr.)	Auto Expense (Dr.)	Auto Expense (Cr.)	Stat. & Off. Supplies Exp. (Dr.)	Stat. & Off. Supplies Exp. (Cr.)	Misc. Exp. (Dr.)	Misc. Exp. (Cr.)
	-	+		+		+	
	44.50	2.00		30.00		12.50	

3G. *You began a business giving swimming lessons. Record the following in their accounts; but remember that petty cash spent is not recorded in the accounts until the end of the month when, after making out the Petty Cash Statement, a check is written to put the used up money back in the petty cash drawer. Use your own name as the name of the firm on the Trial Balance.*

6/13 *You began a business teaching swimming lessons without investing any money. On 6/13 you gave three lessons and got $12, which you put in the bank.*
6/14 *You decided you needed some cash handy and set up an $8 petty cash fund.*
6/15 *You needed a life preserver so you bought one at the store and charged it. The price was $5.*
6/18 *You gave five more lessons at $4 each, depositing the money in the bank.*
6/19 *You bought a rubber ring for $1.50 cash, taking it out of the petty cash fund.*
6/22 *You spent $1 for Cokes for the swimming students. This came out of petty cash; and, since it was for the students, it was recorded as a business expense.*
6/27 *The bill from the store came and you paid it.*
6/28 *Took $1.50 out of the bank for lunch.*
6/29 *Billy bit the life preserver, and it is now worthless.*
6/29 *Billy paid $5 for his lesson.*
6/30 *Made out a check to Petty Cash in order to replace the money spent. (Be sure to also make out your Petty Cash Statement.)*

Cash in Bank

Store Payable

Capital

Withdrawals

Income

Misc. Expense

Petty Cash

Life Preserver

Rubber Ring

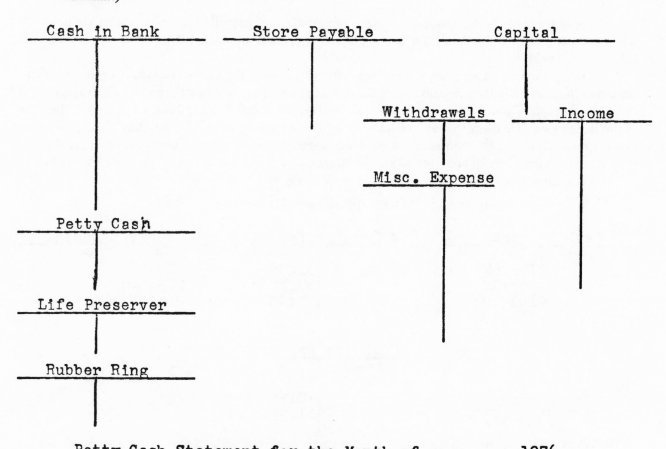

Petty Cash Statement for the Month of ______, 1976

Rubber Ring
Withdrawals
Miscellaneous Expense ______
Total

Make out Trial Balance below.

Accounting for Payroll

Records are made in the accounts for three things affecting payroll: (1) when salaries are paid, (2) when taxes and other deductions from the employees' paychecks are paid, (3) when the employer's payroll taxes are paid.

(1) When the salaries are paid, the net pay (after deductions) is given to the employees in cash. This decreases the cash left in the company. All of the deductions are now owed by the employer who took them out of the employees' paychecks. The owner's cash asset is decreased. His liabilities are increased (because of the deductions). He owns less, and of what's left, he owes more; so the whole salary reduces what he owns free and clear, and the entire gross salary is an expense, Salary Expense. After the paychecks of problem 2G in chapter 2 had been recorded, the accounts would have appeared as those shown below. Payable is a name given to liability accounts, since they will have to be paid.

Accounts after problem 2G is recorded:

Cash in Bank	
+	−
	153.54
	165.32
	163.40

Fed Inc Tax Payable	
−	+
	35.00
	37.10
	28.90

Salary Expense	
+	−
200.25	
215.00	
204.25	

FICA Tax Payable	
−	+
	11.71
	12.58
	11.95

(2) When paying the deductions held out of the employees' paychecks, a check is written for the whole amount owed to an agency. Therefore, Cash in Bank is credited. The amount is then no longer owed, so the Tax or Deduction Payable account is debited to decrease the liability. When making out the check in problem 2H, Federal Income Tax Payable would be debited for $101.00 and FICA Tax Payable would be debited for $36.24 (the part that has been owed ever since it was deducted from the employees' paychecks.)

Accounts after problems 2G & 2H are recorded:

Cash in Bank

+	—
	153.54
	165.32
	163.40
	173.48--2H

Fed Inc Tax Payable

—	+
2H--101.00	35.00
	37.10
	28.90

Salary Expense

+	—
200.25	
215.00	
204.25	

FICA Tax Payable

—	+
2H-- 36.24	11.71
	12.58
	11.95

Employer's Payroll Tax Exp

+	—
2H--36.24	

(3) The employer's share of the FICA tax is another expense to him. It reduces cash without giving something of value and must be debited to the expense account, Employer's Payroll Tax Expense, in order to decrease owner's equity. This is true of both of the unemployment compensation taxes, also. In problem 2H, the employer's share of the FICA is debited to Employer's Payroll Tax Expense and it is credited to Cash. After problems 2G and 2H had both been recorded in the accounts, they would show the amounts illustrated above.

3H. Based on the Total Payroll Record sheets in the Problems on page 50, record the following in the accounts below: the payrolls of 12/10, 12/17, 12/24, and 12/31. Then record the payment of the federal income tax and the total FICA tax. Record the payment of the city tax, also.

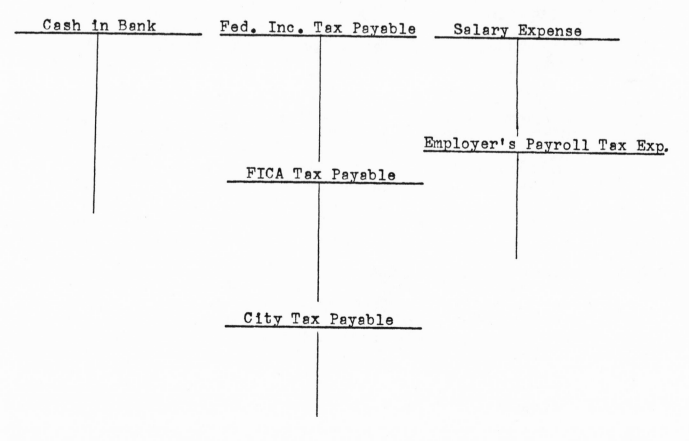

Cash in Bank

Fed. Inc. Tax Payable

Salary Expense

Employer's Payroll Tax Exp.

FICA Tax Payable

City Tax Payable

Accounting for Sales Tax

Occasionally a service-type firm sells a few items. Since such a small part of the business involves retail sales, the method of bookkeeping explained here (called the Cash Basis of bookkeeping) can be used. However, state retail sales tax must be collected on those items sold, and later, the tax must be paid to the state government.

A separate income account should be kept for the items sold. When an article is sold, this Sales Income account is credited for the entire price of the article plus the sales tax. Of course, cash is debited for the whole amount.

At the end of the month (or in some cases at the end of the year) the state government sends a form to be used in figuring out the amount of the state's sales tax which has been collected and is now owed. If there is any question about how to arrive at the amount owed, call or visit the state Internal Revenue office; they will be happy to be of help. A check is then made out for the total sales tax owed. When this check is recorded in the books, Cash in Bank is credited and Sales Tax Expense is debited.

Payment of an Installment Loan

When making installment or mortgage payments to the bank, part of the regular monthly payment is interest and part is payment on the loan. The interest is an expense, and the payment on the loan reduces what is still owed. The entire amount is credited to Cash. If the monthly interest rate on a $10,000 loan were 0.8% and the monthly payment were $150: $10,000 × 0.008 = $80, $150 – $80 = $70. Interest Expense would be debited for the $80, Mortgage Payable would be debited for $70, and Cash would be credited for $150. The bank will tell you the monthly interest rate.

Since the interest is always figured on the unpaid balance of the loan, the portion of the regular payment that is interest decreases each month and the amount repaying the loan then increases.

Financial Statements

Owners are very interested in two important facts: has the company made a profit and what is the condition of the company's finances today. (How much does it own, how much does it owe, and how much is free of debt.)

Although all of the money is listed in the accounts and is shown on the Trial Balance, it needs to be arranged in the form of financial statements to be understood clearly. These financial statements are called the Income and Expense Statement and the Balance Sheet.

Before beginning to prepare the statements, all known information must be recorded in the accounts. The accounts are then totaled and balanced, and a Trial Balance is prepared. Statements are usually prepared in rough draft and then typed, with a copy made for the file. Each account listed on the Trial Balance will be shown on one of these statements; no account appears on both statements. Each of the financial statements has a three line title: (1) the name of the company, (2) the name of the statement, (3) the date.

INCOME AND EXPENSE STATEMENT

The Income and Expense Statement (sometimes called Profit and Loss Statement) shows what has happened to owner's equity as a result of the company's operations. It lists all of the Income accounts, with the total balance of each (taken from the Trial Balance) and all of the Expense accounts, with their totals. If the total of all income was greater than the total of all the expenses, what is owned free of debt has increased; and the company has a Net Income. But if expenses were greater than all of the income, the amount owned free and clear has decreased; and this is called a Net Loss. Only the income accounts and the expense accounts are shown on the Income and Expense Statement.

If you read that our company has a Net Income of $3,000, this doesn't mean much without knowing how long it took us to earn it. A $3,000 Net Income earned in a month is fine, but it wouldn't be a very good profit for a year. Therefore, the date line of the Income and Expense Statement must show how long a time it covers, how long it has been since the last Income and Expense Statement was made out.

George's Lawn Care
Income & Expense Statement
for Month Ending May 30, 1976

Incomes:		
Mowing Income	$26.00	
Raking Income	5.00	
Total Income		$31.00
Expenses:		
Gas Expense	$ 1.00	
Repair Expense	7.00	8.00
Total Expense		$23.00
Net Income		

Above is an example of the Income and Expense Statement for problem 3E. (Financial statements were made out at the end of last month.) There are no debit or credit columns used on financial statements. The reason for two columns is so that amounts can be added in the first column and the totals shown in the far column.

3I. Prepare an Income and Expense Statement for problem 3F.

3J. Prepare an Income and Expense Statement for problem 3G.

BALANCE SHEET

The Balance Sheet is simply the account balances (taken from the Trial Balance) written in the form of the Bookkeeping Equation, showing how the equation balances. (This is why it is called the Balance Sheet.)

Assets	**Liabilities**
(List each Asset account and its balance)	(List each Liability account and its balance.)
	Owner's Equity

In showing the owner's equity, first the owner's account (where his investments are recorded) is listed. Then the Net Income or Net Loss is shown. It is taken from the Income and Expense Statement and shows whether his ownership was increased by Net Income or decreased by a Net Loss. The other owner's account, Withdrawals, is then listed. Any withdrawals always take from owner's equity and are subtracted from a net income. Then the portion of the business that is owned free and clear of debt is known.

The total liabilities are added to the total owner's equity. The two sides—Assets and Liabilities plus Owner's Equity—must total the same amount, and these totals are double underlined to show that they are in balance.

George's Lawn Care
Balance Sheet
May 30, 1976

Assets			Liabilities		
Cash	$ 4.00		Store Payable	0	
Lawn Mower	50.00		Total Liabilities		0
Grass Catcher	16.00				
			Owner's Equity		
			George:		
			Investments	$50.00	
			Plus Net Income	23.00	
			Less Withdrawals	- 3.00	
			Capital, May 30		$70.00
Total Assets		$70.00	Total Liab. & Equity		$70.00

The Balance Sheet shown above is for problem 3E. Remember that the first money column is used to list amounts to be added so their totals can be placed in the second column.

3K. Make out a Balance Sheet for problem 3F.

3L. Make out a Balance Sheet for problem 3G.

PUTTING IT ALL TOGETHER

Chapter Summary Problems

A. WHAT KIND?

Please show all of the kinds of accounts, and indicate on which side each is increased.

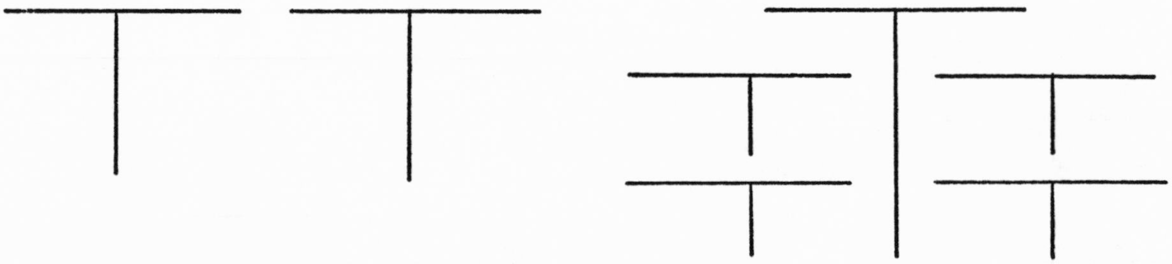

B. WHAT IS IT?

Please fill in the blanks with the correct words from those listed below:

debit	owner's equity
Balance Sheet	Income and Expense Statement
Net Loss	accounts
asset	bookkeeping equation
Withdrawals	increases
credit	decreases
liability	Capital
Trial Balance	Net Income

1. All that is owned free and clear of debt is called ________________________.
2. The ________________________ is sometimes called a Profit and Loss Statement.
3. ________________________ means the right side of an account.
4. Debiting an expense account ________________________ that account.
5. Everything that a company owns is called a ________________________.
6. Assets equal liabilities plus owner's equity is called the ________________________.
7. The ________________________ shows the above in financial statement form.
8. If the expenses are greater than the income this is a ________________________.
9. ________________________ is another name for the owner's account and is used to show investments.
10. A ________________________ checks that debits equal the credits.

11. Debiting a liability account ______________________ that account.
12. ______________________ is something that a company owes.
13. ______________________ is added to the investments in the owner's equity section of the Balance Sheet.
14. ______________________ take from owner's equity and are debits.
15. ______________________ are the forms used to show increases and decreases in the value of assets, liabilities, and owner's equity.
16. ______________________ means the left side of an account.

C. USING WHAT YOU KNOW

You have been hired to keep the books for North's Pole, Ski, and Snowmobile Rentals. Please record the following. Then prepare a Trial Balance and financial statements. Use tax tables shown in Chapter 2 for payrolls. There are no state or local withholding taxes.

1. 11/15/76 Mr. North invested $10,000 cash in the business.
2. 11/16/76 He purchased $3,000 worth of ski equipment and paid for it.
3. 11/16/76 Purchased $25,000 worth of snowmobiles and charged them.
4. 11/19/76 Purchased $1,000 worth of office equipment and paid for it.
5. 11/20/76 Set up a $100 petty cash fund.
6. 11/20/76 Paid November rent of $300.
7. 11/21/76 Took $5 out of petty cash to buy rental agreement forms (office supplies).
8. 11/21/76 Earned $200 from rental of ski equipment.
9. 11/22/76 Earned $150 from snowmobile rental.
10. 11/23/76 Paid first week salaries—Paul R. Bare worked 30 hours and earns $6 per hour. (He has 1 exemption.) Sam T. Claus worked 32 hours and earns $6.10 per hour. (He has 3 exemptions.) You earn $4.50 per hour and worked 40 hours (You have 1 exemption.)
11. 11/26/76 Took $10 out of petty cash to pay for envelopes and typing paper.
12. 11/26/76 Received $220 for snowmobile rental.
13. 11/27/76 Had a snowmobile repaired and charged the $50 repair bill.
14. 11/28/76 Paid $8 out of petty cash for ski magazine subscription.
15. 11/28/76 Mr. North withdrew $180 to go to Florida.
16. 11/29/76 Received $250 from ski equipment rentals.
17. 11/30/76 Paid the 11/27 $50 snowmobile repair bill.
18. 11/30/76 Paid $400 on what is owed on the snowmobiles.
19. 11/30/76 Paid second week salaries. Mr. Bare worked 36 hours, Mr. Claus worked 30 hours, and you worked 45 hours.
20. 11/30/76 Paid $40 to the electric company.
21. 11/30/76 Paid the FICA and federal income taxes for November.
22. 11/30/76 Made out a check to put the used-up part back into petty cash.

North's Pole, Ski, & Snowmobile Rentals

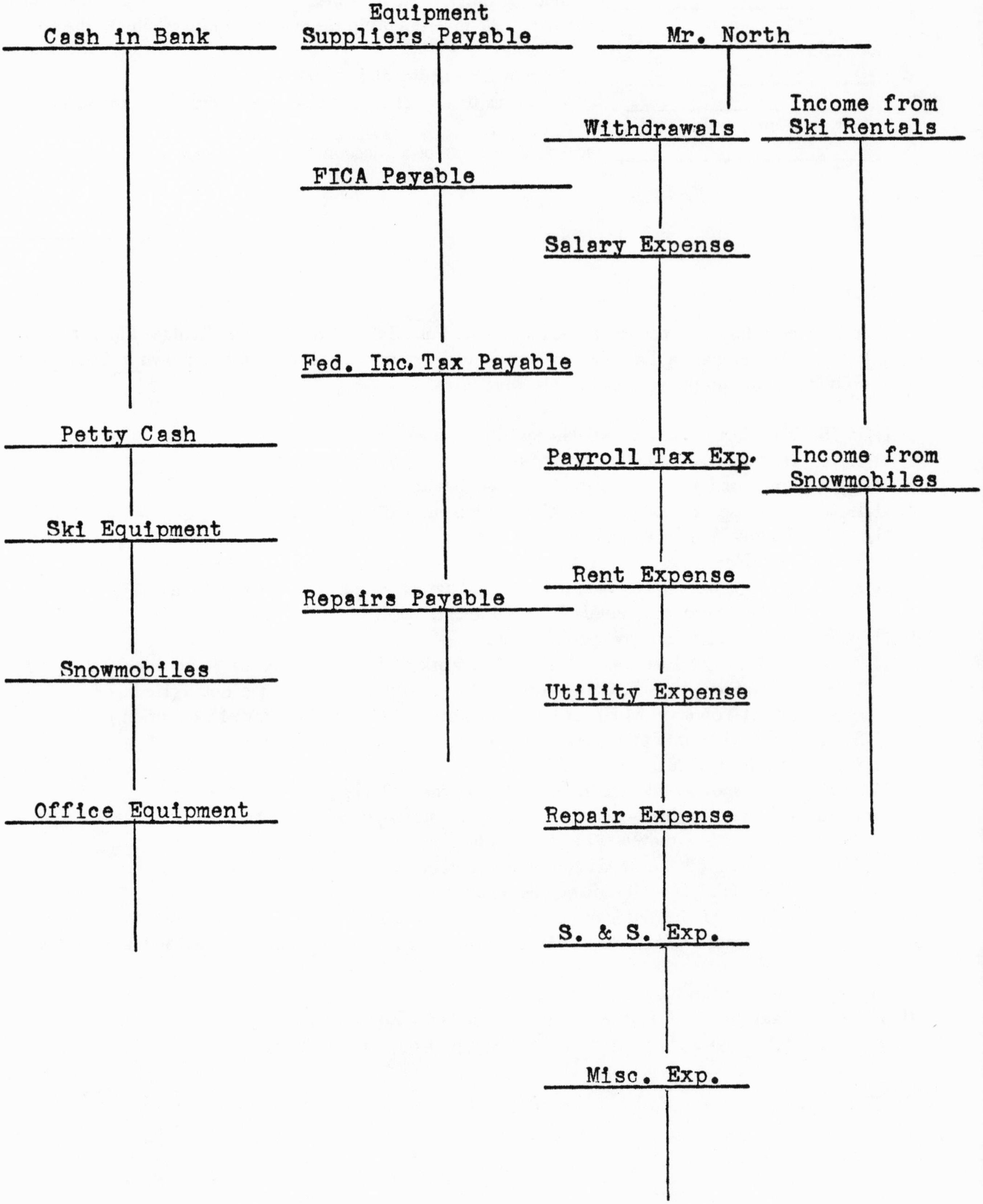

Make out Trial Balance below.

Make out Income and Expense Statement below.

No.________ $________

RECEIVED OF PETTY CASH

DATE________19____

FOR________________

____

CHARGE TO________________
ACCOUNT

____
APPROVED BY RECEIVED BY

________ ________
TOPS FORM 3008

No.________ $________

RECEIVED OF PETTY CASH

DATE________19____

FOR________________

____

CHARGE TO________________
ACCOUNT

____
APPROVED BY RECEIVED BY

________ ________
TOPS FORM 3008

No.________ $________

RECEIVED OF PETTY CASH

DATE________19____

FOR________________

____

CHARGE TO________________
ACCOUNT

____
APPROVED BY RECEIVED BY

________ ________
TOPS FORM 3008

Show Petty Cash Statement Here

Make out Balance Sheet below.

4
USING THE CORRECT FORMS

You may have noticed from the problems in Chapter 3 that if amounts are put directly into the accounts, it is easy to forget either the debit or the credit part of the entry. Therefore, bookkeepers use a planning sheet before making entries in the accounts. This planning sheet is called a Journal.

Original Papers

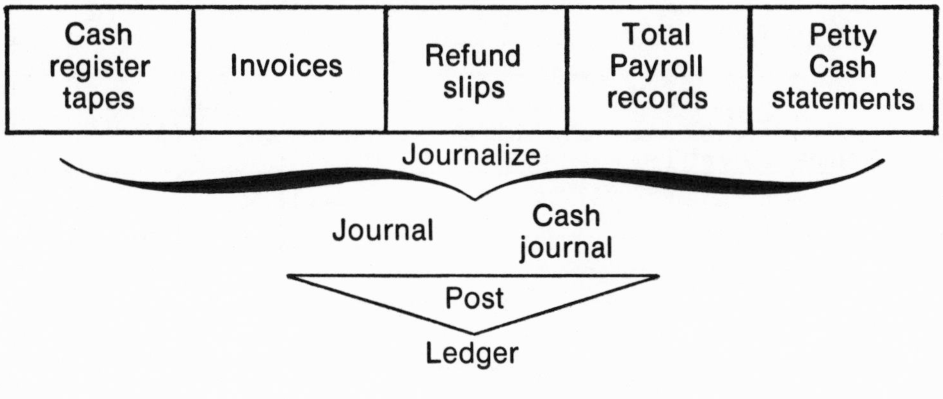

The Journal

Whenever something happens that is to be recorded in the company's books, it is first entered in the journal. The date used is always today's date: the day this journal entry is being made. The column marked "Account Title" is for the names of the accounts to be debited and credited. On the same line with the date, write the exact title of the account you plan to debit. Its amount goes in the Debit column.

On the next line, the exact title of the account to be credited is written in the Account Title column, with its amount in the Credit column. If more than one account is to be debited or credited, each account title and amount is shown on a separate line, always with debits shown first and credits under the debits. The last line of the entry is an explanation of what happened, and this is written in the Account Title column.

For each journal entry the reasoning is the same as that learned in Chapter 3: (1) what is one thing affected? (2) what kind of account is it? (3) did it increase or decrease? (4) on which side (debit or credit) do I increase or decrease this kind of account? If you want to debit, put the account title on the first line of the entry and the amount in the Debit column. If you want to credit, put the title on the second line and its amount in the Credit column. Then reason in the same manner for the other account affected, record its title and amount, and write the explanation.

The next entry is then put on the next line of the same page. You can tell that it is a new entry because it has a date. If there isn't enough room at the bottom of the page for a whole journal entry, put all of it on the next page rather than split up a journal entry between pages. When a page is filled, check your accuracy by totaling the Debit column to be certain that it agrees with the total of the Credit column. The column marked "Posted" is not filled in at this time.

Journal entries for problem 3E in chapter 3 would have looked like those in the journal below.

Date	Account Title	Post	Debit		Credit	
May 8	Lawn Mower		50	00		
	George				50	00
	Investment					
9	Cash		8	00		
	Mowing Income				8	00
	Mr. Brown's yard					
11	Cash		15	00		
	Mowing Income				10	00
	Raking Income				5	00
	Mrs. Fall's yard					
13	Withdrawals		3	00		
	Cash				3	00
	Went to movie					
15	Grass Catcher		16	00		
	Store Payable				16	00
	Charged at Sears					
16	Repair Expense		7	00		
	Cash				7	00
	Lawn mower fixed					
20	Cash		8	00		
	Mowing Income				8	00
	Mrs. Smith's yard					
21	Gas Expense		1	00		
	Cash				1	00
	Mower gas					
25	Store Payable		16	00		
	Cash				16	00
	Paid Sears					

4A. You have been asked to keep the records for Charlie Brown's baseball team. Record the following material in the journal below. The titles of the accounts are listed.

6/20 Charlie Brown invested $10 of his summer camp money in the baseball team.
6/25 He spent $6 for a new bat and ball.
6/26 The team charged admission for their first game and made $2.
6/28 During practice the shortstop hit a homerun through Charlie Brown's window, and the team now owes Mr. Brown $5 for a new window.
6/29 Charlie Brown paid his dad the $5.
6/30 He withdrew $1 to buy a kite.

Accounts

Cash	Charlie Brown
Equipment	Withdrawals
Dad Payable	Income
	Miscellaneous Expense

page 1

Date	Account Title	Post	Debit		Credit	

POSTING FROM THE JOURNAL

At the end of the week, the amounts put in the journal can be recorded in their accounts. The book of accounts is called a ledger, and the act of recording the journal entries in the ledger of accounts is called posting.

The regular form for an account is much like that used in Chapter 3. The date used is the same date that was entered in the journal. In addition to the date and amount, each side of the account has an Items column where you can note anything affecting the entry that you wish to remember (such as names of the individual stores owed in the Accounts or Stores Payable account). There is also a column marked "Posted" to show the number of the journal page from which the entry was posted. Then, if there is need to look it up at any time, the account will show on just what page the original journal entry can be found.

Each account is assigned a certain number when the bookkeeping system is first set up, and the accounts are kept in numerical order in the ledger. After the journal entry has been posted to the correct account, that account number is placed in the Posted column of the *journal*. Then if the telephone rings or a customer comes in while you are in the middle of posting, you will always know that if a number is in the journal's Posted column, that amount has already been posted in the ledger. In this way nothing will be overlooked or posted twice. This also shows exactly where the journal entry can be found in the ledger.

After being posted to the ledger, problem 3E (the journal entry shown on page 80) would appear like the accounts below.

Accounts

Cash — Account No. 10

Date	Items	Post	Debit	Date	Items	Post	Credit
May 9		1	8 00	May 13		1	3 00
11		1	15 00	16		1	7 00
20		1	8 00	21		1	1 00
				25		1	16 00
	4.00		31 00				27 00

Lawn Mower — Account No. 11

Date	Items	Post	Debit	Date	Items	Post	Credit
May 8		1	50 00				

Grass Catcher — Account No. 12

Date	Items	Post	Debit	Date	Items	Post	Credit
May 15		1	16 00				

Store Payable — Account No. 30

Date	Items	Post	Debit	Date	Items	Post	Credit
May 25	Sears	1	16 00	May 15	Sears	1	16 00

George — Account No. 40

Date	Items	Post	Debit	Date	Items	Post	Credit
				May 8		1	50 00

Withdrawals — Account No. 040

Date	Items	Post	Debit		Date	Items	Post	Credit	
May 13		1	3	00					

Mowing Income — Account No. 50

Date	Items	Post	Debit		Date	Items	Post	Credit	
					May 9		1	8	00
					11		1	10	00
					20		1	8	00
								26	00

Raking Income — Account No. 51

Date	Items	Post	Debit		Date	Items	Post	Credit	
					May 11		1	5	00

Repair Expense — Account No. 60

Date	Items	Post	Debit		Date	Items	Post	Credit	
May 16		1	7	00					

Gas Expense — Account No. 61

Date	Items	Post	Debit		Date	Items	Post	Credit	
May 21		1	1	00					

4B. *Post problem 4A to the ledger accounts below. Be certain to fill in the Posted column of the journal in problem 4A with the correct account number as each account is posted. Total and balance the accounts.*

Cash — Account No. 11

Date	Items	Post	Debit	Date	Items	Post	Credit

Equipment — Account No. 12

Date	Items	Post	Debit	Date	Items	Post	Credit

Dad Payable — Account No. 21

Date	Items	Post	Debit	Date	Items	Post	Credit

Charlie Brown — Account No. 31

Date	Items	Post	Debit	Date	Items	Post	Credit

Withdrawals — Account No. 031

Date	Items	Post	Debit	Date	Items	Post	Credit

Income — Account No. 41

Date	Items	Post	Debit	Date	Items	Post	Credit

Miscellaneous Expense — Account No. 51

Date	Items	Post	Debit	Date	Items	Post	Credit

The Cash Journal

Since most of the business that a company has involves cash, a cash journal is often used, instead of the regular journal, for those entries involving cash. In it, there are two pages opposite each other. All increases in cash are recorded on the left page which is called the Cash Receipts page; and all decreases in cash are listed on the right page, called the Cash Disbursements or Expenditures page. Whenever cash is increased or decreased during the month, it is immediately recorded in this cash journal instead of being put in the regular journal.

Every time that Cash in Bank is affected, some other account is affected also. When Cash is debited, a different account will be credited. So in the cash journal, the Cash Receipts page has a place to list the name of the account you plan to credit; and it has a column to show the amount of money involved. The Cash Disbursements page (which will all be credited to Cash) has a place to list the names of the accounts you plan to debit, as well as an amount column.

Cash Journal

Cash Receipts

Date	Account Credited	Posted	Amount
June 13	Income		12.00
18	Income		20.00
29	Income		5.00
	Total		37.00

Cash Disbursements

Date	Account Debited	Posted	Check No.	Amount
June 14	Petty Cash		1	8.00
27	Store Payable		2	5.00
28	Withdrawals		3	1.50
30	Rubber Ring		4	1.50
	Misc. Expense		4	1.00
	Total			17.00

Journal page 1

Date	Account Title	Post	Debit	Credit
June 15	Life Preserver		5 00	
	Store Payable			5 00
	Charged at Sports, Inc.			
29	Miscellaneous Expense		5 00	
	Life Preserver			5 00
	Billy bit life preserver			

If problem 3G from the last chapter had been recorded in a cash journal, it would have looked like the illustration above. Notice that no journal entry was made on 6/19 or on 6/22, since (as you learned in Chapter 3) no entry is made for money taken out of petty cash until the end of the month. Also, no record was made on 6/15 or on 6/29. Neither of these debited or credited cash, so they cannot be put in a cash journal and must be recorded in a regular journal as shown.

4C. *A friend named Lucy has asked you to keep the books for her psychiatry office. Please record the following in the cash journal. The account titles in your books are listed above the journal.*

2/5 Received $50 from medical fees.
2/6 Purchased $20 worth of stationery supplies. Made out Check Number 101.
2/10 Received $80 medical fees.

2/12 Paid janitor $25. Check #102.
2/13 Lucy invested $500.
2/15 Bought a new couch for $150, Check #103.
2/18 Paid $21 for a new "Doctor Is In" sign, Check #104.
2/23 Received $95 from fees.
2/25 Lucy withdrew $5 to attend a friend's piano concert, Check #105.
2/28 Paid a $30 utility bill, Check #106.

Accounts

Cash	Withdrawals
Furniture	Income from Fees
Signs	Office Supplies Expense
Lucy	Janitorial Expense
	Utility Expense

Cash Journal

Cash Receipts				Cash Disbursements				
Date	Account Credited	Posted	Amount	Date	Account Debited	Posted	Check No.	Amount

POSTING FROM THE CASH JOURNAL

At the end of the month, the Cash Receipts (the left page of the cash journal) are totaled. This total is then posted on the debit side of the Cash in Bank account. The date used for this posting is the last day of the month. CJ (which stands for Cash Journal) is put in the Posted column. Then the Cash Disbursements page is added and its total is credited to the Cash in Bank account as of the last day of the month, with a CJ in the Posted column. The Cash in Bank account number is then written in the Posted column on both pages of the cash journal, opposite the totals that were posted. This posting of only the totals to Cash in Bank saves a considerable amount of time, and this is the main reason for the use of a cash journal.

The accounts to be credited that are listed on the Cash Receipts page are then each posted individually, using their journal date and putting a CJ in the Posted column of the accounts. As each is posted, the account's number is recorded in the Posted column of the cash journal to show that it has been posted to the ledger. Then the amounts shown on the Cash Disbursements page of the cash journal are each posted to the debit side of their accounts.

The posting of problem 3G (the cash journal illustrated on page 85) would appear in the ledger accounts as those shown on the following pages.

Cash in Bank — Account No. 11

Date	Items	Post	Debit		Date	Items	Post	Credit	
June 30		CJ	37	00	June 30		CJ	17	00
	20.00								

Petty Cash — Account No. 12

Date	Items	Post	Debit		Date	Items	Post	Credit	
June 14		CJ	8	00					

Life Preserver — Account No. 13

Date	Items	Post	Debit		Date	Items	Post	Credit	
June 15		J1	5	00	June 29		J1	5	00

Rubber Ring — Account No. 14

Date	Items	Post	Debit		Date	Items	Post	Credit	
June 30		CJ	1	50					

Store Payable — Account No. 21

Date	Items	Post	Debit		Date	Items	Post	Credit	
June 27		CJ	5	00	June 15		J1	5	00

Capital — Account No. 31

Date	Items	Post	Debit		Date	Items	Post	Credit	

Withdrawals — Account No. 031

Date	Items	Post	Debit		Date	Items	Post	Credit	
June 28		CJ	1	50					

Income — Account No. 41

Date	Items	Post	Debit		Date	Items	Post	Credit	
					June 13		CJ	12	00
					18		CJ	20	00
					29		CJ	5	00
								37	00

Miscellaneous Expense — Account No. 51

Date	Items	Post	Debit		Date	Items	Post	Credit	
June 20		J1	5	00					
30		CJ	1	00					
			6	00					

4D. *Post the cash journal of problem 4C to the accounts below. Note that the accounts already have some amounts in them, as recorded by the former bookkeeper. These should also be added when totaling and balancing the accounts. Be certain to fill in both the journal and the ledger Posted columns.*

Ledger

Cash — Account No. 11

Date	Items	Post	Debit		Date	Items	Post	Credit	
Jan 31	Balance	✓	1000	00					

Furniture — Account No. 12

Date	Items	Post	Debit		Date	Items	Post	Credit	
Jan 31	Balance	✓	600	00					

Signs — Account No. 13

Date	Items	Post	Debit		Date	Items	Post	Credit	

Lucy — Account No. 31

Date	Items	Post	Debit		Date	Items	Post	Credit	
					1975 Jan 31	Balance	✓	1200	00

Withdrawals — Account No. 031

Date	Items	Post	Debit		Date	Items	Post	Credit	

Income from Fees — Account No. 41

Date	Items	Post	Debit		Date	Items	Post	Credit	
					Jan 31	Balance	✓	580	00

Office Supplies Expense — Account No. 51

Date	Items	Post	Debit		Date	Items	Post	Credit	
Jan 31	Balance	✓	50	00					

Janitorial Expense — Account No. 52

Date	Items	Post	Debit		Date	Items	Post	Credit	
Jan 31	Balance	✓	50	00					

Utility Expense — Account No. 53

Date	Items	Post	Debit		Date	Items	Post	Credit	
Jan 31	Balance	✓	80	00					

Trial Balance

The Trial Balance has a three-line title: (1) name of the company, (2) name of the paper (Trial Balance), (3) date. As shown in Chapter 3, all accounts and their debit or credit balances are listed and totaled. The debit and credit totals agreeing, both are double underlined to show that they balance. Sometimes an account number column is used on the Trial Balance.

The Trial Balance for problem 3G (the ledger illustrated on pages 87 and 88) would appear as shown below.

Your Name
Trial Balance
June 30, 1976

Account Title	No.	Debit	Credit
Cash in Bank	11	20.00	
Petty Cash	12	8,00	
Rubber Ring	14	1.50	
Withdrawals	031	1.50	
Income	41		37.00
Miscellaneous Expense	51	6.00	
		37.00	37.00

4E. Mr. Schroeder has hired you to do the bookkeeping for his piano tuning firm. Please journalize and post the following entries. Then prepare a Trial Balance. Use the cash journal whenever possible.

1/5/76	Bought a new car to be used in the business for $3,000 cash, Check #1.
1/10/76	Paid $50 for an ad in the telephone directory, Check #2.
1/12/76	Received $30 from piano tuning.
1/15/76	Bought $30 worth of tuning equipment, and charged it to Beethoven's Fifth Music Company.
1/16/76	Bought $75 worth of stationery and office supplies, Check #3.
1/18/76	Paid $5 for gas for the car, Check #4.
1/18/76	Earned $40 from piano tuning.
1/18/76	Had repairs on the car charged at Bach's Garage. They amounted to $15.
1/25/76	Received $50 from piano tuning.
1/26/76	Sold some old tools for $10.
1/27/76	Paid the music company the $30, Check #5.
1/27/76	Mr. Schroeder withdrew $40 to buy a complete biography of his favorite composer, Check #6.

Cash Journal

Cash Receipts				Cash Disbursements				
Date	Account Credited	Posted	Amount	Date	Account Debited	Posted	Check No.	Amount

Journal

Date	Account Title	Post	Debit	Credit

Ledger for Schroeder's Tune Ups

Cash in Bank — Account No. 101

Date	Items	Post	Debit		Date	Items	Post	Credit	
Jan 1	Balance	✓	5000	00					

Car — Account No. 102

Date	Items	Post	Debit		Date	Items	Post	Credit	

Car Depreciation — Account No. 0102

Date	Items	Post	Debit		Date	Items	Post	Credit	

Tools & Equipment — Account No. 103

Date	Items	Post	Debit		Date	Items	Post	Credit	
Jan 1	Balance	✓	500	00					

Supplies — Account No. 104

Date	Items	Post	Debit		Date	Items	Post	Credit	

Accounts Payable — Account No. 202

Date	Items	Post	Debit		Date	Items	Post	Credit	

Mr. Schroeder — Account No. 301

Date	Items	Post	Debit		Date	Items	Post	Credit	
					1973 Jan 1	Balance	✓	5500	00

Withdrawals — Account No. 0301

Date	Items	Post	Debit		Date	Items	Post	Credit	

Income — Account No. 401

Date	Items	Post	Debit		Date	Items	Post	Credit	

Advertising Expense — Account No. 501

Date	Items	Post	Debit		Date	Items	Post	Credit	

Office Supplies Expense — Account No. 502

Date	Items	Post	Debit		Date	Items	Post	Credit	

Car Expense — Account No. 503

Date	Items	Post	Debit		Date	Items	Post	Credit	

Depreciation Expense — Account No. 504

Date	Items	Post	Debit		Date	Items	Post	Credit	

Account Title	No.	Debit	Credit

Preparing to Make out Financial Statements

Monthly Bookkeeping Cycle

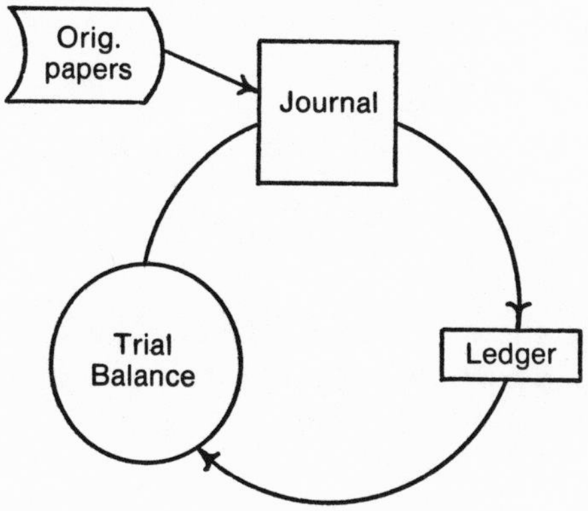

Bookkeeping Cycle When Closing the Books

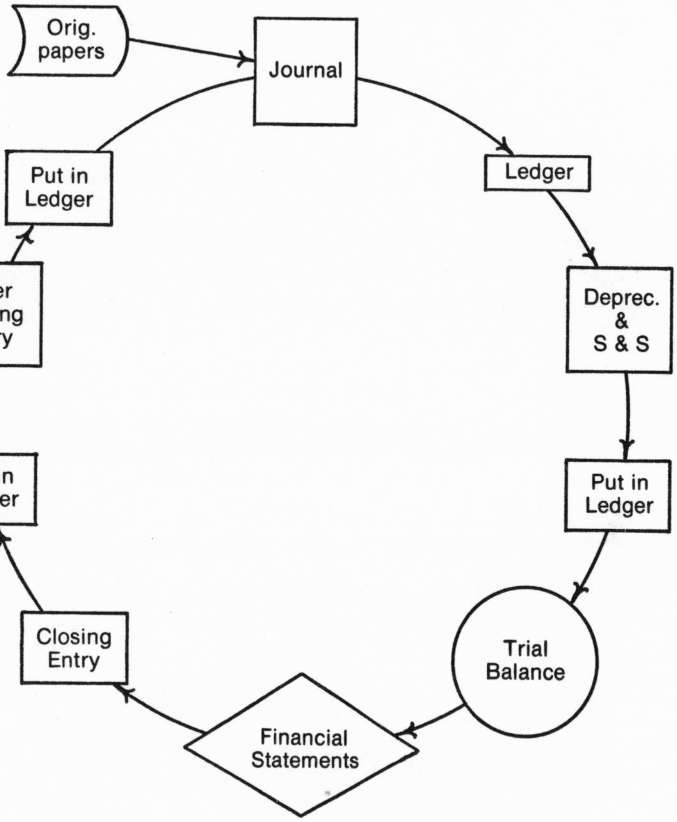

DEPRECIATION

In problem 4E, Mr. Schroeder bought a new car for $3,000. By the end of the year, it will no longer be worth $3,000. Such assets as buildings, cars, and machines lose value due to age or use. This loss of value is called depreciation. Since the asset is no longer worth as much, and there is nothing to show for this, depreciation is an expense. Mr. Schroeder's car really loses a little value each day, but this depreciation is not recorded until the bookeeper is ready to make out financial statements. Since depreciation is an expense, it must be included with the other expenses before profit can be accurately stated on the Income and Expense Statement.

The amount of depreciation is first figured, then the journal entry is made and posted. If Mr. Schroeder expects to use his car in the business for about ten years and it cost $3,000, this means that it loses value at the rate of about $300 per year. (Mr. Schroeder expects the car to be worthless at the end of the ten years.) To figure yearly depreciation on an asset, divide the amount of value it will lose by the expected life.

In making the journal entry, Depreciation Expense will be debited for $300 to take the expense from what he owns free and clear since value has been lost. Because it is not worth as much, the asset Car will be decreased by crediting Car Depreciation. This account takes away from the asset Car. It is a separate account so that the Balance Sheet will show both the car at its original cost and the car's total depreciation.

If on June 1, I bought an $8,100 machine to stamp out shoe tongues and paid for it, my journal entry would be:

		Debit	*Credit*
6/1/76	Machinery	8,100	
	Cash in Bank		8,100
	(a cash journal could have been used)		

By December 31, the machine would have lost value due to depreciation. If I expect the machine to last ten years and then be worth $100 scrap value, it loses $800 value per year. As I've had it half a year, the machine has depreciated by $400. Therefore, my journal entry before preparing financial statements is:

		Debit	*Credit*
12/31/76	Depreciation Expense	400	
	Machine Depreciation		400

This entry is then posted and a Trial Balance is prepared before making out the financial statements. Depreciation Expense is included with all of the expenses on the Income and Expense Statement. The Asset section of the Balance Sheet would show, among the other assets:

	(figuring column)	
Machinery	$8,100	
Less total Machine Depreciation	400	
Current Value		$7,700

At the end of the following year, this machine would have lost an additional $800 due to deprceiation, since it loses value at the rate of $800 per year; and the journal entry would debit Depreciation Expense and credit Machine Depreciation for that amount. The Income and Expense Statement for the year would include the $800 Depreciation Expense that had built up during 1976. The Balance Sheet would include among the assets:

Machinery	$8,100	
Less total Machine Depreciation	1,200	
Current Value		$6,900

Since the machine is $1\frac{1}{2}$ years old it is worth $1,200 less than when it was new. $400 was entered in Machine Depreciation at the end of 1976 and $800 at the end of 1977.

UNUSED SUPPLIES

All of the supplies were recorded in an expense account as they were purchased. Any supplies that have not been used are not really expenses, and should not reduce the profit shown on the Income and Expense Statement. Unused supplies are something of value owned.

Before making out financial statements, count all of the supplies left (this is known as taking inventory) and estimate their value. This value of supplies in stock is then taken out of the expenses so it will not deduct from the profit, and it is put in an asset account to add to the value of the things owned.

If I purchased $200 worth of office supplies on 6/19 for cash, my journal entry would be:

		Debit	Credit
6/19	Office Supplies Expense	200	
	Cash in Bank		200

Before making out financial statements at the end of the year, I took an inventory and found that I had $50 worth of supplies left. My journal entry would be:

12/31	Office Supplies	50	
	Office Supplies Expense		50

The office Supplies Expense account would then show a $150 balance (since $150 worth of supplies had been used up) on the Income and Expense Statement, and $50 worth of stationery and Office Supplies that are on hand would be included in the asset section of the Balance Sheet.

4F. *Below, make the journal entries for problem 4E (pages 91-94) that would be necessary before making out financial statements on December 31, 1975. Mr. Schroeder expects the car to last six years and then have no value. There are $20 worth of stationery and office supplies left in stock.*

page 2

Date	Account Title	Post	Debit	Credit

4G. *Post these journal entries to Mr. Schroeder's accounts on pages 91 through 93. Make out a new Trial Balance and an Income and Expense Statement and a Balance Sheet for him as of 12/31/75. Financial statements were last made out 12/31/74. There have been no other entries made in the accounts between January and the end of December. (Refer to Chapter 3 if you have forgotten how to make out financial statements.)*

Account Title	No.	Debit	Credit

Show Income & Expense Statement here

Balance Sheet

Closing the Owner's Equity Accounts

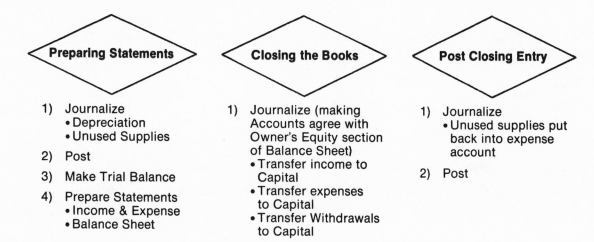

Preparing Statements

1) Journalize
   - Depreciation
   - Unused Supplies
2) Post
3) Make Trial Balance
4) Prepare Statements
   - Income & Expense
   - Balance Sheet

Closing the Books

1) Journalize (making Accounts agree with Owner's Equity section of Balance Sheet)
   - Transfer income to Capital
   - Transfer expenses to Capital
   - Transfer Withdrawals to Capital
2) Post
3) Rule closed accounts

Post Closing Entry

1) Journalize
   - Unused supplies put back into expense account
2) Post

The Owner's Equity section of the Balance Sheet shows the original investment, plus the profit (incomes in excess of expenses), less the withdrawals. This total is the amount that the owner is then reinvesting. The accounts in the ledger should now be changed to show this reinvestment. Of course, journal entries must be made first and then posted to the ledger.

The credit balance of each income account is transferred out of its income account to the credit side of the owner's or capital account. Here it will add to his investment. The debit balance of each expense account is transferred out of its expense account to the debit side of the owner's account, where it will take from the amount he is reinvesting. The debit balance of the Withdrawals account is transferred out of its account to the debit side of the owner's account to take from his reinvestment.

When this is journalized and posted, the owner's account will have the same balance that is shown on the Balance Sheet. All income and expense accounts and the Withdrawals account will have no balances left in them, since their balances were transferred out by debiting to transfer credit balances and crediting to transfer debit balances. This is why, in the example of the machine on page 96, the Depreciation expense account had no money left in it after the end of the first year. Its $400 debit balance had been transferred into the owner's account. Then at the end of the second year, when the 1976 depreciation was recorded in the Depreciation Expense account, this expense of the current year was the only amount in the account. The value in Machine Depreciation continued to build year after year, since it takes from an asset account and is not closed out as owner's equity accounts are.

The closing journal entries for problem 4D would appear as shown below:

		Debit	*Credit*
2/28	Income from Fees	805	
	Lucy		805
2/28	Lucy	70	
	Office Supplies Expense		70
2/28	Lucy	75	
	Janitorial Expense		75
2/28	Lucy	110	
	Utility Expense		110
2/28	Lucy	5	
	Withdrawals		5

When the journal entries are posted, the accounts that have been closed out are double ruled to show that they are in balance. The accounts from problem 4D are shown below.

Lucy — Account No. 31

Date	Items	Post	Debit	Date	Items	Post	Credit
Feb 28		J1	70 00	Jan 31	Balance	✓	1200 00
28		J1	75 00	Feb 13		CJ	500 00
28		J1	110 00	28		J1	805 00
28		J1	5 00				2505 00
			260 00		2245.00		

Withdrawals — Account No. 031

Date	Items	Post	Debit	Date	Items	Post	Credit
Feb 25		CJ	5 00	Feb 28		J1	5 00

Income from Fees — Account No. 41

Date	Items	Post	Debit	Date	Items	Post	Credit
Feb 28		J1	805 00	Jan 31	Balance	✓	580 00
				Feb 5		CJ	50 00
				10		CJ	80 00
				23		CJ	95 00
			805 00				805 00

Office Supplies Expense — Account No. 51

Date	Items	Post	Debit	Date	Items	Post	Credit
Jan 31	Balance	✓	50 00	Feb 28		J1	70 00
Feb 6		CJ	20 00				
			70 00				70 00

Janitorial Expense — Account No. 52

Date	Items	Post	Debit	Date	Items	Post	Credit
Jan 31	Balance	✓	50 00	Feb 28		J1	75 00
Feb 12		CJ	25 00				
			75 00				75 00

Utility Expense — Account No. 53

Date	Items	Post	Debit	Date	Items	Post	Credit
Jan 31	Balance		80 00	Feb 28		J1	110 00
Feb 28		CJ	30 00				
			110 00				110 00

4H. In the journal below, make the journal entries to close Mr. Schroeder's Income, Expense, and Withdrawals accounts. Then post them to his ledger on pages 91-93, rule the closed accounts, and make out a Trial Balance.

Journal

page 3

Date	Account Title	Post	Debit	Credit

Account Title	No.	Debit	Credit

Entry after Closing

Only one more journal entry is needed before recording new business.As you remember, the supplies were transferred out of the expense account where they are usually kept, into an asset account so they would be included with the other things of value on the Balance Sheet. Now that the financial statements are complete, the Supplies asset account is credited to take out the value of the supplies (since the value of supplies is not usually kept there) and the Supplies Expense account is debited to put the value into the account, where it is kept. If before making out statements the journal entry had been made that is illustrated on page 97, debiting Office Supplies for $50 and crediting Office Supplies Expense for $50, the following journal entry would now be needed:

		Debit	*Credit*
1/1	Office Supplies Expense	50	
	Office Supplies		50

41. *Please make the journal entry to put Mr. Schroeder's office supplies back into the account where they are usually kept, and then post the entry to his accounts.*

page 4

~~Date~~	Account Title	Post	Debit	Credit

PUTTING IT ALL TOGETHER

Chapter Summary Problems

A. WHAT IS IT?

Fill in the blanks with the correct words from those listed below:

journalizing	ledger
Posted	Cash Receipts
explanation	journal
depreciation	Cash Disbursements
Supplies	posting
Items	Depreciation Expense
closing	Car Depreciation
Account Title	

1. Transferring the balances of income, expense, and withdrawal accounts into the owner's account is called ______________________ the books.
2. ______________________ is a column in the ledger used to note things you wish to remember.
3. ______________________ is a column which appears in both the journal and ledger and is used for cross reference.
4. The ______________________ is the book of accounts.
5. The ______________________ account is closed after the Income and Expense Statement is prepared.
6. The last line of a journal entry is the ______________________.
7. All bookkeeping information is first recorded in the ______________________.
8. Recording an entry in the journal is called ______________________.
9. Write the explanation in the ______________________ column of a journal.
10. ______________________ is a loss of value due to age or use.
11. ______________________ is recording journal entries in their accounts.
12. The left page of the cash journal is the ______________________ page.
13. Any time money is spent it is recorded on the ______________________ page of the cash journal.
14. After making out financial statments, the value of the unused inventory is taken out of the ______________________ asset account.
15. ______________________ is an account set up to take from an asset account.

B. USING WHAT YOU KNOW

You have been hired to do the bookkeeping for the Snoopy Squadron Flying School. Record the following entries in the journals (use the cash journal whenever possible) and post them. Then make out a Trial Balance and financial statements. Close the owner's equity accounts, and put the value of the gas back in the correct account.

1. 6/1/76 Snoopy invested a plane worth $16,000 and $500 cash in the business. He owed $13,000 on a mortgage on the plane. (Use the regular journal since there are two debits.)
2. 6/2/76 He paid one month's rent on the hangar, Check #1 for $200.
3. 6/5/76 Bought $120 worth of gas, Check #2.
4. 6/6/76 Earned $50 from giving lessons.
5. 6/8/76 Earned $30 from lessons.
6. 6/15/76 Withdrew $15 to buy a silk scarf and some goggles, Check #3.
7. 6/18/76 Withdrew $5 to buy the Red Cross girls some root beer, Check #4.
8. 6/20/76 Earned $35 giving lessons.
9. 6/22/76 Paid $300 on what he owed on the plane mortgage, Check #5. $50 of this was interest.
10. 6/24/76 Had $100 worth of repairs done on the plane after the Red Baron damaged it. Charged it to The Doghouse Hangar.
11. 6/25/76 Earned $80.
12. 6/30/76 Before you make out financial statements, Snoopy found that he had $50 worth of gas still on hand. Please prepare for financial statements by journalizing this.
13. 6/30/76 He figures that the plane will last eight years. Please allow for depreciation.
14. 6/30/76 Post all journal entries to the accounts; total and balance them.
15. 6/30/76 Make out a Trial Balance and financial statements.
16. 6/30/76 Make journal entries to close the income, expense, and withdrawals accounts. Post and rule them.
17. 7/1/76 Make the necessary entry to put the unused gas back into its expense account. Post this.

Cash Journal

Cash Receipts				Cash Disbursements				
Date	Account Credited	Posted	Amount	Date	Account Debited	Posted	Check No.	Amount

Journal

Date	Account Title	Post	Debit	Credit

Cash in Bank — Account No. 11

Date	Items	Post	Debit	Date	Items	Post	Credit

Gas Supplies — Account No. 12

Date	Items	Post	Debit	Date	Items	Post	Credit

Plane — Account No. 13

Date	Items	Post	Debit	Date	Items	Post	Credit

Plane Depreciation — Account No. 012

Date	Items	Post	Debit	Date	Items	Post	Credit

Mortgage Payable — Account No. 21

Date	Items	Post	Debit	Date	Items	Post	Credit

Accounts Payable — Account No. 22

Date	Items	Post	Debit	Date	Items	Post	Credit

Snoopy — Account No. 31

Date	Items	Post	Debit	Date	Items	Post	Credit

Withdrawals Account No. 031

Date	Items	Post	Debit	Date	Items	Post	Credit

Income Account No. 41

Date	Items	Post	Debit	Date	Items	Post	Credit

Rent Expense Account No. 51

Date	Items	Post	Debit	Date	Items	Post	Credit

Gas Expense Account No. 52

Date	Items	Post	Debit	Date	Items	Post	Credit

Miscellaneous Expense Account No. 53

Date	Items	Post	Debit	Date	Items	Post	Credit

Depreciation Expense Account No. 54

Date	Items	Post	Debit	Date	Items	Post	Credit

Account Title	No.	Debit	Credit

Show Trial Balance

Show Income & Expense Statement

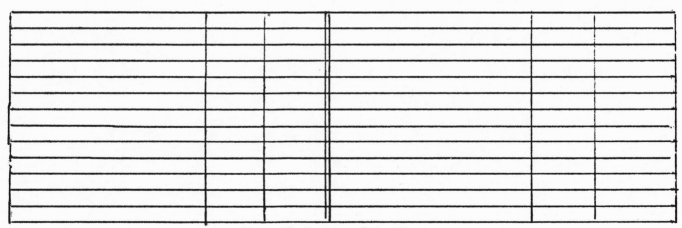

Show Balance Sheet

FINAL SUMMARY PROBLEM Chapters 1-4

Charlie Brown's father has asked you to keep the books for Brown's Barber Shop, because his bookkeeper is on vacation. The shop has been closed from December 1 through December 11. They maintain a petty cash fund of $50. They have two barbers (in addition to Mr. Brown, who does not receive a salary). Red Bard is paid $5 per hour and Curly Hart is paid $5.50 per hour. Both men have one exemption. Use the tax tables in Chapter 2 to figure payrolls. There are no city or state income taxes.

1. 12/12/76 Pay $150 rent.
2. 12/13/76 Pay $30 for subscriptions to magazines.
3. 12/15/76 Buy new equipment for $300, charging it to Daniel Druff Distributors.
4. 12/16/76 Deposit this week's earnings in the bank—$405 in bills plus $30 in change. $425 of it was for haircuts, shaves, etc. $10 was received from selling shampoos and other products. Sales tax is included in the $10. (This entry can be put on two separate lines of the cash journal since the entire amount is a debit to cash.)
5. 12/16/76 Pay newsboy $3 out of petty cash.
6. 12/16/76 Pay Red his salary for 36 hours work and Curly for 35 hours. (Use the regular journal for this entry since accounts other than cash are also credited.)
7. 12/19/76 Pay $8 out of petty cash for window washing.
8. 12/21/76 Buy $90 worth of shampoo and other supplies to use in the shop.
9. 12/22/76 Give Mr. Brown a check for $200, since he is withdrawing that money to send his son to camp.
10. 12/23/76 Deposit this week's earnings—$565 in bills, $10 in change. $20 of this was income from the sale of products.
11. 12/23/76 Pay Red and Curly. Each worked 40 hours.

12. 12/26/76 Take $10 out of petty cash to buy some more shampoo.
13. 12/27/76 Give Mr. Brown a check for the $150 he is withdrawing.
14. 12/28/76 Pay the janitor $180.
15. 12/29/76 Pay $100 on the bill from Daniel Druff Distributors.
16. 12/30/76 Deposit $540 in bills, $32 in change. $22 of this was from the sale of products.
17. 12/30/76 Pay Red for 38 hours work and Curly for 36 hours.
18. 12/31/76 Make out a Petty Cash Statement for the month, and make out a check to put the money spent back into the petty cash drawer. Record this in the books.
19. 12/31/76 Pay state sales tax to the state Internal Revenue Service. They collect 5% of this month's total sales income.
20. 12/31/76 Pay the Federal Internal Revenue Service all that is owed for Red and Curly's federal income tax and the total FICA tax owed (their share plus the employer's).
21. 12/31/76 Make out a bank reconciliation for December. No checks were written nor deposits made until December 12. Remember to record the service charge.
22. 12/31/76 The equipment is expected to last 10 years. Make a journal entry for this year's depreciation. The equipment he has had less than one-half month has not depreciated.
23. 12/31/76 $60 worth of barber shop supplies are left in stock. Make a journal entry for this.
24. 12/31/76 Make out the Trial Balance and financial statements. The last statements were made out one year ago.
25. 12/31/76 Close the owner's equity accounts, and make a Trial Balance to check your accuracy.
26. 1/1/77 Put the value of the supplies back into the correct account.

113 $
19
TO
	DOLLARS	CENTS
BAL. FOR'D		
DEPOSITS		
"		
TOTAL		
THIS CHECK		
OTHER DEDUCTIONS		
BAL. FOR'D		

113
2-52
710
19
PAY TO THE ORDER OF $
DOLLARS
NATIONAL BOULEVARD BANK OF CHICAGO
SAMPLE-VOID
DELUXE CHECK PRINTERS, INC.
MEMO
⑆0710⑉0052⑆ ⑈123456 7⑈ 0113
DELUXE CHECK PRINTERS • RJ-1

114 $________

________________ 19____

TO________________

	DOLLARS	CENTS
BAL. FOR'D		
DEPOSITS		
"		
TOTAL		
THIS CHECK		
OTHER DEDUCTIONS		
BAL. FOR'D		

114

2-52/710

________________ 19____

PAY TO THE ORDER OF________________________________ $________

____ DOLLARS

NATIONAL BOULEVARD BANK OF CHICAGO

SAMPLE-VOID
DELUXE CHECK PRINTERS, INC.

MEMO________________________ ________________________

⑆0710⑉0052⑆ ⑈123456 7⑈ 0114

DELUXE CHECK PRINTERS • RJ-1

115 $________

________________ 19____

TO________________

	DOLLARS	CENTS
BAL. FOR'D		
DEPOSITS		
"		
TOTAL		
THIS CHECK		
OTHER DEDUCTIONS		
BAL. FOR'D		

115

2-52/710

________________ 19____

PAY TO THE ORDER OF________________________________ $________

____ DOLLARS

NATIONAL BOULEVARD BANK OF CHICAGO

SAMPLE-VOID
DELUXE CHECK PRINTERS, INC.

MEMO________________________ ________________________

⑆0710⑉0052⑆ ⑈123456 7⑈ 0115

DELUXE CHECK PRINTERS • RJ-1

116 $________

________________ 19____

TO________________

	DOLLARS	CENTS
BAL. FOR'D		
DEPOSITS		
"		
TOTAL		
THIS CHECK		
OTHER DEDUCTIONS		
BAL. FOR'D		

116

2-52/710

________________ 19____

PAY TO THE ORDER OF________________________________ $________

____ DOLLARS

NATIONAL BOULEVARD BANK OF CHICAGO

SAMPLE-VOID
DELUXE CHECK PRINTERS, INC.

MEMO________________________ ________________________

⑆0710⑉0052⑆ ⑈123456 7⑈ 0116

DELUXE CHECK PRINTERS • RJ-1

117 $______

______19____

TO______

	DOLLARS	CENTS
BAL. FOR'D		
DEPOSITS		
"		
TOTAL		
THIS CHECK		
OTHER DEDUCTIONS		
BAL. FOR'D		

117

2-52/710

______19____

PAY TO THE ORDER OF______ $______

______DOLLARS

NATIONAL BOULEVARD BANK OF CHICAGO

SAMPLE-VOID
DELUXE CHECK PRINTERS, INC.

MEMO______

⑆0710⑈0052⑆ ⑈123456 7⑈ 0117

DELUXE CHECK PRINTERS • RJ-1

118 $______

______19____

TO______

	DOLLARS	CENTS
BAL. FOR'D		
DEPOSITS		
"		
TOTAL		
THIS CHECK		
OTHER DEDUCTIONS		
BAL. FOR'D		

118

2-52/710

______19____

PAY TO THE ORDER OF______ $______

______DOLLARS

NATIONAL BOULEVARD BANK OF CHICAGO

SAMPLE-VOID
DELUXE CHECK PRINTERS, INC.

MEMO______

⑆0710⑈0052⑆ ⑈123456 7⑈ 0118

DELUXE CHECK PRINTERS • RJ-1

119 $______

______19____

TO______

	DOLLARS	CENTS
BAL. FOR'D		
DEPOSITS		
"		
TOTAL		
THIS CHECK		
OTHER DEDUCTIONS		
BAL. FOR'D		

119

2-52/710

______19____

PAY TO THE ORDER OF______ $______

______DOLLARS

NATIONAL BOULEVARD BANK OF CHICAGO

SAMPLE-VOID
DELUXE CHECK PRINTERS, INC.

MEMO______

⑆0710⑈0052⑆ ⑈123456 7⑈ 0119

DELUXE CHECK PRINTERS • RJ-1

120 $ ________

________ 19____

TO ________

	DOLLARS	CENTS
BAL. FOR'D		
DEPOSITS		
"		
TOTAL		
THIS CHECK		
OTHER DEDUCTIONS		
BAL. FOR'D		

120

2-52
710

________ 19____

PAY TO THE ORDER OF ________ $ ________

________ DOLLARS

NATIONAL BOULEVARD BANK OF CHICAGO

SAMPLE-VOID
DELUXE CHECK PRINTERS, INC.

MEMO ________

⑆0710⑉00521⑆ ⑈123456 7⑈ 0120

DELUXE CHECK PRINTERS • RJ-1

121 $ ________

________ 19____

TO ________

	DOLLARS	CENTS
BAL. FOR'D		
DEPOSITS		
"		
TOTAL		
THIS CHECK		
OTHER DEDUCTIONS		
BAL. FOR'D		

121

2-52
710

________ 19____

PAY TO THE ORDER OF ________ $ ________

________ DOLLARS

NATIONAL BOULEVARD BANK OF CHICAGO

SAMPLE-VOID
DELUXE CHECK PRINTERS, INC.

MEMO ________

⑆0710⑉00521⑆ ⑈123456 7⑈ 0121

DELUXE CHECK PRINTERS • RJ-1

122 $ ________

________ 19____

TO ________

	DOLLARS	CENTS
BAL. FOR'D		
DEPOSITS		
"		
TOTAL		
THIS CHECK		
OTHER DEDUCTIONS		
BAL. FOR'D		

122

2-52
710

________ 19____

PAY TO THE ORDER OF ________ $ ________

________ DOLLARS

NATIONAL BOULEVARD BANK OF CHICAGO

SAMPLE-VOID
DELUXE CHECK PRINTERS, INC.

MEMO ________

⑆0710⑉00521⑆ ⑈123456 7⑈ 0122

DELUXE CHECK PRINTERS • RJ-1

No.__________ $__________

RECEIVED OF PETTY CASH

DATE________________19____

FOR________________________________

CHARGE TO__________________________
ACCOUNT

APPROVED BY RECEIVED BY

TOPS FORM 3008

No.__________ $__________

RECEIVED OF PETTY CASH

DATE________________19____

FOR________________________________

CHARGE TO__________________________
ACCOUNT

APPROVED BY RECEIVED BY

TOPS FORM 3008

No.__________ $__________

RECEIVED OF PETTY CASH

DATE________________19____

FOR________________________________

CHARGE TO__________________________
ACCOUNT

APPROVED BY RECEIVED BY

TOPS FORM 3008

CHECKING ACCOUNT DEPOSIT TICKET

CASH	CURRENCY		
	COIN		
CHECKS			
TOTAL FROM OTHER SIDE			
TOTAL			
LESS CASH RECEIVED			
NET DEPOSIT			

[redacted]

2-52/710

USE OTHER SIDE FOR ADDITIONAL LISTING

BE SURE EACH ITEM IS PROPERLY ENDORSED

DATE ______________________ 19____

____

NATIONAL BOULEVARD BANK OF CHICAGO

SAMPLE-VOID
DELUXE CHECK PRINTERS, INC.

⑆123456 7⑆

DELUXE JD-3 CHECKS AND OTHER ITEMS ARE RECEIVED FOR DEPOSIT SUBJECT TO THE TERMS AND CONDITIONS OF THIS BANK'S COLLECTION AGREEMENT.

CHECKING ACCOUNT DEPOSIT TICKET

CASH	CURRENCY		
	COIN		
CHECKS			
TOTAL FROM OTHER SIDE			
TOTAL			
LESS CASH RECEIVED			
NET DEPOSIT			

[redacted]

2-52/710

USE OTHER SIDE FOR ADDITIONAL LISTING

BE SURE EACH ITEM IS PROPERLY ENDORSED

DATE ______________________ 19____

____

NATIONAL BOULEVARD BANK OF CHICAGO

SAMPLE-VOID
DELUXE CHECK PRINTERS, INC.

⑆123456 7⑆

DELUXE JD-3 CHECKS AND OTHER ITEMS ARE RECEIVED FOR DEPOSIT SUBJECT TO THE TERMS AND CONDITIONS OF THIS BANK'S COLLECTION AGREEMENT.

CHECKING ACCOUNT DEPOSIT TICKET

CASH	CURRENCY		
	COIN		
CHECKS			
TOTAL FROM OTHER SIDE			
TOTAL			
LESS CASH RECEIVED			
NET DEPOSIT			

[redacted]

2-52/710

USE OTHER SIDE FOR ADDITIONAL LISTING

BE SURE EACH ITEM IS PROPERLY ENDORSED

DATE ______________________ 19____

____

NATIONAL BOULEVARD BANK OF CHICAGO

SAMPLE-VOID
DELUXE CHECK PRINTERS, INC.

⑆123456 7⑆

DELUXE JD-3 CHECKS AND OTHER ITEMS ARE RECEIVED FOR DEPOSIT SUBJECT TO THE TERMS AND CONDITIONS OF THIS BANK'S COLLECTION AGREEMENT.

305

DATE ____________________ 19____

TO ____________________

FOR ____________________

BAL. FOR'D		
DEP.		
TOTAL		
THIS CHECK		
BALANCE		

TOTAL WAGES		
SOCIAL SEC. TAX		
U. S. INC. TAX		
STATE INC. TAX		
TOTAL DED.		
CHECK		

DETACH BEFORE CASHING CHECK

STATEMENT OF EARNINGS AND DEDUCTIONS FOR EMPLOYEE'S RECORD COVERING PAY PERIOD TO AND INCLUDING DATE SHOWN BELOW

DATE ____________________ 19____

TO ____________________

TOTAL WAGES		
SOCIAL SECURITY TAX		
WITHHOLDING U. S. INCOME TAX		
STATE INCOME TAX		
TOTAL DEDUCTIONS		
AMOUNT THIS CHECK		

306

DATE ____________________ 19____

TO ____________________

FOR ____________________

BAL. FOR'D		
DEP.		
TOTAL		
THIS CHECK		
BALANCE		

TOTAL WAGES		
SOCIAL SEC. TAX		
U. S. INC. TAX		
STATE INC. TAX		
TOTAL DED.		
CHECK		

DETACH BEFORE CASHING CHECK

STATEMENT OF EARNINGS AND DEDUCTIONS FOR EMPLOYEE'S RECORD COVERING PAY PERIOD TO AND INCLUDING DATE SHOWN BELOW

DATE ____________________ 19____

TO ____________________

TOTAL WAGES		
SOCIAL SECURITY TAX		
WITHHOLDING U. S. INCOME TAX		
STATE INCOME TAX		
TOTAL DEDUCTIONS		
AMOUNT THIS CHECK		

307

DATE ____________________ 19____

TO ____________________

FOR ____________________

BAL. FOR'D		
DEP.		
TOTAL		
THIS CHECK		
BALANCE		

TOTAL WAGES		
SOCIAL SEC. TAX		
U. S. INC. TAX		
STATE INC. TAX		
TOTAL DED.		
CHECK		

DETACH BEFORE CASHING CHECK

STATEMENT OF EARNINGS AND DEDUCTIONS FOR EMPLOYEE'S RECORD COVERING PAY PERIOD TO AND INCLUDING DATE SHOWN BELOW

DATE ____________________ 19____

TO ____________________

TOTAL WAGES		
SOCIAL SECURITY TAX		
WITHHOLDING U. S. INCOME TAX		
STATE INCOME TAX		
TOTAL DEDUCTIONS		
AMOUNT THIS CHECK		

305

______________ 19____ 2-52/710

PAY TO THE ORDER OF ______________________________ $__________

______________________________ DOLLARS

NATIONAL BOULEVARD BANK OF CHICAGO

SAMPLE-VOID
DELUXE CHECK PRINTERS, INC.

____

⑈000305⑈ ⑆07100052⑆ ⑈123456 7⑈

DELUXE CHECK PRINTERS PS-3

306

______________ 19____ 2-52/710

PAY TO THE ORDER OF ______________________________ $__________

PAYROLL

______________________________ DOLLARS

NATIONAL BOULEVARD BANK OF CHICAGO

SAMPLE-VOID
DELUXE CHECK PRINTERS, INC.

____

⑈000306⑈ ⑆07100052⑆ ⑈123456 7⑈

DELUXE CHECK PRINTERS PS-3

307

______________ 19____ 2-52/710

PAY TO THE ORDER OF ______________________________ $__________

PAYROLL

______________________________ DOLLARS

NATIONAL BOULEVARD BANK OF CHICAGO

SAMPLE-VOID
DELUXE CHECK PRINTERS, INC.

____

⑈000307⑈ ⑆07100052⑆ ⑈123456 7⑈

DELUXE CHECK PRINTERS PS-3

308

DATE ______________________ 19 ____

TO ______________________

FOR ______________________

BAL. FOR'D		
DEP.		
TOTAL		
THIS CHECK		
BALANCE		

TOTAL WAGES		
SOCIAL SEC. TAX		
U. S. INC. TAX		
STATE INC. TAX		
TOTAL DED.		
CHECK		

DETACH BEFORE CASHING CHECK

STATEMENT OF EARNINGS AND DEDUCTIONS FOR EMPLOYEE'S RECORD COVERING PAY PERIOD TO AND INCLUDING DATE SHOWN BELOW

DATE ______________________ 19 ____

TO ______________________

TOTAL WAGES		
SOCIAL SECURITY TAX		
WITHHOLDING U. S. INCOME TAX		
STATE INCOME TAX		
TOTAL DEDUCTIONS		
AMOUNT THIS CHECK		

309

DATE ______________________ 19 ____

TO ______________________

FOR ______________________

BAL. FOR'D		
DEP.		
TOTAL		
THIS CHECK		
BALANCE		

TOTAL WAGES		
SOCIAL SEC. TAX		
U. S. INC. TAX		
STATE INC. TAX		
TOTAL DED.		
CHECK		

DETACH BEFORE CASHING CHECK

STATEMENT OF EARNINGS AND DEDUCTIONS FOR EMPLOYEE'S RECORD COVERING PAY PERIOD TO AND INCLUDING DATE SHOWN BELOW

DATE ______________________ 19 ____

TO ______________________

TOTAL WAGES		
SOCIAL SECURITY TAX		
WITHHOLDING U. S. INCOME TAX		
STATE INCOME TAX		
TOTAL DEDUCTIONS		
AMOUNT THIS CHECK		

310

DATE ______________________ 19 ____

TO ______________________

FOR ______________________

BAL. FOR'D		
DEP.		
TOTAL		
THIS CHECK		
BALANCE		

TOTAL WAGES		
SOCIAL SEC. TAX		
U. S. INC. TAX		
STATE INC. TAX		
TOTAL DED.		
CHECK		

DETACH BEFORE CASHING CHECK

STATEMENT OF EARNINGS AND DEDUCTIONS FOR EMPLOYEE'S RECORD COVERING PAY PERIOD TO AND INCLUDING DATE SHOWN BELOW

DATE ______________________ 19 ____

TO ______________________

TOTAL WAGES		
SOCIAL SECURITY TAX		
WITHHOLDING U. S. INCOME TAX		
STATE INCOME TAX		
TOTAL DEDUCTIONS		
AMOUNT THIS CHECK		

308

19___ 2-52/710

PAY TO THE ORDER OF ___ $ ___

PAYROLL

___ DOLLARS

NATIONAL BOULEVARD BANK OF CHICAGO

SAMPLE-VOID
DELUXE CHECK PRINTERS, INC.

⑈000308⑈ ⑆0710⑉0052⑆ ⑈123456 7⑈

DELUXE CHECK PRINTERS PS-3

309

19___ 2-52/710

PAY TO THE ORDER OF ___ $ ___

PAYROLL

___ DOLLARS

NATIONAL BOULEVARD BANK OF CHICAGO

SAMPLE-VOID
DELUXE CHECK PRINTERS, INC.

⑈000309⑈ ⑆0710⑉0052⑆ ⑈123456 7⑈

DELUXE CHECK PRINTERS PS-3

310

19___ 2-52/710

PAY TO THE ORDER OF ___ $ ___

PAYROLL

___ DOLLARS

NATIONAL BOULEVARD BANK OF CHICAGO

SAMPLE-VOID
DELUXE CHECK PRINTERS, INC.

⑈000310⑈ ⑆0710⑉0052⑆ ⑈123456 7⑈

DELUXE CHECK PRINTERS PS-3

Total Payroll Record
Brown's Barber Shop
Payroll for week ending ________

Name	Reg Hours	O.T. Hours	Reg Pay	O.T. Pay	Gross Pay	Fed Inc. Tax	FICA Tax	Net Pay
Total								

Total Payroll Record
Brown's Barber Shop
Payroll for week ending ________

Name	Reg Hours	O.T. Hours	Reg Pay	O.T. Pay	Gross Pay	Fed Inc. Tax	FICA Tax	Net Pay
Total								

Total Payroll Record
Brown's Barber Shop
Payroll for week ending ________

Name	Reg Hours	O.T. Hours	Reg Pay	O.T. Pay	Gross Pay	Fed Inc. Tax	FICA Tax	Net Pay
Total								

Individual Employee's Earnings Record

Name Red Bard

week ending	reg. pay	o.t. pay	gross pay	cumulative pay	fed inc tax	FICA tax	net pay
				$8100.00			
total							

Individual Employee's Earnings Record

Name Curly Hart

week ending	reg. pay	o.t. pay	gross pay	cumulative pay	fed inc tax	FICA tax	net pay
				$7900.00			
total							

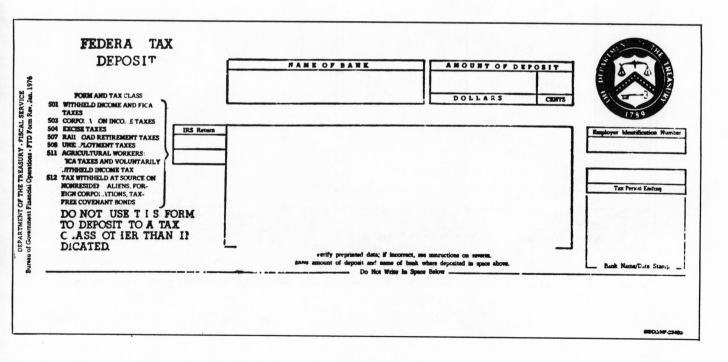

FEDERA TAX DEPOSIT

DEPARTMENT OF THE TREASURY - FISCAL SERVICE
Bureau of Government Financial Operations - FTD Form Rev. Jan. 1976

FORM AND TAX CLASS
501 WITHHELD INCOME AND FICA TAXES
503 CORPO A ON INCO E TAXES
504 EXCISE TAXES
507 RAIL OAD RETIREMENT TAXES
508 UNE PLOYMENT TAXES
511 AGRICULTURAL WORKERS: ICA TAXES AND VOLUNTARILY ITHHELD INCOME TAX
512 TAX WITHHELD AT SOURCE ON NONRESIDEN ALIENS, FOREIGN CORPO ATIONS, TAX-FREE COVENANT BONDS

DO NOT USE T I S FORM TO DEPOSIT TO A TAX C ASS OT IER THAN I DICATED.

NAME OF BANK

AMOUNT OF DEPOSIT

DOLLARS | CENTS

IRS Return

THE DEPARTMENT OF THE TREASURY 1789

Employer Identification Number

Tax Period Ending

Bank Name/Date Stamp

verify preprinted data; if incorrect, see instructions on reverse.
amount of deposit and name of bank where deposited in space above.

Do Not Write In Space Below

NATIONAL BOULEVARD BANK OF CHICAGO
400-410 N. MICHIGAN AVE., 237 E. GRAND AVE.,
PHONE (312) 467-4100 • MEMBER FDIC

Brown's Barber Shop
6 S. Sussex Street

ACCOUNT NUMBER
123456 - 7
DATE OF STATEMENT
12/31/76

BEGINNING BALANCE	NUMBER	TOTAL CHECKS & DEBITS	NUMBER	TOTAL DEPOSITS & CREDITS	SERVICE CHARGE	ENDING BALANCE
4000.00	11	1508.14	2	1010.00	.85	3501.01

DATE	CHECKS AND DEBITS		DEPOSITS & CREDITS	BALANCE
12/16	30.00		435.00	4405.00
12/17	138.67	148.34		4117.99
12/18	150.00			3967.99
12/22	200.00			3767.99
12/23	167.83		575.00	4175.16
12/28	150.00	.85 SC		4024.31
12/29	90.00	153.30		
	180.00	100.00		3501.01

LP - LIST OF CHECKS
OD - OVERDRAWN
RT - RETURNED ITEM
SC - SERVICE CHARGE

CC - CERTIFIED CHECK
CM - CREDIT MEMO
DM - DEBIT MEMO
MC - MISC. CHARGE

PLEASE EXAMINE AT ONCE
REPORT ALL EXCEPTIONS TO OUR AUDIT DEPT.
WITHIN 10 DAYS.

MONTH____________________ 19 ________

THIS FORM IS PROVIDED TO HELP YOU BALANCE YOUR BANK STATEMENT

CHECKS OUTSTANDING - NOT CHARGED TO ACCOUNT

NO.	$	
TOTAL	$	

BANK BALANCE SHOWN ON THIS STATEMENT $____________

ADD +

DEPOSITS NOT CREDITED IN THIS STATEMENT (IF ANY) $____________

SUB-TOTAL $____________

SUBTRACT —

CHECKS OUTSTANDING $____________

BALANCE $____________

SHOULD AGREE WITH CHECK BOOK BALANCE AFTER DEDUCTING SERVICE CHARGE (IF ANY) SHOWN ON THIS STATEMENT FOR PRESENT MONTH.

Each depositor insured to $40,000

FDIC

FEDERAL DEPOSIT INSURANCE CORPORATION

Petty Cash Statement
for the Month of ________, 1976

Journal

Date	Account Title	Post	Debit	Credit

Journal

Date	Account Title	Post	Debit		Credit	

Cash Journal

Cash Receipts				Cash Disbursements				
Date	Account Credited	Post	Amount	Date	Account Debited	Post	Check No.	Amount

Cash in Bank — Account No. 11

Date	Items	Post	Debit	¢	Date	Items	Post	Credit	¢
Nov. 30	Balance	✓	4000	00					

Petty Cash — Account No. 12

Date	Items	Post	Debit	¢	Date	Items	Post	Credit	¢
Nov. 30	Balance	✓	50	00					

Equipment — Account No. 13

Date	Items	Post	Debit	¢	Date	Items	Post	Credit	¢
Nov. 30	Balance	✓	6000	00					

Equipment Depreciation — Account No. 013

Date	Items	Post	Debit	¢	Date	Items	Post	Credit	¢
					Nov. 30	Balance	✓	500	00

Supplies — Account No. 14

Date	Items	Post	Debit	¢	Date	Items	Post	Credit	¢

Accounts Payable — Account No. 21

Date	Items	Post	Debit	¢	Date	Items	Post	Credit	¢

Federal Income Tax Payable — Account No. 22

Date	Items	Post	Debit	¢	Date	Items	Post	Credit	¢

FICA Tax Payable — Account No. 23

Date	Items	Post	Debit		Date	Items	Post	Credit	

Mr. Brown — Account No. 31

Date	Items	Post	Debit		Date	Items	Post	Credit	
					Nov 30	Balance		13384	80

Withdrawals — Account No. 031

Date	Items	Post	Debit		Date	Items	Post	Credit	
Nov 30	Balance	✓	1500	00					

Income — Account No. 41

Date	Items	Post	Debit		Date	Items	Post	Credit	
					Nov 30	Balance	✓	19000	00

Sales Income — Account No. 42

Date	Items	Post	Debit		Date	Items	Post	Credit	
					Nov 30	Balance	✓	2062	00

Rent Expense — Account No. 51

Date	Items	Post	Debit		Date	Items	Post	Credit	
Nov 30	Balance	✓	1650	00					

Salary Expense — Account No. 52

Date	Items	Post	Debit	Date	Items	Post	Credit
Nov. 30	Balance	✓	16000 00				

Payroll Tax Expense — Account No. 53

Date	Items	Post	Debit	Date	Items	Post	Credit
Nov. 30	Balance	✓	966 80				

Sales Tax Expense — Account No. 54

Date	Items	Post	Debit	Date	Items	Post	Credit
Nov 30	Balance	✓	103 10				

Supplies Expense — Account No. 55

Date	Items	Post	Debit	Date	Items	Post	Credit
Nov. 30	Balance	✓	800 00				

Janitorial Expense — Account No. 56

Date	Items	Post	Debit	Date	Items	Post	Credit
Nov. 30	Balance		1876 90				

Depreciation Expense — Account No. 57

Date	Items	Post	Debit	Date	Items	Post	Credit

Miscellaneous Expense — Account No. 58

Date	Items	Post	Debit	Date	Items	Post	Credit
Nov. 30	Balance	✓	2000 00				

Trial Balances

Account Title	No.	Debit	Credit

Account Title	No.	Debit	Credit

Income & Expense Statement

Balance Sheet

5

BOOKKEEPING FOR A RETAILER

All of the illustrations used in Chapters 3 and 4 were of firms selling services. In each case, incomes and expenses were not recorded in the books until the money actually changed hands. This is the bookkeeping method used by most service-type firms, and it is known as the Cash Basis of Accounting.

When Incomes and Expenses Are Recorded:

	Accrual Basis	**Cash Basis**
Incomes	When Money EARNED	When Money RECEIVED
Expenses	When Money OWED	When Money PAID

Since a retailer sells merchandise, which he must keep in stock, and, because so much of his business is done on credit, merchants generally prefer to use the Accrual Basis of Accounting. Using this method, incomes are recorded as soon as they are earned, whether the money has been received or not; and expenses are shown at the time they are owed, regardless of whether they have been paid for.

Since Cash can't always be debited when money is earned, an account called Accounts Receivable is used to record money owed to the firm that will be received in the future. Since expenses must be recorded at times before they are paid, the liability account Accounts Payable is credited to add to what is owed and must be paid in the future.

Recording Inventory and Purchases

The value of the merchandise in stock is an asset. Whenever the merchandise in stock is counted, its value is figured (the method will be described later in this chapter) and recorded on the debit side of the Inventory account. This account is not changed until another physical inventory is taken.

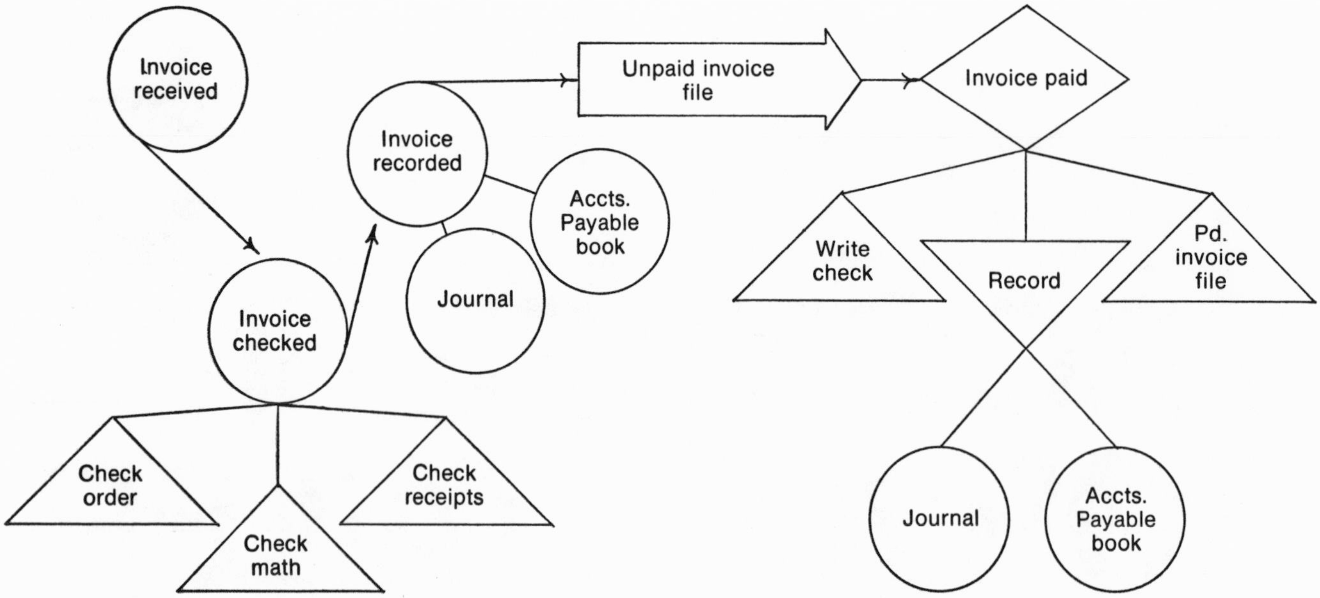

As merchandise intended for resale is received, its purchase price (the wholesale cost) is recorded in the Purchases account. This is an expense account, since it takes from the income made on sales. If the merchandise is paid for at once, cash is credited; if it is charged, Accounts Payable is credited to add to what is owed.

Since a retailer purchases merchandise on account so frequently, it saves time to set up special columns in the journal to debit Purchases and to credit Accounts Payable. Problem 5A would appear as shown at the bottom right, if such columns were used.

PURCHASE RETURNS

At times, merchandise is returned for a credit. Then it is taken out of the Purchases account by crediting, and out of Accounts Payable by debiting. If a refund is received, this takes from the purchases and adds to the cash.

5A. The Hook n Hanger, a men's clothing store, has employed you as a part-time bookkeeper. Journalize the following:

11/8 Purchased $300 worth of shirts on account from the Bow Shirt Company Invoice 125.
11/12 Purchased $1,000 of Johnny Cavett suits on account, Invoice 103.
11/15 Returned two of the suits for $200—Credit Memo 54.
11/19 Bought $100 worth of Count Dracula ties on account, Invoice 519
11/20 Returned $50 worth of shirts to Bow Shirt Company and got credit for them, Credit Memo 12.

GENERAL JOURNAL

DATE	ACCOUNT TITLE	POST	DEBIT	CREDIT

Journal

Date	Account Title	Post	Debit		Credit	
			Purchases	Other	Accts Pay	Other
Nov 8	Purchases-inv 125		300.00			
	Accts Pay-Bow Shirt				300.00	
12	Purchases-inv 103		1000.00			
	Accts Pay-J. Cavett				1000.00	
15	Accts Pay-J. Cavett			200.00		
	Purchases-CM 54					200.00
19	Purchases-inv 519		100.00			
	Accts Pay-Ct Dracula				100.00	
20	Accts Pay-Bow Shirt			50.00		
	Purchases-CM 12					50.00
	Totals		1400.00	250.00	1400.00	250.00

$1650 = $1650

FREIGHT BILLS ON PURCHASES.

Sometimes the retailer has to pay the freight charges on his purchases. This adds to the cost of the merchandise, and it is debited to Purchases and credited to Cash or to Accounts Payable.

ACCOUNTS PAYABLE BOOK

It's important to know just how much is owed to each supplier. This is easy to keep track of by using an Accounts Payable Book. Each supplier who is owed is listed on a separate page, and they are kept in alphabetical order. As the invoices and credit memos are being journalized, they should also be entered in the Accounts Payable Book. The invoices are then filed alphabetically in an Unpaid Invoices file. Credit memos are attached to the invoice showing the original purchase of the returned merchandise.

Accounts Payable Book

Bow Shirt Co.
25 E. Main St., City

DATE	NUMBER	CHARGES	PAYMENTS	BALANCE
Nov 8	Inc. 125	300.00		300.00
20	C M 12		50.00	250.00

The Bow Shirt Company page of the Accounts Payable Book from problem 5A is shown above.

List of Accounts Payable. At the end of the month a list of accounts payable and the amount owed to each can be prepared from the Accounts Payable Book. The total of this list should agree with the balance of the Accounts Payable ledger account.

Paying an Account Payable. When money is paid on account, it is journalized in the Cash Journal and recorded in the Accounts Payable Book. The invoice is then pulled out of the Unpaid Invoice file. The check number is recorded on it, and it is filled alphabetically in a Paid Invoice file.

Since money is paid on account so often, a special column debiting Accounts Payable can be shown on the Cash Disbursements page. This will save time, since only the totals need to be posted to Accounts Payable and to Cash at the end of the month. Any other accounts must still be posted individually.

5B. Please record the following:

11/30 Paid Bow Shirt Company the balance owed on account, Check # 501.
11/30 Paid Johnny Cavett Suit Company the balance owed, Check # 502.

Cash Journal

Cash Disbursements

Date	Account Debited	Post	Ck. No.	Debit Accts. Pay	Other	Credit Cash

PURCHASE DISCOUNTS

Cash discounts are often given when an account is paid promptly. This is a form of income to the merchant, for it reduces the amount he must pay.

If a cash discount is being offered, it is shown on the invoices. Some common terms are 2/10; n/30 (2% of the invoice total can be deducted if it is paid within 10 days of the invoice date; if not the entire amount—net—is due within 30 days of the invoice date), 2%–10 (2% may be deducted if paid by the 10th of the month), 2/30; n/60 (2% deducted if paid within 30 days, if not total is due within 60 days.)

If a 1% discount had been offered by the Bow Shirt Company, and a 2% discount was granted by Johnny Cavett Suits, and both were paid on time, the journal entry recording payments would have appeared like this:

Cash Disbursements

Date	Accounts to be debited	Ck. No.	Debit Accts.Pay.	Debit Other	Credit Cash	Credit Disc.Inc.
Nov 30	Bow Shirt Co.	501	250.00		247.50	2.50
30	Johnny Cavett Suits	502	800.00		784.00	16.00

5C. *Journalize and post the following. Also record the entries in the Accounts Payable Book and prepare a list of the accounts payable at the end of the month.*

Dec. 1	Purchased 50 pairs of slacks on account from Sack Slack Company at $17 each, Invoice 201.
Dec. 5	Got 20 pairs of shoes on account from Penguin Shoe Company at $20 each, Invoice 305.
Dec. 8	Bought $95 worth of shoes from a new supplier—Still Dogs Shoes. Paid for them with Check # 106.
Dec. 10	Paid Sack Slack Company. Terms were 2/10; n/30, Check # 107.
Dec. 12	Returned two pairs of shoes to Penguin Shoe Company for credit, Credit Memo 26.
Dec. 14	Bought 10 pairs of Haggard Slacks at $12 each, Invoice 503.
Dec. 14	Received Invoice 35 from Trusty Truck lines for $20 owed for freight on purchases.
Dec. 14	Paid Penguin Shoes—terms 1/10; n/30, Check # 108.
Dec. 20	Bought $55 worth of slacks from Haggard, Invoice 549.
Dec. 23	Paid Trusty Truck Lines, terms net 90 days, Check # 109.
Dec. 25	Paid Haggard Slacks total owed. Terms on both invoices were 2/10; n/30, Check # 110.
Dec. 26	Purchased 30 pairs Penguin shoes at $22 each, Invoice 395.
Dec. 28	Received invoice for $50 from Trusty Truck Lines, Invoice 23.

Journal

Date	Account Title	Post	Debit Purchases	Debit Other	Credit Accts. Pay	Credit Other

Cash Disbursements

Date	Account Debited	Post	Ck. No.	Debit Accts. Pay.	Debit Other	Credit Cash	Credit Disc. Inc.

Ledger

Cash — Account No. 10

Date	Items	Post	Debit	Date	Items	Post	Credit

Accounts Payable — Account No. 20

Date	Items	Post	Debit	Date	Items	Post	Credit

Discount Income — Account No. 41

Date	Items	Post	Debit	Date	Items	Post	Credit

Purchases — Account No. 50

Date	Items	Post	Debit	Date	Items	Post	Credit

Accounts Payable Book

Haggard Slacks
100 Well Fair Road

Date	Number	Charges	Payments	Balance

Penguin Shoe Co.
22 Gnaw Bone Bend

Date	Number	Charges	Payments	Balance

Sack Slack Co.
59 Petunia Point

Date	Number	Charges	Payments	Balance

Trusty Truck Lines
66 Spooky Hollow

Date	Number	Charges	Payments	Balance

List Accounts Payable here.

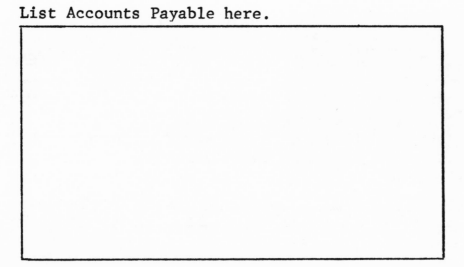

Recording Sales

Sales is the income account for a retailer, and the retail price of the merchandise sold is recorded in it. If money is received, Cash is debited. If the sale is charged, this promise—that the customer will pay in the future—is something of value. The asset Accounts Receivable is debited.

Cash sales are rung up on the cash register. A tape of the total cash sales is gotten at the end of each day. These totals are recorded in the cash journal, and the tapes are filed by date.

Charge sales and the payments on charge accounts are written up on sales slips which are journalized, recorded in the Accounts Receivable Book, and filed by sales slip number.

SALES TAX

Since most states charge a sales tax, the retailer must collect this tax for the government. The value of the merchandise sold is credited to Sales. The tax on it is now owed to the state; therefore, the liability Sales Tax Payable is added to by crediting. Either Cash or Accounts Receivable is debited for the sale plus tax.

When the sales tax is to be paid at the end of the month, a check is made out for the balance in the Sales Tax Payable account. Cash is credited, while the liability Sales Tax Payable is debited since it is no longer owed.

SALES RETURNS

Occasionally customers return merchandise. Then the values put into accounts at the time of the sale are taken back out. Sales is debited, Sales Tax Payable is debited, and either Cash or Accounts Receivable is credited. If the customer originally charged the merchandise, a Credit Memo is made out and the customer is given a copy. The store's copy is recorded and then filed in numerical order in an Accounts Receivable Credit Memo file.

5D. Record the following sales for the Hook n Hanger. Our state charges 5% sales tax. Note that special columns have been set up in both the journal and the cash journal for the Sales and the Accounts Receivable accounts which are used so frequently. Add sales tax to each sale.

11/10 Sold Mr. I. M. Rich a $500 suit. He charged it, Sales Slip 104.
11/10 B. Good bought $25 on account, Sales Slip 105.
11/10 At the end of the day, the cash register showed sales of $300, tax $15, cash receipts $315.
11/11 Sold Mr. Brown a pair of $25 shoes. He charged them, Sales Slip 106.
11/11 Mr. B. Good, who bought a shirt for $10 yesterday (sales tax 50¢), returned it for a credit, CM 14.
11/11 Cash sales for the day $400, tax $20, total $420.
11/12 Ben Good bought $100 worth of merchandise on account, Sales Slip 107. Figure the tax.
11/12 Mr. Brown returned the shoes purchased yesterday for credit, Credit Memo 15.
11/12 Cash sales $500, tax $25, total receipts $525.

Journal

Date	Account Title	Post	Debit			Credit			
			Purch	Acc Rec	Other	Acc Pay	Sales	S. Tax	Other

Cash Book

Cash Receipts

Date	Account Credited	Post	Debit Cash	Credit		
				Sales	S. Tax	Other

CASH SHORT AND OVER

Sometimes incorrect change is made during the day so that the totals of the cash register tapes don't agree with what is in the drawer. If the money in the drawer is short, this is an expense. Miscellaneous Expense should be debited and Cash credited for the shortage. If the amount in the drawer is more than the total on the tape, add to the Cash by debiting and take from the day's expenses by crediting Miscellaneous Expense.

ACCOUNTS RECEIVABLE BOOK

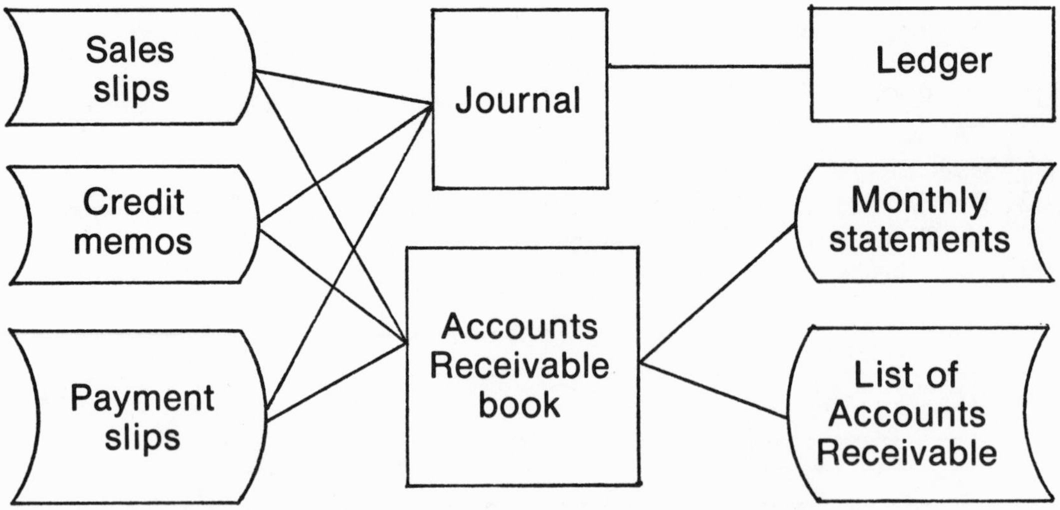

An accurate record of how much is owed by each charge customer must be kept in a book or in a card file. A separate page is used for each individual, showing her or his name and address. All sales slips, credit memos, and payments are recorded in the Accounts Receivable Book as well as in the correct journal. The page for Mr. Brown in problem 5D is shown below.

Accounts Receivable Book

R. Brown
10½ D Street, City

Date	Number	Charges	Payments	Balance
Nov 11	ss#106	25.00		25.00
12	CM #15		25.00	--

BILLING ACCOUNTS RECEIVABLE

At the end of the month, the Accounts Receivable Book is used to prepare bills to be sent to each customer who owes a balance.

These same customers are listed and the balances owed are shown on an Accounts Receivable List. The list is made out at the end of each month. The total of this list should agree with the Accounts Receivable ledger account.

5E. *Journalize and post the following. Also record the entries in the Accounts Receivable Book and prepare a list of the accounts receivable at the end of the month. Add 5% sales tax to each sale.*

12/25 Sold Guy Sharp $35 merchandise on account, SS # 119.
12/25 Sold Abe Abel $86 merchandise on account, SS # 120.
12/25 Cash sales for the day $519 plus sales tax.
12/26 Guy Sharp bought a sport coat for $85, SS # 121.
12/26 Homer Lee purchased $150 worth of merchandise and charged it, SS # 122.
12/26 Cash sales $501 plus tax.
12/29 Guy Sharp bought a pair of slacks for $28, SS # 123.
12/29 Homer Lee paid his account in full.
12/29 Cash sales for the day $580 plus sales tax.
12/30 Icabod Kane charged $250 worth of merchandise, SS # 124.
12/30 Cash sales $498 plus tax.
12/30 Cash drawer was $3.20 over the register tape total.
12/31 Abe Abel paid $50 on account.
12/31 Homer Lee bought $40 worth on account, SS # 125.
12/31 Cash sales for the day $799.
12/31 Cash drawer was $1.25 over.

JOURNAL

DATE	ACCOUNT TITLE	POST	DEBIT			CREDIT			
			PURCHASES	ACCTS REC.	OTHER	ACCTS PAY.	SALES	SALES TAX	OTHER

CASH BOOK

CASH RECEIPTS

DATE	ACCOUNT CREDITED	POST	DEBIT CASH	CREDIT SALES	CREDIT SALES TAX	CREDIT OTHER

List of Accounts Receivable

LEDGER

Cash Account No. 11

DATE	ITEMS	POST	DEBIT	DATE	ITEMS	POST	CREDIT

Accounts Receivable Account No. 12

DATE	ITEMS	POST	DEBIT	DATE	ITEMS	POST	CREDIT

Sales Tax Payable Account No. 23

DATE	ITEMS	POST	DEBIT	DATE	ITEMS	POST	CREDIT

Sales Account No. 41

DATE	ITEMS	POST	DEBIT	DATE	ITEMS	POST	CREDIT

Miscellaneous Expense Account No. 57

DATE	ITEMS	POST	DEBIT	DATE	ITEMS	POST	CREDIT

Accounts Receivable Book

Abe Abel
88 Abner Alley

DATE	NUMBER	CHARGES	PAYMENTS	BALANCE

Icabod Kane
1313 Slippy Hollow

DATE	NUMBER	CHARGES	PAYMENTS	BALANCE

Homer Lee
1 Home Town Lane

DATE	NUMBER	CHARGES	PAYMENTS	BALANCE

Guy Sharp
2 Dead End Road

DATE	NUMBER	CHARGES	PAYMENTS	BALANCE

Bad Debts

Any time a retailer grants credit, there is the possibility that a customer may not pay. Often these overdue bills are turned over to a collection agency. If collected, the agency's fee is an expense. Accounts Receivable would be credited for the entire amount, since it is no longer owed. Cash is debited for the amount received, and Miscellaneous Expense is debited for the part kept by the collection agency. Occasionally, an account is uncollectable. Then the amount owed is taken out of Accounts Receivable, out of Sales, and out of the Sales Tax Payable account (as a return would be).

The Retailer's Gross Profit

The Income Dollar

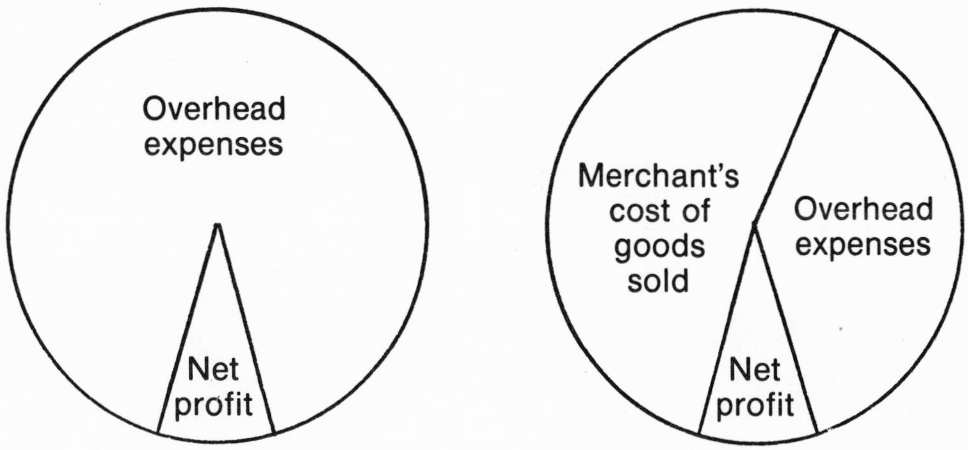

Service Firm — Merchandising Firm

For a service-type firm as illustrated in Chapters 3 and 4, the entire income is gross profit. But a retailer's sales are not all his gross profit because he must pay for those goods which he sells. Therefore, a retailer's gross income is the difference between the wholesale prices he paid for the goods sold and the retail price which he received for them. This is called markup.

The Sales account shows the retail price of the sales. The wholesale or cost price of those goods that were sold must be calculated before the markup can be known.

FIGURING COST OF GOODS SOLD

If everything in the store had been sold and the walls were bare, this would mean that the beginning inventory plus all the purchases received had been sold. (Both Inventory and Purchases accounts are kept at wholesale or cost figures.) This is the very most that could possibly be sold. Unfortunately, it didn't all sell. So what is left is counted and its cost figured and subtracted from what was available for sale. The result is the portion of the merchandise stock which did sell, and it's at wholesale prices.

Beginning Inventory
+ Purchases
Goods Available for Sale
–Ending Inventory
= Cost of Goods Sold

(This ending inventory becomes the beginning inventory the next time Cost of Goods is figured.)

PRICING INVENTORY

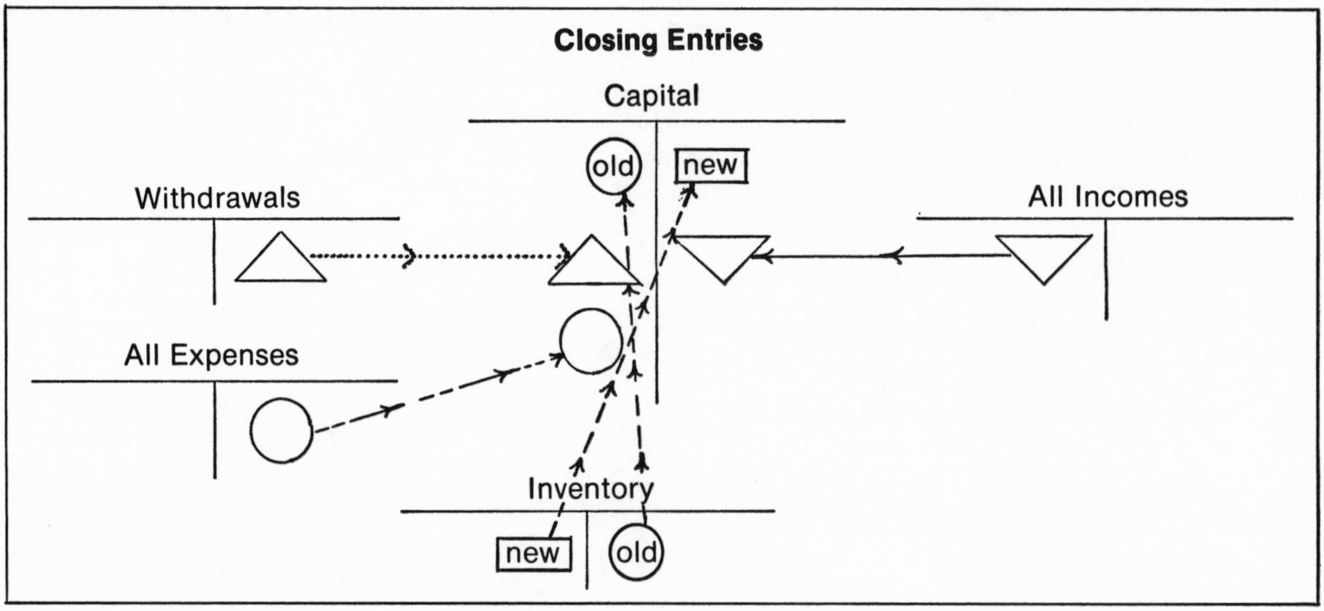

If five boxes of Z were purchased and one is left, there would be no problem pricing the one left if the same price had been paid for all five. However, if prices increased so that two were bought at one price per box and three were purchased at a higher cost, which price should be given to the box of Z on the shelf? There are several approved methods for pricing inventory.

Some stores can set up a code to show the purchase price on the sales ticket or article without it being obvious to the customer. If this is possible, it is then easy to add all of these prices to arrive at a figure for ending inventory. If this is not possible, the easiest method is to price each item at its current market cost.

JOURNALIZING THE CHANGE IN INVENTORY

The old, beginning inventory which has been carried in the Inventory asset account, since a physical inventory was last taken, is no longer accurate. Before the Income and Expense Statement can be prepared, two journal entries must be made and posted to correct this Inventory account. The beginning inventory is credited to Inventory to take it out of this asset account, and it is debited to the account named Beginning Inventory (an Owner's Equity account, thus taking from Owner's Equity since it is an asset no longer owned.) The value of the present, ending inventory is now entered in the Inventory asset account by debiting and added to the Owner's Equity section by crediting the account Ending Inventory. These two journal entries are make before making out the Trial Balance when preparing financial statements, just as the entries allowing for depreciation and unused supplies are (see Chapter 4).

When closing the Owner's Equity accounts, the debit balance in Beginning Inventory will be transferred into Capital, and the credit balance in Ending Inventory will be transferred into Capital.

5F. The Hook n Hanger had an inventory at the end of last year of $50,000. This year their inventory is worth $70,000. They purchased $300,000 worth of merchandise at wholesale prices during the year, and their sales for the year totaled $500,000. Figure their gross income.

Financial Statements

The Cost of Goods Sold and the Gross Income are shown on the Income and Expense Statement as follows:

Sales		$89,950
Purchase Discount Income		50
Total Income		$90,000
Less Cost of Goods Sold:		
Beginning Inventory	$14,000	
+ Purchases	50,000	
Goods Available for Sale	$64,000	
Less Ending Inventory	12,000	52,000
Gross Income		$38,000
Less Overhead Expenses:		
Utility Expense	2,000	
Salary Expense	25,000	27,000
Net Income		$11,000

5G. *Make a complete Income and Expense Statement on this page, using the figures on the Trial Balance shown. Statements were last made out 6/30/76.*

The Hook n Hanger
Trial Balance
December 31, 1976

	Debits	Credits
Cash	10,000	
Petty Cash	100	
Accounts Receivable	15,000	
Inventory	16,000	
Store Equipment	7,000	
Accounts Payable		18,800
Sales Tax Payable		500
Capital, Cap Hook		10,000
Withdrawals, Hook	1,000	
Capital, Brent Hanger		10,000
Withdrawals, Hanger	500	
Sales		124,900
Purchases Discount Income		100
Purchases	80,000	
Beginning Inventory	19,000	
Ending Inventory		16,000
Rent Expense	3,400	
Utilities Expense	2,100	
Salary Expense	25,000	
Miscellaneous Expense	1,200	
	180,300	180,300

5H. *Below the Trial Balance, show the Balance Sheet. Because the Hook n Hanger is a partnership, both owners will be shown in the Owner's Equity section. Each man's withdrawals will take only from his own capital account. Since it is an equal partnership, they will share the net income equally.*

PUTTING IT ALL TOGETHER

Chapter Summary Problems

A. *WHAT IS IT?*

Please fill in the blanks with the correct words from those listed below:

refund	collection fees
Inventory	Sales
credit memos	Accounts Receivable Book
sales slips	Cash Basis of Accounting
Purchases	cash discounts
Accrual Basis of Accounting	Accounts Payable Book
Accounts Payable	gross income
bad debts	Purchases Discounts

1. Freight bills on goods received are charged to the ________________________ account.
2. The total of the Accounts Payable List must agree with the balance of the ________________________ account in the ledger.
3. ________________________, recording sales on account, are filed in numerical order.
4. ________________________ are an expense that should be charged to Miscellaneous Expense.
5. Sales returns which had been charged are recorded in the same way that ________________________ are.
6. ________________________ are issued when goods that had been charged are returned.
7. The ________________________ records an expense as soon as it is owed.
8. In the ________________________ an income is journalized only when money is received.
9. ________________________ is an asset needed to figure Cost of Goods Sold.
10. When money is collected to pay an account, it is recorded in the cash journal and in the ________________________.
11. The Cash Disbursements page is credited for ________________________.
12. A ________________________ is issued when merchandise purchased for cash is returned.
13. To find Gross Income subtract Cost of Goods Sold from ________________________.
14. Markup is another name for ________________________.
15. All purchases of goods on account are recorded in the ________________________.

B. *USING WHAT YOU KNOW*

Holly Haus and Fanny Feffer have an equal partnership in the Haus and Feffer Cookie House. You have been hired as their bookkeeper on a trial basis. They have no salaries, because the owners are the only workers, and they withdraw money as needed. A 5% sales tax is charged on all sales. Use the following forms.

1. 12/24/76 Purchased $50 worth of candy from Sweet Candy Company, Invoice # 509.
2. 12/24/76 Paid $10 to trucking firm out of cash, Check # 501.
3. 12/24/76 Sold $100 worth of cookies on account to the Group Coop nursery. Add on the tax, Sales Slip # 101.
4. 12/24/76 Cash sales $100 plus sales tax.
5. 12/24/76 Cash drawer was short by $1.

6. 12/25/76 Paid Knurtz Nuts the money owed. Their $600 invoice was dated 12/19, terms 2/10; n/30. Check #502.
7. 12/25/76 Sold $200 on account to the Old Woman's Shoe nursery. Add the tax. SS #102.
8. 12/25/76 A cash customer returned a $5 box of candy that was spoiled. Give her a refund. Ck. #503.
9. 12/25/76 Write off the candy as spoilage expense. (This reduces the amount of purchases available for resale. Only its wholesale cost of $4 is an expense to you.)
10. 12/25/76 Cash sales $150 plus tax.
11. 12/26/76 Paid Bob's Gas Station $25 for gasoline for the truck, Ck. #504.
12. 12/26/76 Charged $100 worth of cookies purchased from Mrs. Leapober.
13. 12/26/76 Sold $50 worth of cookies to the Group Coop on account, SS #103.
14. 12/26/76 Returned $50 worth of candy to Sweet Candy Company for credit, CM 55.
15. 12/26/76 Cash sales $195 plus tax.
16. 12/29/76 Received $200 worth of nuts from Knurtz, Inv. #251.
17. 12/29/76 The $100 owed by Spill & Spot Cleaners had been turned over to a collection agency. They now have collected it and given you $60, keeping $40 as their fee. (Because of the Collection Expense use the Journal instead of the Cash Journal.)
18. 12/29/76 Sold $300 worth to Holiday Party Service and charged it, SS #104.
19. 12/29/76 Sold $25 worth of cookies to the Group Coop, SS #105.
20. 12/29/76 Cash sales $130 plus tax.
21. 12/30/76 Holiday Party Services returned $55 worth for credit, CM 22.
22. 12/30/76 Paid $85 on account to Mrs. Leapober, terms 30 days, Ck. #505.
23. 12/30/76 Holiday Party Service paid the balance owed on account.
24. 12/30/76 Cash sales $110.
25. 12/31/76 Pay all of the sales tax owed—$165.00, Ck. #506.
26. 12/31/76 Send out statements to accounts receivable. Prepare the Accounts Receivable List and the Accounts Payable List.
27. 12/31/76 Make a journal entry to record depreciation. They expect to use the truck about five years, at which time it will be worth about $400. Depreciation was last figured and recorded on 6/30/76.
28. 12/31/76 Make journal entries to take the beginning inventory out of the asset account and to record the present ending inventory of $5,000.00.
29. 12/31/76 Total the journals and make certain that on each journal the total debits equal the total credits. (If they don't, check that debits equal credits on each of the individual entries.) Post all of the individual amounts from the "Others" column of the journals. Also post the totals from the special columns to their accounts. Total and balance the ledger accounts.
30. 12/31/76 Make out the Trial Balance.
31. 12/31/76 Make out the financial statements.
32. 12/31/76 Journalize and post the closing entries needed to make the balances of the ledger Capital accounts agree with the Owner's Equity section of the Balance Sheet.

Good job—you're hired!

JOURNAL

DATE	ACCOUNT TITLE	POST	DEBIT			CREDIT			
			PURCHASES	ACCTS REC.	OTHER	ACCTS PAY.	SALES	SALES TAX	OTHER

Cash Book
Cash Receipts

Date	Account Credited	Post	Debit Cash	Credit Sales	S. Tax	Other

Accounts Receivable Book

The Group Coop
300 Boling Alley

Date	Number	Charges	Payments	Balance
Dec 23	Balance			500.00

The Holiday Party Service
5 Poverty Gulch

Date	Number	Charges	Payments	Balance
Dec 23	Balance			500.00

The Old Women's Shoe
12 Rimes Rd.

Date	Number	Charges	Payments	Balance
Dec 23	Balance			900.00

The Spill & Spot Cleaner
2 Possum Trot Trail

Date	Number	Charges	Payments	Balance
Dec 23	Balance			100.00

Cash Disbursements

Date	Account Debited	Post	Ck. No.	Debit Accts. Pay	Debit Other	Credit Cash	Credit Disc. Inc

Accounts Payable Book

Oscar B. Sweet Candy Co.
5 Pound Pl.

DATE	NUMBER	CHARGES	PAYMENTS	BALANCE
Dec 23	Balance			500.00

Knurtx Nuts
33 Tree Pt.

DATE	NUMBER	CHARGES	PAYMENTS	BALANCE
Dec 23	Balance			600.00

Appelohnia Leapober
102 Frog Pond Blvd.

DATE	NUMBER	CHARGES	PAYMENTS	BALANCE
Dec 23	Balance			100.00

Accounts Receivable List

Accounts Payable List

Ledger

Cash — Account No. 10

Date	Items	Post	Debit		Date	Items	Post	Credit	
Dec 23	Balance		14100	00					

Accounts Receivable — Account No. 11

Date	Items	Post	Debit		Date	Items	Post	Credit	
Dec 23	Balance		2000	00					

Inventory — Account No. 12

Date	Items	Post	Debit		Date	Items	Post	Credit	
Dec 23	Balance		3000	00					

Truck — Account No. 13

Date	Items	Post	Debit		Date	Items	Post	Credit	
Dec 23	Balance		8400	00					

Truck Depreciation Account No. 013

Date	Items	Post	Debit		Date	Items	Post	Credit	
					Dec 23	Balance		800	00

Accounts Payable Account No. 20

Date	Balance	Post	Debit		Date	Items	Post	Credit	
					Dec 23	Balance		1200	00

Sales Tax Payable Account No. 21

Date	Items	Post	Debit		Date	Items	Post	Credit	
					Dec 23	Balance		100	00

Haus, Capital Account No. 30

Date	Items	Post	Debit		Date	Items	Post	Credit	
					Dec 23	Balance		13800	00

Haus, Withdrawals Account No. 030

Date	Items	Post	Debit		Date	Items	Post	Credit	
Dec 23	Balance		2400	00					

Feffer, Capital Account No. 31

Date	Items	Post	Debit		Date	Items	Post	Credit	
					Dec 23	Balance		13800	00

Feffer, Withdrawals Account No. 031

Date	Items	Post	Debit		Date	Items	Post	Credit	
Dec 23	Balance		2500	00					

Sales — Account No. 40

Date	Items	Post	Debit	Date	Items	Post	Credit
				Dec 23	Balance		19000 00

Purchase Discount Income — Account No. 41

Date	Items	Post	Debit	Date	Items	Post	Credit
				Dec 23	Balance		200 00

Purchases — Account No. 50

Date	Items	Post	Debit	Date	Items	Post	Credit
Dec 23	Balance		13000 00				

Beginning Inventory — Account No. 51

Date	Items	Post	Debit	Date	Items	Post	Credit

Ending Inventory — Account No. 52

Date	Items	Post	Debit	Date	Items	Post	Credit

Rent Expense — Account No. 60

Date	Items	Post	Debit	Date	Items	Post	Credit
Dec. 23	Balance		1200 00				

Spoilage Expense — Account No. 61

Date	Items	Post	Debit	Date	Items	Post	Credit
Dec. 23	Balance		200 00				

Truck Expense — Account No. 62

Date	Items	Post	Debit	Date	Items	Post	Credit
Dec. 23	Balance		600 00				

Depreciation Expense — Account No. 63

Date	Items	Post	Debit		Date	Items	Post	Credit	

Utility Expense — Account No. 64

Date	Items	Post	Debit		Date	Items	Post	Credit	
Dec. 23	Balance		900	00					

Miscellaneous Expense — Account No. 65

Date	Items	Post	Debit		Date	Items	Post	Credit	
Dec. 23	Balance		600	00					

Statement

The Haus and Feffer Cookie House

Send To:

Date:

Terms: 30 days net

Date	Description	Charges	Payments	Balance

Account Title	No.	Debit	Credit

Statement

The Haus and Feffer Cookie House

Send To:

Date:

Terms: 30 days net

Date	Description	Charges	Payments	Balance

Haus and Feffer Cookie House
Income & Expense Statement
For the Six Months Ending Dec. 31, 1976

Sales......................		$
Purchases Discount Income..		
Total Income............		
Less Cost of Goods Sold:		
Inventory 6/30..........	$	
Plus Purchases..........		
Available for Sale.....	$	
Less Inventory 12/31.....		
Gross Income..............		$
Less Overhead Expenses:		
Rent Expense............	$	
Spoilage Expense........		
Truck Expense...........		
Depreciation Expense.....		
Utility Expense..........		
Miscellaneous Expense....		
Net Income................		$

Haus and Feffer Cookie House
Balance Sheet
December 31, 1976

Assets			Liabilities		
Cash................		$	Accounts Payable....		$
Accounts Receivable...					
Inventory............			Owner's Equity		
Truck................	$		Haus, Capital....	$	
Less Depreciation...			+ Net Income....		
			- Withdrawals...		
			Feffer, Capital..	$	
			+ Net Income....		
			- Withdrawals...		
Total Assets		$	Total Liab. + O.E.		$

ANSWER KEY
Chapter 1

JOINT ACCOUNT-3

Nelson O. Fault Insurance Company

The undersigned hereby agree to the rules, regulations and by-laws of the NATIONAL BOULEVARD BANK OF CHICAGO, to the Co-Depositor Clause below and to the clauses on the reverse hereof relating to collections and to examination of returned statements and cancelled checks.

Sign Here { *Nelson O. Fault* / *Your Signature* / ______

CO-DEPOSITOR CLAUSE

All moneys now on deposit, or at any time deposited by us or either of us, with said Bank to the credit of this account, or in accounts in continuation hereof, are and shall be so deposited by us and received by said Bank upon the following terms and conditions of repayment, viz:

That the amount thereof, or any part, and any interest thereon shall be paid by said Bank to us, or either of us, whether the other or others be living or not, or to the heirs, executors, administrators, or assigns of the survivor of us, or upon the written order of any person or persons so entitled to payment. Payment of funds to survivor contingent upon release from Inheritance Tax Office.

We further agree that any of us, may deposit and endorse for deposit in this account and in accounts in continuation hereof, checks, drafts, notes and orders belonging or payable to any of us, and may cash and endorse for negotiation any of the same. Said Bank shall have the right to charge against this account and accounts in continuation hereof any liabilities, at any time existing, of any of the undersigned to you. Our intention is to create a joint tenancy in this account, and in accounts in continuation hereof, with the right of survivorship

DATE *current date* ACCEPTED ______

FORM 368 10M 4-73 BANK OFFICIAL

①A

CHECKING ACCOUNT DEPOSIT TICKET

CASH	CURRENCY	78	00
	COIN	5	40
CHECKS	*Deeds*	98	00
	Kidd	47	90
	Clean	54	20
TOTAL FROM OTHER SIDE			
TOTAL		283	50
LESS CASH RECEIVED			
NET DEPOSIT		283	50

[redacted]

2-52
710

USE OTHER SIDE FOR ADDITIONAL LISTING

BE SURE EACH ITEM IS PROPERLY ENDORSED

DATE *current date* 19____

Nelson O. Fault Insurance Co.

NATIONAL BOULEVARD BANK OF CHICAGO

SAMPLE-VOID
DELUXE CHECK PRINTERS, INC.

⑈123456 7⑈

DELUXE JD-3 CHECKS AND OTHER ITEMS ARE RECEIVED FOR DEPOSIT SUBJECT TO THE TERMS AND CONDITIONS OF THIS BANK'S COLLECTION AGREEMENT.

①B

(1)C

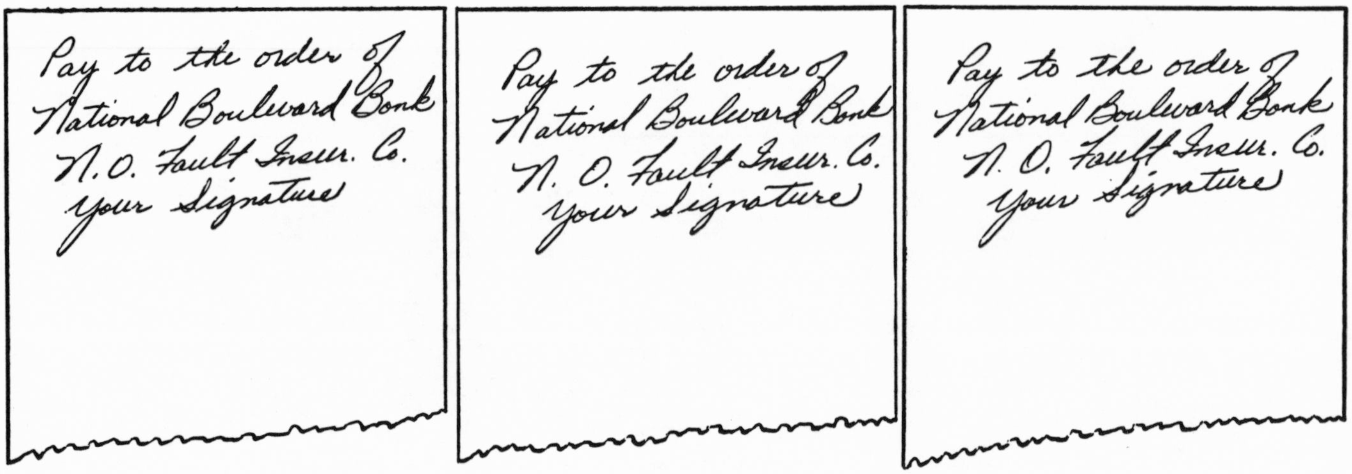
Pay to the order of
National Boulevard Bank
N. O. Fault Insur. Co.
your Signature
Pay to the order of
National Boulevard Bank
N. O. Fault Insur. Co.
Your Signature
Pay to the order of
National Boulevard Bank
N. O. Fault Insur. Co.
Your Signature

101 $ 95 62/00
current date 19
TO Linus Blanket Company
DOLLARS CENTS
BAL. FOR'D 855 00
DEPOSITS
TOTAL
THIS CHECK 95 62
OTHER DEDUCTIONS
BAL. FOR'D 759 38
101
current date 19
2-52/710
PAY TO THE ORDER OF Linus Blanket Company $ 95 62/00
Ninety-five and 62/00 DOLLARS
NATIONAL BOULEVARD BANK OF CHICAGO
SAMPLE-VOID
DELUXE CHECK PRINTERS, INC.
MEMO
Your Signature
⑆0710⑉0052⑆ ⑈123456 7⑈ 0151
DELUXE CHECK PRINTERS • RJ-1

(1)D

①E

MONTH *current month* 19 ______

THIS FORM IS PROVIDED TO HELP YOU BALANCE YOUR BANK STATEMENT

CHECKS OUTSTANDING - NOT CHARGED TO ACCOUNT

NO.	$	
174	16	35
177	8	19
178	20	42
179	83	00
TOTAL	$ 127	96

BANK BALANCE SHOWN ON THIS STATEMENT $ 788.36

ADD +

DEPOSITS NOT CREDITED IN THIS STATEMENT (IF ANY) $ 322.24

SUB-TOTAL $ 1110.60

SUBTRACT −

CHECKS OUTSTANDING $ 127.96

BALANCE $ 982.64

SHOULD AGREE WITH CHECK BOOK BALANCE AFTER DEDUCTING SERVICE CHARGE (IF ANY) SHOWN ON THIS STATEMENT FOR PRESENT MONTH.

Check stub balance $985.53
less S.C. − 2.89
$982.64

①F

PETTY CASH

6 $2 00/00

For Car wash

Charge to Account Auto Expense

Signed your signature

Date January—

Rediform 9G 009

PETTY CASH

7 $2 50/00

For Subscription to Picayune Tribune

Charge to Account Miscellaneous Expense

Signed your signature

Date January—

Rediform 9G 009

PETTY CASH

8 $30 00/00

For Typewriter erasers

Charge to Account Stationery & Office Supplies Ex.

Signed your signature

Date January—

Rediform 9G 009

(1) F

PETTY CASH

9 $10 00/00

For Took Miss Trixie La Moore to lunch

Charge to Account Miscellaneous Expense

Signed your signature

Date January –

Rediform 9G 009

(1) G

Petty Cash Statement for the Month of January, 1976

Auto Expense	$ 2.00
Stationery & Office Supplies Ex.	30.00
Miscellaneous Expense	12.50
Total spent	$ 44.50
Amount left	5.50
January 1 total	$50.00

(1) H

102 $ 44 50/00

Jan 31 19 76

TO Petty Cash

	DOLLARS	CENTS
BAL. FOR'D	759	38
DEPOSITS		
"		
TOTAL		
THIS CHECK	44	50
OTHER DEDUCTIONS		
BAL. FOR'D	714	88

102

January 31 19 76 — 2-52/710

PAY TO THE ORDER OF Petty Cash $ 44 50/00

Forty-four and 50/00 DOLLARS

NATIONAL BOULEVARD BANK OF CHICAGO

SAMPLE-VOID
DELUXE CHECK PRINTERS, INC.

MEMO

Your Signature

⑆0710⑉0052⑆ ⑈123456 7⑈ 0152

DELUXE CHECK PRINTERS • RJ-1

Summary Problems

A. What is it?

1. night deposit
2. dishonored check
3. canceled check
4. voucher
5. late deposit
6. voided
7. bank statement
8. cashier's check
9. service charge
10. endorsed
11. deposit slip
12. petty cash fund
13. reconciling
14. Currency
15. check stub
16. signature card
17. outstanding checks

B. Using What You Know

(1)

JOINT ACCOUNT-3

Nelson O. Fault Insurance Company

The undersigned hereby agree to the rules, regulations and by-laws of the NATIONAL BOULEVARD BANK OF CHICAGO, to the Co-Depositor Clause below and to the clauses on the reverse hereof relating to collections and to examination of returned statements and cancelled checks.

Sign Here: Nelson O. Fault
your Signature

CO-DEPOSITOR CLAUSE

All moneys now on deposit, or at any time deposited by us or either of us, with said Bank to the credit of this account, or in accounts in continuation hereof, are and shall be so deposited by us and received by said Bank upon the following terms and conditions of repayment, viz:

That the amount thereof, or any part, and any interest thereon shall be paid by said Bank to us, or either of us, whether the other or others be living or not, or to the heirs, executors, administrators, or assigns of the survivor of us, or upon the written order of any person or persons so entitled to payment. Payment of funds to survivor contingent upon release from Inheritance Tax Office.

We further agree that any of us, may deposit and endorse for deposit in this account and in accounts in continuation hereof, checks, drafts, notes and orders belonging or payable to any of us, and may cash and endorse for negotiation any of the same. Said Bank shall have the right to charge against this account and accounts in continuation hereof any liabilities, at any time existing, of any of the undersigned to you. Our intention is to create a joint tenancy in this account, and in accounts in continuation hereof, with the right of survivorship

DATE Sept 1, 1976 ACCEPTED ____________

FORM 368 10M 4-73 BANK OFFICIAL

103 $135 04/00
Sept 5 1976
TO George Winstead
on account

	DOLLARS	CENTS
BAL. FOR'D	1519	40
DEPOSITS		
"		
TOTAL		
THIS CHECK	135	04
OTHER DEDUCTIONS		
BAL. FOR'D	1384	36

103

Sept 5 1976 2-52/710

PAY TO THE ORDER OF George Winstead $135 04/00

One hundred thirty-five and 04/00 DOLLARS

NATIONAL BOULEVARD BANK OF CHICAGO

SAMPLE-VOID
DELUXE CHECK PRINTERS, INC.

MEMO

Your Signature

⑆0710⑉0052⑆ ⑈123456 7⑈ 0103

DELUXE CHECK PRINTERS • RJ-1

(2)

PETTY CASH

1 $8.50

For Window Washing

Charge to Account Miscellaneous Expense

Signed your signature

Date Sept 6, 1976

Rediform 9C009

(3)

(4)

104 $91.95/00
Sept 6 1976
TO Smith Furniture Co
office chair

	DOLLARS	CENTS
BAL. FOR'D	1384	36
DEPOSITS		
"		
TOTAL		
THIS CHECK	91	95
OTHER DEDUCTIONS		
BAL. FOR'D	1292	41

104

Sept 6 1976 2-52/710

PAY TO THE ORDER OF Smith Furniture Store $91 95/00

Ninety-one and 95/00 DOLLARS

NATIONAL BOULEVARD BANK OF CHICAGO

SAMPLE-VOID
DELUXE CHECK PRINTERS, INC.

MEMO

Your Signature

⑆0710⑉0052⑆ ⑈123456 7⑈ 0104

DELUXE CHECK PRINTERS • RJ-1

(5)

105 $ 57 30/00

Sept 6 19 76

TO Office Supplies stationery Inc

	DOLLARS	CENTS
BAL. FOR'D	1292	41
DEPOSITS		
"		
TOTAL		
THIS CHECK	57	30
OTHER DEDUCTIONS		
BAL. FOR'D	1235	11

105

Sept 6 19 76 — 2-52/710

PAY TO THE ORDER OF Office Supplies Inc. $ 57 30/00

Fifty-seven and 30/00 DOLLARS

NATIONAL BOULEVARD BANK OF CHICAGO

SAMPLE-VOID
DELUXE CHECK PRINTERS, INC.

MEMO

Your Signature

⑆0710⑉0052⑆ ⑈123456 7⑈ 0105

DELUXE CHECK PRINTERS • RJ-1

DATE Sept 10 19 76

Checks and other items are received for deposit subject to the terms and conditions of this bank's collection agreement.

CURRENCY, COUPONS AND BONDS SHOULD BE SENT BY REGISTERED MAIL INSURED.
PLEASE PRINT MAILING ADDRESS IF NOT SHOWN BELOW

NATIONAL BOULEVARD BANK
OF CHICAGO
WRIGLEY BUILDING
410 N. MICHIGAN AVE • CHICAGO, ILLINOIS 60611

Nelson O. Fault Insurance Co.
707 N. 9th St.
Chicago, Illinois

CHECKS		CHECKS		CHECKS	
				59	20
				119	00

TOTAL FROM ABOVE	178	20
CURRENCY	519	00
COIN	3	25
TOTAL	700	45
LESS CASH		
TOTAL DEPOSIT	700	45

SPACE FOR ADDITIONAL LISTINGS ON REVERSE SIDE

ENDORSE ALL CHECKS. (YOUR NAME)
PAY TO THE ORDER OF NATIONAL BOULEVARD BANK
1: SEND BOTH COPIES TO BANK WITH YOUR DEPOSIT
2: RECEIPT WILL BE RETURNED TO YOU
3: REVERSE CARBON BEFORE USING REVERSE SIDE

(6)

Pay to the order of
National Boulevard Bank
For Deposit Only
N.O. Fault Insur. Co.
Your Signature

Pay to the order of
National Boulevard Bank
For Deposit Only
N.O. Fault Insur. Co.
Your Signature

PETTY CASH

2 $ 24 00/00

For Newspaper subscription - 4 mos.

Charge to Account Miscellaneous Expense

Signed your signature

Date Sept. 11, 1976

Rediform 9G009

(7)

---

(8)

106 $ 19 88/00

Sept 15 19 76

TO Taylor Garage

car repairs

	DOLLARS	CENTS
BAL. FOR'D	1235	11
DEPOSITS	700	45
"		
TOTAL	1935	56
THIS CHECK	19	88
OTHER DEDUCTIONS		
BAL. FOR'D	1915	68

106

Sept 15 19 76 2-52/710

PAY TO THE ORDER OF Taylor Garage $ 19 88/00

Nineteen and 88/00 DOLLARS

NATIONAL BOULEVARD BANK OF CHICAGO

SAMPLE-VOID
DELUXE CHECK PRINTERS, INC.

MEMO

Your Signature

⑆0710⑉0052⑆ ⑈123456 7⑈ 0106

DELUXE CHECK PRINTERS • RJ-1

---

(9)

107 $ 100 00/00

Sept 18 19 76

TO N. O. Fault

personal use

	DOLLARS	CENTS
BAL. FOR'D	1915	68
DEPOSITS		
"		
TOTAL		
THIS CHECK	100	00
OTHER DEDUCTIONS		
BAL. FOR'D	1815	68

107

Sept 18 19 76 2-52/710

PAY TO THE ORDER OF Nelson O. Fault $ 100 00/00

One-hundred and 00/00 DOLLARS

NATIONAL BOULEVARD BANK OF CHICAGO

SAMPLE-VOID
DELUXE CHECK PRINTERS, INC.

MEMO

Your Signature

⑆0710⑉0052⑆ ⑈123456 7⑈ 0107

DELUXE CHECK PRINTERS • RJ-1

(10)

PETTY CASH

3 $2 20/00

For Paper clips

Charge to Account Stationery & Office Supplies Exp

Signed your signature

Date Sept 23, 1976

Rediform 9C009

DATE Sept 23 1976

Checks and other items are received for deposit subject to the terms and conditions of this bank's collection agreement.

CURRENCY, COUPONS AND BONDS SHOULD BE SENT BY REGISTERED MAIL INSURED.
PLEASE PRINT MAILING ADDRESS IF NOT SHOWN BELOW

NATIONAL BOULEVARD BANK
OF CHICAGO
WRIGLEY BUILDING
410 N. MICHIGAN AVE • CHICAGO, ILLINOIS 60611

Nelson O. Fault Insurance Co
707 N. 9th St.
Chicago, Illinois

CHECKS		CHECKS		CHECKS	
				17	80

TOTAL FROM ABOVE	17	80
CURRENCY	455	00
COIN	5	90
TOTAL	478	70
LESS CASH		
TOTAL DEPOSIT	478	70

SPACE FOR ADDITIONAL LISTINGS ON REVERSE SIDE

ENDORSE ALL CHECKS (YOUR NAME)
PAY TO THE ORDER OF NATIONAL BOULEVARD BANK
1: SEND BOTH COPIES TO BANK WITH YOUR DEPOSIT
2: RECEIPT WILL BE RETURNED TO YOU
3: REVERSE CARBON BEFORE USING REVERSE SIDE

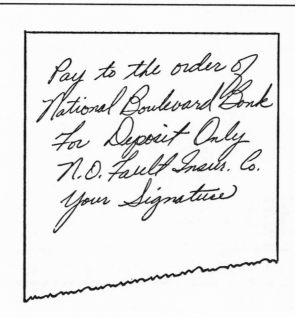

(11)

Pay to the order of
National Boulevard Bank
For Deposit Only
N.O. Fault Insur. Co.
Your Signature

108 $56 00/100

Sept 27 1976

Janitorial Serv.

cleaning carpet

	DOLLARS	CENTS
BAL. FOR'D	1815.	68
DEPOSITS	478	70
"		
TOTAL	2294	38
THIS CHECK	56	00
OTHER DEDUCTIONS		
BAL. FOR'D	2238	38

108

Sept 27 1976 2-52/710

PAY TO THE ORDER OF Janitorial Services, Inc $56 00/100

Fifty-six and 00/100 ———— DOLLARS

NATIONAL BOULEVARD BANK OF CHICAGO

SAMPLE-VOID
DELUXE CHECK PRINTERS, INC.

MEMO ____ Your Signature

⑆0710⑉0052⑆ ⑈123456 7⑈ 0108

DELUXE CHECK PRINTERS • RJ-1

(12)

PETTY CASH

4 $3 60/100

For Stamps

Charge to Account Postage Expense

Signed your signature

Date Sept 29, 1976

Rediform 9G 009

(13)

(14)

DATE Sept 30 1976

Checks and other items are received for deposit subject to the terms and conditions of this bank's collection agreement.

CURRENCY, COUPONS AND BONDS SHOULD BE SENT BY REGISTERED MAIL INSURED.
PLEASE PRINT MAILING ADDRESS IF NOT SHOWN BELOW

NATIONAL BOULEVARD BANK
OF CHICAGO
WRIGLEY BUILDING
410 N. MICHIGAN AVE • CHICAGO, ILLINOIS 60611

Nelson O. Fault Insurance Co
707 N. 9th St.
Chicago, Illinois

CHECKS		CHECKS		CHECKS	

TOTAL FROM ABOVE		
CURRENCY	98	00
COIN	2	25
TOTAL	100	25
LESS CASH		
TOTAL DEPOSIT	100	25

SPACE FOR ADDITIONAL LISTINGS ON REVERSE SIDE

ENDORSE ALL CHECKS (YOUR NAME)
PAY TO THE ORDER OF NATIONAL BOULEVARD BANK
1. SEND BOTH COPIES TO BANK WITH YOUR DEPOSIT
2. RECEIPT WILL BE RETURNED TO YOU
3. REVERSE CARBON BEFORE USING REVERSE SIDE

(15)

Petty Cash Statement
for the Month of *Sept.*, 1976

Stationery & Office Supplies Expense	*$2.20*
Postage Expense	*3.60*
Miscellaneous Expense	*32.50*
Total Spent	*$38.30*
Amount Left	*12.70*
September 1 Total	*$50.00*

109 $ *38 30/00*

Sept 30 19*76*

TO *Petty Cash*

	DOLLARS	CENTS
BAL. FOR'D	*2238*	*38*
DEPOSITS	*100*	*25*
"		
TOTAL	*2338*	*63*
THIS CHECK	*38*	*30*
OTHER DEDUCTIONS *SC*	*2*	*00*
BAL. FOR'D	*2298*	*33*

109

Sept 30 19*76* 2-52/710

PAY TO THE ORDER OF *Petty Cash* $ *38 30/00*

Thirty-eight and 30/00 DOLLARS

NATIONAL BOULEVARD BANK OF CHICAGO

SAMPLE-VOID
DELUXE CHECK PRINTERS, INC.

MEMO

Your Signature

⑆0710⑉0052⑆ ⑈123456 7⑈ 0109

DELUXE CHECK PRINTERS • RJ-1

(16)

(17)

MONTH September 19 76

THIS FORM IS PROVIDED TO HELP YOU BALANCE YOUR BANK STATEMENT

CHECKS OUTSTANDING - NOT CHARGED TO ACCOUNT

NO.	$	
104	91	95
109	38	30
TOTAL	$ 130	25

BANK BALANCE SHOWN ON THIS STATEMENT $ 2328.33

ADD +

DEPOSITS NOT CREDITED IN THIS STATEMENT (IF ANY) $ 100.25

SUB-TOTAL $ 2428.58

SUBTRACT —

CHECKS OUTSTANDING $ 130.25

BALANCE $ 2298.33

SHOULD AGREE WITH CHECK BOOK BALANCE AFTER DEDUCTING SERVICE CHARGE (IF ANY) SHOWN ON THIS STATEMENT FOR PRESENT MONTH.

Each depositor insured to $40,000

FDIC

FEDERAL DEPOSIT INSURANCE CORPORATION

ANSWER KEY
Chapter 2

(2)F

293

DATE Jan 28 1976
TO Columbone
FOR

		TOTAL WAGES	200 25
		SOCIAL SEC. TAX	11 71
BAL. FOR'D	1051 00	U. S. INC. TAX	35 00
DEP.		STATE INC. TAX	
TOTAL			
THIS CHECK	153 54	TOTAL DED.	46 71
BALANCE	897 46	CHECK	153 54

DETACH BEFORE CASHING CHECK
STATEMENT OF EARNINGS AND DEDUCTIONS FOR EMPLOYEE'S RECORD COVERING PAY PERIOD TO AND INCLUDING DATE SHOWN BELOW

DATE Jan 28 1976
TO Columbone

TOTAL WAGES	200 25
SOCIAL SECURITY TAX	11 71
WITHHOLDING U. S. INCOME TAX	35 00
STATE INCOME TAX	
TOTAL DEDUCTIONS	46 71
AMOUNT THIS CHECK	153 54

293

Jan 28 1976 2-52/710

PAY TO THE ORDER OF Columbone $153 54/100

One-hundred fifty-three and 54/00 DOLLARS

NATIONAL BOULEVARD BANK OF CHICAGO

SAMPLE-VOID
DELUXE CHECK PRINTERS, INC.

Your Signature

⑈000350⑈ ⑆0710⑉0052⑆ ⑈123456 7⑈

294

DATE Jan 28 1976
TO Mc Clown
FOR

		TOTAL WAGES	215 00
		SOCIAL SEC. TAX	12 58
BAL. FOR'D	897 46	U. S. INC. TAX	37 10
DEP.		STATE INC. TAX	
TOTAL			
THIS CHECK	165 32	TOTAL DED.	49 68
BALANCE	732 14	CHECK	165 32

DETACH BEFORE CASHING CHECK
STATEMENT OF EARNINGS AND DEDUCTIONS FOR EMPLOYEE'S RECORD COVERING PAY PERIOD TO AND INCLUDING DATE SHOWN BELOW

DATE Jan 28 1976
TO Mc Clown

TOTAL WAGES	215 00
SOCIAL SECURITY TAX	12 58
WITHHOLDING U. S. INCOME TAX	37 10
STATE INCOME TAX	
TOTAL DEDUCTIONS	49 68
AMOUNT THIS CHECK	165 32

294

Jan 28 1976 2-52/710

PAY TO THE ORDER OF Mc Clown $165 32/100

One hundred sixty-five and 32/00 DOLLARS

NATIONAL BOULEVARD BANK OF CHICAGO

SAMPLE-VOID
DELUXE CHECK PRINTERS, INC.

Your Signature

⑈000351⑈ ⑆0710⑉0052⑆ ⑈123456 7⑈

295

DATE Jan 28 1976
TO Darnabee Smith
FOR

		TOTAL WAGES	204 25
		SOCIAL SEC. TAX	11 95
BAL. FOR'D	732 14	U. S. INC. TAX	28 90
DEP.		STATE INC. TAX	
TOTAL			
THIS CHECK	163 40	TOTAL DED.	40 85
BALANCE	568 74	CHECK	163 40

DETACH BEFORE CASHING CHECK
STATEMENT OF EARNINGS AND DEDUCTIONS FOR EMPLOYEE'S RECORD COVERING PAY PERIOD TO AND INCLUDING DATE SHOWN BELOW

DATE Jan 28 1976
TO Darnabee Smith

TOTAL WAGES	204 25
SOCIAL SECURITY TAX	11 95
WITHHOLDING U. S. INCOME TAX	28 90
STATE INCOME TAX	
TOTAL DEDUCTIONS	40 85
AMOUNT THIS CHECK	163 40

295

Jan 28 1976 2-52/710

PAY TO THE ORDER OF Darnabee Smith $163 40/00

One hundred sixty-three and 40/00 DOLLARS

NATIONAL BOULEVARD BANK OF CHICAGO

SAMPLE-VOID
DELUXE CHECK PRINTERS, INC.

Your Signature

⑈000352⑈ ⑆0710⑉0052⑆ ⑈123456 7⑈

(2) G

Total Payroll Record
Jane's Pond Detective Agency
Payroll for week ending 1/28/76

Name	Reg Hours	O.T. Hours	Reg Pay	O.T. Pay	Gross Pay	Fed Inc Tax	FICA	Net Pay
Columbone	40	3	180.00	20.25	200.25	35.00	11.71	153.54
McClown	40	2	200.00	15.00	215.00	37.10	12.58	165.32
Smith	40	5	172.00	32.25	204.25	28.90	11.95	163.40
			552.00	67.50	619.50	101.00	36.24	482.26

Individual Employee's Earnings Record

employee Columbone
number 007

Week Ending	Reg Pay	O.T. Pay	Gross Pay	Cumulative Pay	Fed Inc Tax	FICA Tax	Net Pay
1-7-76	180	0	180.00	180.00	30.80	10.53	138.67
1-14-76	180	6.75	186.75	366.75	30.80	10.92	145.03
1-21-76	180	6.75	186.75	553.50	30.80	10.92	145.03
1-28-76	180	20.25	200.25	753.75	35.00	11.71	153.24
Jan. total	720	33.75	753.75		127.40	44.08	582.27

Individual Employee's Earnings Record

employee McClown
number 001

Week Ending	Reg Pay	O.T. Pay	Gross Pay	Cumulative Pay	Fed Inc Tax	FICA Tax	Net Pay
1-7-76	200	0	200.00	200.00	35.00	11.70	153.30
1-14-76	200	0	200.00	400.00	35.00	11.70	153.30
1-21-76	200	10.00	210.00	610.00	37.10	12.29	160.61
1-28-76	200	15.00	215.00	825.00	37.10	12.58	165.32
Jan. total	800	25.00	825.00		144.20	48.27	632.53

Individual Employee's Earnings Record

employee Darnabee Smith
number 0013

Week Ending	Reg Pay	O.T. Pay	Gross Pay	Cumulative Pay	Fed Inc Tax	FICA Tax	Net Pay
1-7-76	172	12.90	184.90	184.90	24.70	10.82	149.38
1-14-76	172	12.90	184.90	369.80	24.70	10.82	149.38
1-21-76	172	12.90	184.90	554.70	24.70	10.82	149.38
1-28-76	172	32.25	204.25	758.95	28.90	11.95	163.40
Jan. total	688	70.95	758.95		103.00	44.41	611.54

2H

110

PAY TO THE ORDER OF *National Boulevard Bank* — Jan 31 1976 — 2-52/710

$ *648 12/00*

Six hundred forty-eight and 12/00 ——— DOLLARS

NATIONAL BOULEVARD BANK OF CHICAGO

SAMPLE-VOID
DELUXE CHECK PRINTERS, INC.

MEMO *FICA + w/h - 1/76* *Your Signature*

⑆0710⑉0052⑆ ⑈123456 7⑈ 0160

DELUXE CHECK PRINTERS • RJ-1

FEDERA TAX DEPOSIT

DEPARTMENT OF THE TREASURY - FISCAL SERVICE
Bureau of Government Financial Operations - FTD Form Rev. Jan. 1976

FORM AND TAX CLASS
501 WITHHELD INCOME AND FICA TAXES
503 CORPO. A .ON INCO. .E TAXES
504 EXCISE TAXES
507 RAIL OAD RETIREMENT TAXES
508 UNE. PLOYMENT TAXES
511 AGRICULTURAL WORKERS: FICA TAXES AND VOLUNTARILY WITHHELD INCOME TAX
512 TAX WITHHELD AT SOURCE ON NONRESIDEN ALIENS, FOREIGN CORPOI..ATIONS, TAX-FREE COVENANT BONDS

DO NOT USE T I S FORM TO DEPOSIT TO A TAX C .ASS OT IER THAN II - DICATED

NAME OF BANK: *National Boulevard*

AMOUNT OF DEPOSIT: DOLLARS *648* CENTS *12*

IRS Return

Jane's Pond Detective Agency
101 Thieve's Alley
Los Angeles California

Employer Identification Number: *23-027123*

March 1976
Tax Period Ending

Bank Name/Date Stamp

verify preprinted data; if incorrect, see instructions on reverse.
Enter amount of deposit and name of bank where deposited in space above.

Do Not Write In Space Below

NBCC/HP-22483

2I

Columbone

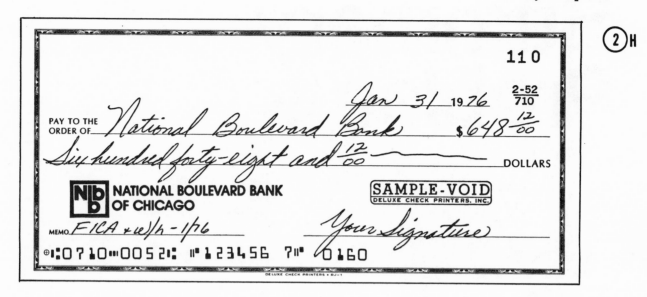

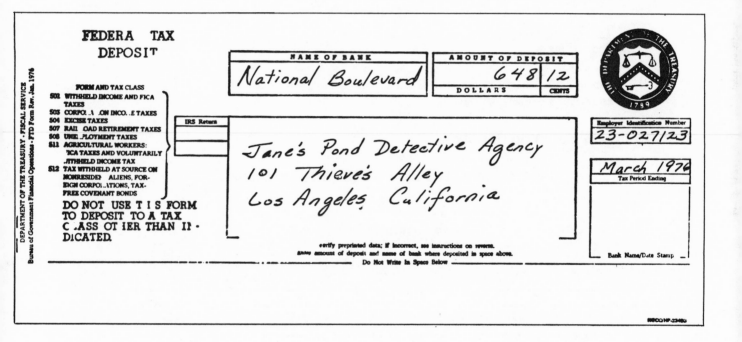

$2340	.0328	$2340	$4200 (maximum charged)
x .027	-.027	x 4	x.0058
$63.18 State UC	.0058	$9340	$24.36 Federal UC

McClown

$2600		$2600	$4200 (maximum amount
x .027		x 4	x.0058 charged)
$70.20 State UC		$10400	$24.36 Federal UC

Summary Problems

A. What is it?

1. overtime
2. gross pay
3. W-2 form
4. Federal Tax Deposit form
5. FICA
6. unemployment compensation
7. time card
8. W-4 form
9. Individual Employee's Earnings Record
10. Federal unemployment compensation
11. Total Payroll Record
12. deductions
13. net pay
14. Employer's Quarterly Federal Tax Return
15. employer's payroll tax expense

B. Using What You Know

Individual Employee's Earnings Record

Name Val N. Tyne

	week ending	reg pay	o.t. pay	gross pay	cumulative pay	fed inc tax	FICA tax	city tax	net pay
1	12-10	180.75	0	180.95	180.95	30.80	10.59	1.81	137.75
2	12-17	188.00	17.63	205.63	386.58	35.00	12.03	2.06	156.54
3	12-24	188.00	31.73	219.73	606.31	37.10	12.85	2.20	167.58
4	12-31	188.00	28.20	216.20	822.51	37.10	12.65	2.16	164.29
5	Total	744.95	77.56	822.51		140.00	48.12	8.23	626.16

Individual Employee's Earnings Record

Name Hal O. Whean

	week ending	reg pay	o.t. pay	gross pay	cumulative pay	fed inc tax	FICA tax	city tax	net pay
1	12-10	160.00	21.00	181.00	181.00	30.80	10.59	1.81	137.80
2	12-17	160.00	42.00	202.00	383.00	35.00	11.82	2.02	153.16
3	12-24	160.00	42.00	202.00	585.00	35.00	11.82	2.02	153.16
4	12-31	160.00	24.00	184.00	769.00	30.80	10.76	1.84	140.60
5	Total	640.00	129.00	769.00		131.60	44.99	7.69	584.72

296

Dec 10 1976

Val N Tyne

BAL. FOR'D	2298 33	TOTAL WAGES	180 95
		SOCIAL SEC. TAX	10 59
		U.S. INC. TAX	30 80
		STATE INC. TAX	
		City	1 81
TOTAL			
THIS CHECK	137 75	TOTAL DED.	43 20
BALANCE	2160 58	CHECK	137 75

DETACH BEFORE CASHING CHECK
STATEMENT OF EARNINGS AND DEDUCTIONS FOR EMPLOYEE'S RECORD COVERING PAY PERIOD TO AND INCLUDING DATE SHOWN BELOW

DATE Dec 10 1976

TO Val N. Tyne

TOTAL WAGES	180 95
SOCIAL SECURITY TAX	10 59
WITHHOLDING U.S. INCOME TAX	30 80
STATE INCOME TAX	
City	1 81
TOTAL DEDUCTIONS	43 20
AMOUNT THIS CHECK	137 75

296

Dec 10 1976 $\frac{2-52}{710}$

PAY TO THE ORDER OF Miss Val N. Tyne $137 75/00

One hundred thirty-seven and 75/00 DOLLARS

NATIONAL BOULEVARD BANK OF CHICAGO

SAMPLE-VOID
DELUXE CHECK PRINTERS, INC.

Your Signature

⑈000341⑈ ⑆0710⑉0052⑆ ⑈123456 7⑈

297

Dec 10 1976

Hal O. Whean

BAL. FOR'D	2160 58	TOTAL WAGES	181 00
		SOCIAL SEC. TAX	10 59
		U.S. INC. TAX	30 80
		STATE INC. TAX	
		City	1 81
TOTAL			
THIS CHECK	137 80	TOTAL DED.	43 20
BALANCE	2022 78	CHECK	137 80

DETACH BEFORE CASHING CHECK
STATEMENT OF EARNINGS AND DEDUCTIONS FOR EMPLOYEE'S RECORD COVERING PAY PERIOD TO AND INCLUDING DATE SHOWN BELOW

DATE Dec 10 1976

TO Hal O Whean

TOTAL WAGES	181 00
SOCIAL SECURITY TAX	10 59
WITHHOLDING U.S. INCOME TAX	30 80
STATE INCOME TAX	
City	1 81
TOTAL DEDUCTIONS	43 20
AMOUNT THIS CHECK	137 80

297

Dec 10 1976 $\frac{2-52}{710}$

PAY TO THE ORDER OF Mr. Hal O. Whean $137 80/00

One hundred thirty-seven and 80/00 DOLLARS

NATIONAL BOULEVARD BANK OF CHICAGO

SAMPLE-VOID
DELUXE CHECK PRINTERS, INC.

Your Signature

⑈000342⑈ ⑆0710⑉0052⑆ ⑈123456 7⑈

(1) (2)

298

Dec 17 1976

Val N. Tyne

BAL. FOR'D	2022 78	TOTAL WAGES	205 63
		SOCIAL SEC. TAX	12 03
		U.S. INC. TAX	35 00
		STATE INC. TAX	
		City	2 06
TOTAL			
THIS CHECK	156 54	TOTAL DED.	49 09
BALANCE	1866 24	CHECK	156 54

DETACH BEFORE CASHING CHECK
STATEMENT OF EARNINGS AND DEDUCTIONS FOR EMPLOYEE'S RECORD COVERING PAY PERIOD TO AND INCLUDING DATE SHOWN BELOW

DATE Dec 17 1976

TO Val N Tyne

TOTAL WAGES	205 63
SOCIAL SECURITY TAX	12 03
WITHHOLDING U.S. INCOME TAX	35 00
STATE INCOME TAX	
City	2 06
TOTAL DEDUCTIONS	49 09
AMOUNT THIS CHECK	156 54

298

Dec 17 1976 $\frac{2-52}{710}$

PAY TO THE ORDER OF Miss Val N. Tyne $156 54/00

One hundred fifty-six and 54/00 DOLLARS

NATIONAL BOULEVARD BANK OF CHICAGO

SAMPLE-VOID
DELUXE CHECK PRINTERS, INC.

Your Signature

⑈000343⑈ ⑆0710⑉0052⑆ ⑈123456 7⑈

299

Dec 17 1976

Hal O Whean

BAL. FOR'D	1866 24	TOTAL WAGES	202 00
		SOCIAL SEC. TAX	11 82
		U.S. INC. TAX	35 00
		STATE INC. TAX	
		City	2 02
TOTAL			
THIS CHECK	153 16	TOTAL DED.	48 84
BALANCE	1713 08	CHECK	153 16

DETACH BEFORE CASHING CHECK
STATEMENT OF EARNINGS AND DEDUCTIONS FOR EMPLOYEE'S RECORD COVERING PAY PERIOD TO AND INCLUDING DATE SHOWN BELOW

DATE Dec 17 1976

TO Hal O Whean

TOTAL WAGES	202 00
SOCIAL SECURITY TAX	11 82
WITHHOLDING U.S. INCOME TAX	35 00
STATE INCOME TAX	
City	2 02
TOTAL DEDUCTIONS	48 84
AMOUNT THIS CHECK	153 16

299

Dec 17 1976 $\frac{2-52}{710}$

PAY TO THE ORDER OF Mr Hal O. Whean $153 16/00

One hundred fifty-three and 16/00 DOLLARS

NATIONAL BOULEVARD BANK OF CHICAGO

SAMPLE-VOID
DELUXE CHECK PRINTERS, INC.

Your Signature

⑈000344⑈ ⑆0710⑉0052⑆ ⑈123456 7⑈

300

DATE Dec 24 1976

TO Val N. Tyne

FOR

BAL. FOR'D	1713 08	TOTAL WAGES	219 73
DEP.		SOCIAL SEC. TAX	12 85
		U. S. INC. TAX	37 10
		STATE INC. TAX	
		City	2 20
TOTAL			
THIS CHECK	167 58	TOTAL DED.	52 15
BALANCE	1545 50	CHECK	167 58

DETACH BEFORE CASHING CHECK
STATEMENT OF EARNINGS AND DEDUCTIONS FOR EMPLOYEE'S RECORD COVERING PAY PERIOD TO AND INCLUDING DATE SHOWN BELOW

DATE Dec 24 1976

TO Val N Tyne

TOTAL WAGES	219 73
SOCIAL SECURITY TAX	12 85
WITHHOLDING U. S. INCOME TAX	37 10
STATE INCOME TAX	
City	2 20
TOTAL DEDUCTIONS	52 15
AMOUNT THIS CHECK	167 58

300

Dec 24 1976 2-52/710

PAY TO THE ORDER OF Miss Val N. Tyne $167 58/00

One hundred sixty-seven and 58/00 DOLLARS

NATIONAL BOULEVARD BANK OF CHICAGO

SAMPLE-VOID DELUXE CHECK PRINTERS, INC.

Your Signature

⑈000345⑈ ⑆0710⑉0052⑆ ⑈123456 7⑈

DELUXE CHECK PRINTERS PS-3

301

DATE Dec 24 1976

TO Hal O Whean

FOR

BAL. FOR'D	1545 50	TOTAL WAGES	202 00
DEP.		SOCIAL SEC. TAX	11 82
		U. S. INC. TAX	35 00
		STATE INC. TAX	
		City	2 02
TOTAL			
THIS CHECK	153 16	TOTAL DED.	48 84
BALANCE	1392 34	CHECK	153 16

DETACH BEFORE CASHING CHECK
STATEMENT OF EARNINGS AND DEDUCTIONS FOR EMPLOYEE'S RECORD COVERING PAY PERIOD TO AND INCLUDING DATE SHOWN BELOW

DATE Dec 24 1976

TO Hal O Whean

TOTAL WAGES	202 00
SOCIAL SECURITY TAX	11 82
WITHHOLDING U. S. INCOME TAX	35 00
STATE INCOME TAX	
City	2 02
TOTAL DEDUCTIONS	48 84
AMOUNT THIS CHECK	153 16

301

Dec 24 1976 2-52/710

PAY TO THE ORDER OF Mr Hal O Whean $153 16/00

One hundred fifty-three and 16/00 DOLLARS

NATIONAL BOULEVARD BANK OF CHICAGO

SAMPLE-VOID DELUXE CHECK PRINTERS, INC.

Your Signature

⑈000346⑈ ⑆0710⑉0052⑆ ⑈123456 7⑈

DELUXE CHECK PRINTERS PS-3

(3)

(4)

302

DATE Dec 31 1975

TO Val N. Tyne

FOR

BAL. FOR'D	1392 34	TOTAL WAGES	216 20
DEP.		SOCIAL SEC. TAX	12 65
		U. S. INC. TAX	37 10
		STATE INC. TAX	
		City	2 16
TOTAL			
THIS CHECK	164 29	TOTAL DED.	51 91
BALANCE	1228 05	CHECK	164 29

DETACH BEFORE CASHING CHECK
STATEMENT OF EARNINGS AND DEDUCTIONS FOR EMPLOYEE'S RECORD COVERING PAY PERIOD TO AND INCLUDING DATE SHOWN BELOW

DATE Dec 31 1976

TO Val N. Tyne

TOTAL WAGES	216 20
SOCIAL SECURITY TAX	12 65
WITHHOLDING U. S. INCOME TAX	37 10
STATE INCOME TAX	
City	2 16
TOTAL DEDUCTIONS	51 91
AMOUNT THIS CHECK	164 29

302

Dec 31 1976 2-52/710

PAY TO THE ORDER OF Miss Val N. Tyne $164 29/00

One hundred sixty-four and 29/00 DOLLARS

NATIONAL BOULEVARD BANK OF CHICAGO

SAMPLE-VOID DELUXE CHECK PRINTERS, INC.

Your Signature

⑈000347⑈ ⑆0710⑉0052⑆ ⑈123456 7⑈

DELUXE CHECK PRINTERS PS-3

303

DATE Dec 31 1976

TO Hal O Whean

FOR

BAL. FOR'D	1228 05	TOTAL WAGES	184 00
DEP.		SOCIAL SEC. TAX	10 76
		U. S. INC. TAX	30 80
		STATE INC. TAX	
		City	1 84
TOTAL			
THIS CHECK	140 60	TOTAL DED.	43 40
BALANCE	1087 45	CHECK	140 60

DETACH BEFORE CASHING CHECK
STATEMENT OF EARNINGS AND DEDUCTIONS FOR EMPLOYEE'S RECORD COVERING PAY PERIOD TO AND INCLUDING DATE SHOWN BELOW

DATE Dec 31 1976

TO Hal O Whean

TOTAL WAGES	184 00
SOCIAL SECURITY TAX	10 76
WITHHOLDING U. S. INCOME TAX	30 80
STATE INCOME TAX	
City	1 84
TOTAL DEDUCTIONS	43 40
AMOUNT THIS CHECK	140 60

303

Dec 31 1976 2-52/710

PAY TO THE ORDER OF Mr Hal O. Whean $140 60/00

One hundred forty and 60/00 DOLLARS

NATIONAL BOULEVARD BANK OF CHICAGO

SAMPLE-VOID DELUXE CHECK PRINTERS, INC.

Your Signature

⑈000348⑈ ⑆0710⑉0052⑆ ⑈123456 7⑈

DELUXE CHECK PRINTERS PS-3

Total Payroll Record
Holiday Party Service
Payroll for week ending 12-10

(1)

Name	Reg Hours	O.T. Hours	Reg Pay	O.T. Pay	Gross Pay	Fed Inc Tax	FICA Tax	City Tax	Net Pay
V. Tyne	38½	0	180.95	0	180.95	30.80	10.59	1.81	137.75
H. Whean	40	3½	160.00	21.00	181.00	30.80	10.59	1.81	137.80
Total		3½	340.95	21.00	361.95	61.60	21.18	3.62	275.55

Total Payroll Record
Holiday Party Service
Payroll for Week Ending 12-17

(2)

Name	Reg Hours	O.T. Hours	Reg Pay	O.T. Pay	Gross Pay	Fed Inc Tax	FICA Tax	City Tax	Net Pay
V. Tyne	40	2½	188.00	17.63	205.63	35.00	12.03	2.06	156.54
H. Whean	40	7	160.00	42.00	202.00	35.00	11.82	2.02	153.16
Total	80	9½	348.00	59.63	407.63	70.00	23.85	4.08	309.70

Total Payroll Record
Holiday Party Service
Payroll for Week Ending 12-24

(3)

Name	Reg Hours	O.T. Hours	Reg Pay	O.T. Pay	Gross Pay	Fed Inc Tax	FICA Tax	City Tax	Net Pay
V. Tyne	40	4½	188.00	31.73	219.73	37.10	12.85	2.20	167.58
H. Whean	40	7	160.00	42.00	202.00	35.00	11.82	2.02	153.16
Total	80	11½	348.00	73.73	421.73	72.10	24.67	4.22	320.74

Total Payroll Record
Holiday Party Service
Payroll for Week Ending 12-31

(4)

Name	Reg Hours	O.T. Hours	Reg Pay	O.T. Pay	Gross Pay	Fed Inc Tax	FICA Tax	City Tax	Net Pay
V. Tyne	40	4	188.00	28.20	216.20	37.10	12.65	2.16	164.29
H. Whean	40	4	160.00	24.00	184.00	30.80	10.76	1.84	140.60
Total	80	8	348.00	52.20	400.20	67.90	23.41	4.00	304.89

For Official Use Only

Wage and Tax Statement 1975

Holiday Party Service 362436

Type or print EMPLOYER'S name, address, ZIP code and Federal identifying number.

Copy A For Internal Revenue Service Center

Employer's State identifying number: 362436

21 ☐

Employee's social security number	1 Federal income tax withheld	2 Wages, tips, and other compensation	3 FICA employee tax withheld	4 Total FICA wages
395-25-1195	140.00	822.51	48.12	822.51

Type or print Employee's name, address, and ZIP code below. (Name must aline with arrow)

Name ▶ Val N. Tyne

5 Was employee covered by a qualified pension plan, etc.?	6 *	7 *
no		
8 State or local tax withheld	**9 State or local wages**	**10 State or locality**
8.23	822.51	city
11 State or local tax withheld	**12 State or local wages**	**13 State or locality**

* See instructions on back of Copy D

Form W–2 See instructions on Form W–3 and back of Copy D

Department of the Treasury—Internal Revenue Service
GPO: 1975 — 0-575-022 EI-36-2441915

(5)

For Official Use Only

Wage and Tax Statement 1975

Holiday Party Service 362436

Type or print EMPLOYER'S name, address, ZIP code and Federal identifying number.

Copy A For Internal Revenue Service Center

Employer's State identifying number

21 ☐

Employee's social security number	1 Federal income tax withheld	2 Wages, tips, and other compensation	3 FICA employee tax withheld	4 Total FICA wages
457-22-7515	131.60	769.00	44.99	769.00

Type or print Employee's name, address, and ZIP code below. (Name must aline with arrow)

Name ▶ Hal O. Whean

5 Was employee covered by a qualified pension plan, etc.?	6 *	7 *
no		
8 State or local tax withheld	**9 State or local wages**	**10 State or locality**
7.69	769.00	city
11 State or local tax withheld	**12 State or local wages**	**13 State or locality**

* See instructions on back of Copy D

Form W–2 See instructions on Form W–3 and back of Copy D

Department of the Treasury—Internal Revenue Service
GPO: 1975 — 0-575-022 EI-36-2441915

111

Jan 3 1977 2-52/710

PAY TO THE ORDER OF City $15 92/00

Fifteen and 92/00 DOLLARS (6)

NATIONAL BOULEVARD BANK OF CHICAGO

SAMPLE-VOID
DELUXE CHECK PRINTERS, INC.

MEMO City Withholding Tax Your Signature

⑆0710⑉0052⑆ ⑈123456 7⑈ 0161

DELUXE CHECK PRINTERS • RJ-1

FEDERA . TAX
DEPOSIT

DEPARTMENT OF THE TREASURY - FISCAL SERVICE
Bureau of Government Financial Operations - FTD Form Rev. Jan. 1976

FORM AND TAX CLASS
501 WITHHELD INCOME AND FICA TAXES
503 CORPO. \ ON INCO. E TAXES
504 EXCISE TAXES
507 RAI OAD RETIREMENT TAXES
508 UNE. PLOYMENT TAXES
511 AGRICULTURAL WORKERS: 'ICA TAXES AND VOLUNTARILY .JITHHELD INCOME TAX
512 TAX WITHHELD AT SOURCE ON NONRESIDEI ALIENS, FOREIGN CORPO. ATIONS, TAX-FREE COVENANT BONDS

DO NOT USE T I S FORM TO DEPOSIT TO A TAX C .ASS OT IER THAN II DICATED.

NAME OF BANK	AMOUNT OF DEPOSIT	
National Boulevard	457	82
	DOLLARS	CENTS

IRS Return

Holiday Party Service

Employer Identification Number: 362436

Dec. 1976
Tax Period Ending

Bank Name/Date Stamp

Verify preprinted data; if incorrect, see instructions on reverse.
Enter amount of deposit and name of bank where deposited in space above.
Do Not Write In Space Below

---

(7)

112

Jan 3 1977 2-52/710

PAY TO THE ORDER OF National Boulevard Bank $457 82/00

Four hundred fifty-seven and 82/00 DOLLARS

NATIONAL BOULEVARD BANK OF CHICAGO

SAMPLE-VOID
DELUXE CHECK PRINTERS, INC.

MEMO FICA + w/h - Dec, 1976 Your Signature

⑆0710⑉0052⑆ ⑈123456 7⑈ 0162

DELUXE CHECK PRINTERS • RJ-1

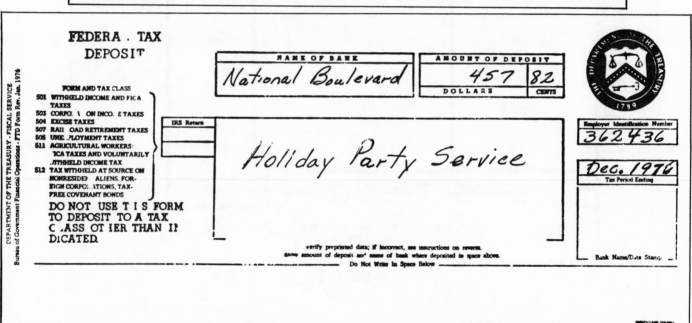

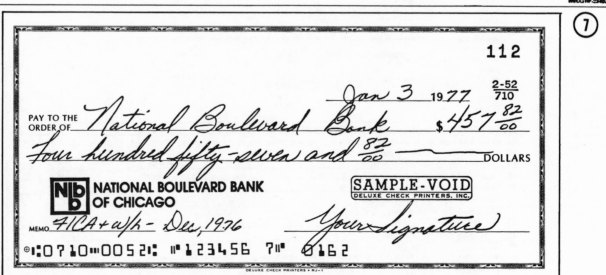

(8)

Please remove this strip at perforation before mailing.

Form 941 (Rev. Oct. 1975) Department of the Treasury Internal Revenue Service

Employer's Quarterly Federal Tax Return

Schedule A—Quarterly Report of Wages Taxable under the Federal Insurance Contributions Act—FOR SOCIAL SECURITY

List for each nonagricultural employee the WAGES taxable under the FICA which were paid during the quarter. If you pay an employee more than $14,100 in a calendar year, report only the first $14,100 of such wages. In the case of "Tip Income," see Instructions on page 4. IF WAGES WERE NOT TAXABLE UNDER THE FICA, MAKE NO ENTRIES IN ITEMS 1 THROUGH 9 AND 14 THROUGH 18.

SSA Use Only

F ☐ 2 ☐ U ☐ E ☐
S ☐ 1 ☐ L ☐ T ☐
X ☐ 0 ☐ V ☐ A ☐

1. Total pages of this return including this page and any pages of Form 941a ▶ 1
2. Total number of employees listed ▶ 2
3. (First quarter only) Number of employees (except household) employed in the pay period including March 12th ▶

4. EMPLOYEE'S SOCIAL SECURITY NUMBER 000 00 0000	5. NAME OF EMPLOYEE (Please type or print)	6. TAXABLE FICA WAGES Paid to Employee in Quarter (Before deductions) Dollars Cents	7. TAXABLE TIPS REPORTED (See page 4) Dollars Cents
395-25-1195	Val N. Tyne	822.51	
457-22-7515	Hal O. Whean	769.00	

If you need more space for listing employees, use Schedule A continuation sheets, Form 941a.

Totals for this page—Wage total in column 6 and tip total in column 7 ⟶ 1591.51

E I NO 31-02714-0

8. TOTAL WAGES TAXABLE UNDER FICA PAID DURING QUARTER. $ 1591.51 ◁

(Total of column 6 on this page and continuation sheets.) Enter here and in item 14 below.

9. TOTAL TAXABLE TIPS REPORTED UNDER FICA DURING QUARTER. $ none ◁

(Total of column 7 on this page and continuation sheets.) Enter here and in item 15 below. (If no tips reported, write "None.")

Employer's name, address, employer identification number, and calendar quarter. (If not correct, please change)

Name (as distinguished from trade name) — Date quarter ended: Dec. 31, 1976

Trade name, if any: Holiday Party Service — Employer Identification No.: 362436

Address and ZIP code

Entries must be made both above and below this line; if address different from previous return check here ☐

Name (as distinguished from trade name) — Date quarter ended: Dec. 31, 1976

Trade name, if any: Holiday Party Service — Employer Identification No.: 362436

Address and ZIP code

T | FP
FF | I
FD | TOT

10. Total Wages And Tips Subject To Withholding Plus Other Compensation ⟶	1591	51
11. Amount Of Income Tax Withheld From Wages, Tips, Annuities, etc. (See instructions)	271	60
12. Adjustment For Preceding Quarters Of Calendar Year	0	
13. Adjusted Total Of Income Tax Withheld ⟶	271	60
14. Taxable FICA Wages Paid (Item 8) $ 1591.51 multiplied by 11.7% = TAX	186	21
15. Taxable Tips Reported (Item 9) $ .... multiplied by 5.85% = TAX	0	
16. Total FICA Taxes (Item 14 plus Item 15) ⟶	186	21
17. Adjustment (See instructions)	0	
18. Adjusted Total Of FICA Taxes ⟶	186	21
19. Total Taxes (Item 13 plus Item 18)	457	81
20. TOTAL DEPOSITS FOR QUARTER (INCLUDING FINAL DEPOSIT MADE FOR QUARTER) AND OVERPAYMENT FROM PREVIOUS QUARTER LISTED IN SCHEDULE B (See instructions on page 4)	457	82
Note: If undeposited taxes at the end of the quarter are $200 or more, the full amount must be deposited with an authorized commercial bank or a Federal Reserve bank. This deposit must be entered in Schedule B and included in item 20.		
21. Undeposited Taxes Due (Item 19 Less Item 20—This Should Be Less Than $200). Pay To Internal Revenue Service And Enter Here ⟶		
22. If Item 20 Is More Than Item 19, Enter Excess Here ▶ $		01

And Check If You Want It ☑ Applied To Next Return, Or ☐ Refunded.

23. If not liable for returns in the future write "FINAL" (See instructions) ▶ Date final wages paid ▶

Under penalties of perjury, I declare that I have examined this return, including accompanying schedules and statements, and to the best of my knowledge and belief it is true, correct and complete.

Date January 3, 1977 Signature Your Signature Title (Owner, etc) Bookkeeper

Form 941 (10-75)

Please remove this strip at perforation before mailing.

(8)

SCHEDULE B—RECORD OF FEDERAL TAX DEPOSITS

Deposit period ending:		A. Tax liability for period	B. Amount deposited	C. Date of deposit
Overpayment from previous quarter				
First month of quarter	1st through 7th day			
	8th through 15th day			
	16th through 22d day			
	23d through last day			
1 First month total	1			
Second month of quarter	1st through 7th day			
	8th through 15th day			
	16th through 22d day			
	23d through last day			
2 Second month total	2			
Third month of quarter	1st through 7th day			
	8th through 15th day	103.96		
	16th through 22d day	117.70		
	23d through last day	236.16	457.82	1-3-77
3 Third month total	3	457.82	457.82	
4 Total for quarter (total of items 1, 2, and 3)		457.82	457.82	
5 Final deposit made for quarter. (Enter zero if the final deposit made for the quarter is included in item 4.)			0	
6 Total deposits for quarter (total of items 4 and 5)—enter here and in item 20, page 1			457.82	

☆ U.S. GOVERNMENT PRINTING OFFICE : 1975—O-591-482

ANSWER KEY
Chapter 3

3A

	Assets	Liabilities	Owner's Equity
1)	$ 1000	$ 800	$ 200
2)	5000	2000	$3000
3)	3000	1000	2000
4)	10000	9000	1000

2 is the best company to own because it has more value clear of debt than the others.

3B

A	Automobile	A	Typewriter
L	Owed to Adams Company	A	Government bonds
L	Unpaid meat bill	L	Any item we owe
A	Office furniture	A	Any item we own
L	Owed to grocery store	OE	The amount of the difference between total assets and total liabilities

3C

Frank N. Stein Costumes

Assets

Cash

+		−	
6/19/76	3000	6/21/76	1000
6/27/76	200	6/30/76	500
6/28/76	100		1500
800	3300		

Costumes

+		−	
6/21/76	1000	6/28/76	100
6/25/76	500		
400	1500		

Liabilities

Costume Suppliers

−		+	
6/30/76	500	6/25/76	500

Owner's Equity

Mr. Stein

−	+	
	6/19/76	3000
	6/27/76	200
		3200

3D

Holme's Sweet Homes

	Debit	Credit
Received cash for sale of old office desk.	A	C
Paid cash to Adams Company in part payment of the cash owed.	E	A
Received cash as commission for the sale of a house.	A	I
Paid cash for rent of office.	K	A
Paid cash for a new automobile.	B	A
Paid cash for gas and oil for auto.	N	A
Owner withdrew money from the business.	H	A
Paid cash for new office machine.	D	A
Received cash from sale of old office machine.	A	D
Paid cash for advertisement in newspaper.	M	A
Paid cash for telephone bill.	L	A
Paid cash for electricity bill.	J	A
Owner invested more money in the business.	A	G

3E

George's Lawn Care

Cash in Bank

Debit		Credit	
5/9	8	5/13	3
5/11	15	5/16	7
5/20	8	5/21	1
4	31	5/25	16
			27

Store Payable

Debit		Credit	
5/25	16	5/15	16

George

Debit		Credit	
		5/8	50

Withdrawals

Debit		Credit	
5/13	3		

Mowing Income

Debit		Credit	
		5/9	8
		5/11	10
		5/20	8
			26

Lawn Mower

Debit		Credit	
5/8	50		

Gas Expense

Debit		Credit	
5/21	1		

Repair Expense

Debit		Credit	
5/16	7		

Raking Income

Debit		Credit	
		5/11	5

Grass Catcher

Debit		Credit	
5/15	16		

George's Lawn Care
Trial Balance
May 30, 1976

	Debit	Credit
Cash in Bank	4	
Lawn Mower	50	
Grass catcher	16	
George		50
Withdrawals	3	
Mowing Income		26
Raking Income		5
Gas Expense	1	
Repair Expense	7	
Total	81	81

3F

Beginner's Piano Lessons
Trial Balance
March 31, 1976

	Debits	Credits
Cash in Bank	45.50	
Book	5.50	
Metronome	18.00	
Piano	300.00	
Owed to Store		18.00
Owed Repair Man		50.00
Capital		320.00
Withdrawals	10.00	
Income		41.00
Miscellaneous Expense	50.00	
	429.00	429.00

Beginner's Piano Lessons

Cash in Bank

3/5	20	3/13	20
3/10	30	3/25	5.50
3/14	5	3/30	10
3/15	20		35.50
3/26	6		
45.50	81		

Owed to Store

3/25	5.50	3/6	5.50
		3/20	18
			23.50 18.00

Capital

		3/5	320

Owed Repair Man

		3/26	50

Income

		3/10	30
		3/14	5
		3/26	6
			41

Book

3/6	5.50		

Withdrawals

3/30	10		

Metronome

3/13	20	3/15	20
3/20	18		
18	38		

Misc. Expense

3/26	50		

Piano

3/5	300		

(3) G

Cash in Bank

6/13 12	6/14 8
6/18 20	6/27 5
6/29 5	6/28 1.50
37	6/30 1.50
	1.00
	17.00

20.00

Store Payable

6/27 5	6/15 5

Capital

Withdrawals

6/28 1.50	

Misc. Expense

6/29 5	
6/30 1	
6	

Income

	6/13 12
	6/18 20
	6/29 5
	37

Petty Cash

6/14 8	

Life Preserver

6/15 5	6/29 5

Rubber Ring

6/30 1.50	

Petty Cash Statement for the month of June, 1976

Rubber Ring	$1.50
Withdrawals	
Miscellaneous Expense	1.00
Total	$2.50

Your Name
Trial Balance
June 30, 1976

	Debit	Credit
Cash in Bank	20.00	
Petty Cash	8.00	
Rubber Ring	1.50	
Withdrawals	1.50	
Income		37.00
Miscellaneous Expense	6.00	
	37.00	37.00

(3) H

Cash in Bank

Debit	Credit
	12/10 275.55
	12/17 309.70
	12/24 320.74
	12/31 304.89
	1/3 15.92
	1/3 457.82
	1684.62

Fed. Inc. Tax Payable

Debit	Credit
1/3 271.60	12/10 61.60
	12/17 70.00
	12/24 72.10
	12/31 67.90
	271.60

FICA Tax Payable

Debit	Credit
1/3 93.11	12/10 21.18
	12/17 23.85
	12/24 24.67
	12/31 23.41
	93.11

City Tax Payable

Debit	Credit
1/3 15.92	12/10 3.62
	12/17 4.08
	12/24 4.22
	12/31 4.00
	15.92

Salary Expense

Debit	Credit
12/10 361.95	
12/17 407.63	
12/24 421.73	
12/31 400.20	
1591.51	

Employer's Payroll Tax Exp

Debit	Credit
1/3 93.11	

(3) I

Beginner's Piano Lessons
Income & Expense Statement
For the Month Ending March 31, 1976

Income	$41.00
Miscellaneous Expense	50.00
Net Loss	$ 9.00

(3) J

Your Name
Income & Expense Statement
For the Month Ending June 30, 1976

Income	$37.00
Miscellaneous Expense	6.00
Net Income	$31.00

(3) K

Beginner's Piano Lessons
Balance Sheet
March 31, 1976

Assets		Liabilities		
Cash in Bank	$ 45.50	Owed to Store	$ 18.00	
Book	5.50	Owed Repair Man	50.00	
Metronome	18.00	Total		$ 68.00
Piano	300.00			
		Owner's Equity		
		Capital:		
		Investments	$320.00	
		Less Net Loss	- 9.00	
		Less Withdrawals	- 10.00	
		Capital, Mar 31		301.00
Total Assets	$369.00	Total Liab & Equity		$369.00

(3) L

Your Name
Balance Sheet
June 30, 1976

Assets		Liabilities		
Cash in Bank	$20.00	Total Liabilities		0
Petty Cash	8.00			
Rubber Ring	1.50	Owner's Equity		
		Capital:		
		Investments	0	
		Plus Net Income	$31.00	
		Less Withdrawals	- 1.50	
		Capital, June 30		$29.50
Total Assets	$29.50	Total Liab & Equity		$29.50

Summary Problems

A. What Kind?

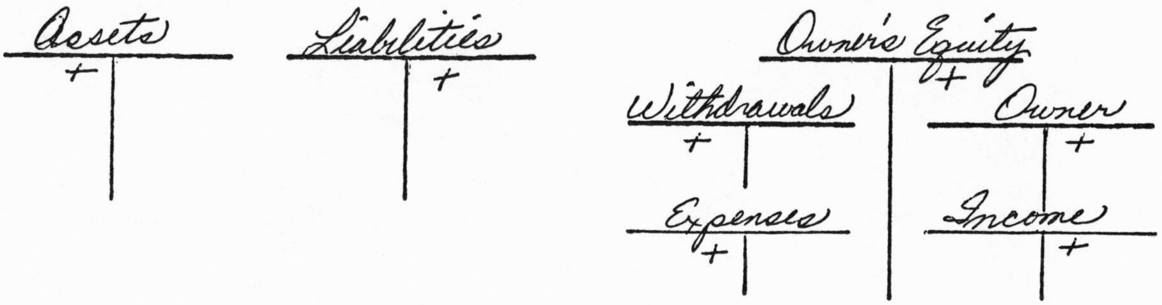

B. What is it?

1. owner's equity
2. Income and Expense Statement
3. credit
4. increases
5. asset
6. bookkeeping equation
7. Balance Sheet
8. Net Loss
9. Capital
10. Trial Balance
11. decreases
12. liability
13. Net Income
14. Withdrawals
15. accounts
16. debit

C. Using What You Know

North's Pole, Ski, & Snowmobile Rentals

Cash in Bank

Ref.	Date	Debit	Date	Credit	Ref.
(1)	11/15	10000	11/16	3000	(2)
(8)	11/21	200	11/19	1000	(4)
(9)	11/22	150	11/20	100	(5)
(12)	11/26	220	11/20	300	(6)
(16)	11/29	250	11/23	138.67	(10)
		10820	11/23	156.98	(10)
			11/23	138.67	(10)
			11/28	180	(15)
			11/30	50	(17)
			11/30	400	(18)
			11/30	166.26	(19)
			11/30	147.59	(19)
			11/30	155.65	(19)
			11/30	40	(20)
			11/30	320.56	(21)
			11/30	23	(22)
4502.62				6317.38	

Petty Cash

Ref.	Date	Debit	Date	Credit	Ref.
(5)	11/20	100			

Ski Equipment

Ref.	Date	Debit	Date	Credit	Ref.
(2)	11/16	3000			

Snowmobiles

Ref.	Date	Debit	Date	Credit	Ref.
(3)	11/16	25,000			

Office Equipment

Ref.	Date	Debit	Date	Credit	Ref.
(4)	11/19	1000			

Suppliers Payable

Ref.	Date	Debit	Date	Credit	Ref.
(18)	11/30	400	11/16	25000	(3)

FICA Payable

Ref.	Date	Debit	Date	Credit	Ref.
(21)	11/30	67.68	11/23	10.53	(10)
			11/23	11.42	(10)
			11/23	10.53	(10)
			11/30	12.64	(19)
			11/30	10.71	(19)
			11/30	11.85	(19)
				67.68	

Fed Inc. Tax Payable

Ref.	Date	Debit	Date	Credit	Ref.
(21)	11/30	185.20	11/23	30.80	(10)
			11/23	26.80	
			11/23	30.80	
			11/30	37.10	
			11/30	24.70	
			11/30	35	
				185.20	

Repairs Payable

Ref.	Date	Debit	Date	Credit	Ref.
(17)	11/30	50	11/27	50	(13)

Mr. North

Ref.	Date	Debit	Date	Credit	Ref.
			11/15	10,000	(1)

Withdrawals

Ref.	Date	Debit	Date	Credit	Ref.
	11/28	180			(15)

Salary Expense

Ref.	Date	Debit	Date	Credit	Ref.
	11/23	180			(10)
	11/23	195.20			(10)
	11/23	180			(10)
	11/30	216			(19)
	11/30	183			(19)
	11/30	202.50			(19)
		1156.70			

Payroll Tax Exp.

Ref.	Date	Debit	Date	Credit	Ref.
	11/30	67.68			(21)

Rent Expense

Ref.	Date	Debit	Date	Credit	Ref.
	11/30	300			(6)

Utility Expense

Ref.	Date	Debit	Date	Credit	Ref.
	11/30	40			(20)

Repairs Expense

Ref.	Date	Debit	Date	Credit	Ref.
	11/27	50			(13)

S. & S. Expense

Ref.	Date	Debit	Date	Credit	Ref.
	11/30	15			(22)

Misc. Expense

Ref.	Date	Debit	Date	Credit	Ref.
	11/30	8			(22)

Ski Rental Income

Ref.	Date	Debit	Date	Credit	Ref.
(8)			11/21	200	
(16)			11/29	250	
				450	

Snowmobile Income

Ref.	Date	Debit	Date	Credit	Ref.
(9)			11/22	150	
(12)			11/26	220	
				370	

North's Pole, Ski, & Snowmobile Rentals
Trial Balance
November 30, 1976

	Debits	Credits
Cash	4502.62	
Petty Cash	100.00	
Ski Equipment	3000.00	
Snowmobiles	25000.00	
Office Equipment	1000.00	
Equipment Supplies Pay		24600.00
Mr. North		10000.00
Withdrawals	180.00	
Income from Ski Equip		450.00
Income from Snowmobiles		370.00
Salary Expense	1156.70	
Payroll Tax Expense	67.68	
Rent Expense	300.00	
Utilities Expense	40.00	
Repairs Expense	50.00	
Stationery & Supplies	15.00	
Miscellaneous Expense	8.00	
	35420.00	35420.00

GENERAL INSTRUCTIONS

North's Pole, Ski, & Snowmobile Rentals
Income & Expense Statement
For Month Ending November 30, 1976

Incomes:		
Income from Ski Rentals	$ 450.00	
Income from Snowmobiles	370.00	$ 820.00
Expenses:		
Salary Expense	$1156.70	
Payroll Tax Expense	67.68	
Rent Expense	300.00	
Utility Expense	40.00	
Repairs Expense	50.00	
Stationery & Supplies Ex	15.00	
Miscellaneous Expense	8.00	1637.38
Net Loss		$ 817.38

(7)

No. 1 $ 5.00

RECEIVED OF PETTY CASH

DATE Nov 21 1976

FOR Rental agreement forms

CHARGE TO Stationery & Supplies Expense ACCOUNT

APPROVED BY

RECEIVED BY Y.J.

TOPS FORM 3008

(11)

No. 2 $ 10.00

RECEIVED OF PETTY CASH

DATE Nov 26 1976

FOR Envelopes & typing paper

CHARGE TO Stationery & Supplies Expense ACCOUNT

APPROVED BY

RECEIVED BY Y.J.

TOPS FORM 3008

(14)

No. 3 $ 8.00

RECEIVED OF PETTY CASH

DATE Nov. 28 1976

FOR Magazine subscription

CHARGE TO Miscellaneous Expense ACCOUNT

APPROVED BY

RECEIVED BY Y.J.

TOPS FORM 3008

Petty Cash Statement
Nov. 30, 1976

Stationery & Supplies Exp.	$15.00
Miscellaneous Expense	8.00
	$23.00
Amount Left	77.00
Nov 1 Total	$100.00

(22)

GENERAL INSTRUCTIONS

North's Pole, Ski & Snowmobile Rentals
Balance Sheet
November 30, 1976

Assets		Liabilities		
Cash	$ 4,502.62	Equipment Suppliers Payable		$24,600.00
Petty Cash	100.00			
Ski Equipment	3,000.00	Owner's Equity		
Snowmobiles	25,000.00	Mr. North:		
Office Equipment	1,000.00	Investments	$10,000.00	
		Less Net Loss	- 817.38	
		Less Withdrawal	- 180.00	9,002.62
Total Assets	$33,602.62	Total Liab. & Equity		$33,602.62

ANSWER KEY
Chapter 4

GENERAL JOURNAL

DATE	ACCOUNT TITLE	POST	DEBIT	CREDIT
June 20	Cash	11	10.00	
	Charlie Brown	31		10.00
	Investment			
25	Equipment	12	6.00	
	Cash	11		6.00
	New bat and ball			
26	Cash	11	2.00	
	Income	41		2.00
	Admission to first game			
28	Miscellaneous Expense	51	5.00	
	Dad Payable	21		5.00
	Owe for broken window			
29	Dad Payable	21	5.00	
	Cash	11		5.00
	Paid for window			
30	Withdrawals	031	1.00	
	Cash	11		1.00
	To buy a kite			
			29.00	29.00
		↑		
	(This column was filled in problem 4B)			

④A

LEDGER

Cash — Account No. 11

DATE	ITEMS	POST	DEBIT	DATE	ITEMS	POST	CREDIT
June 20		1	10.00	June 25		1	6.00
26		1	2.00	29		1	5.00
			12.00	30		1	1.00
							12.00

④B

Equipment — Account No. 12

4 B

DATE	ITEMS	POST	DEBIT	DATE	ITEMS	POST	CREDIT
June 25		1	6.00				

Dad Payable — Account No. 21

DATE	ITEMS	POST	DEBIT	DATE	ITEMS	POST	CREDIT
June 29		1	5.00	June 28		1	5.00

Charlie Brown — Account No. 31

DATE	ITEMS	POST	DEBIT	DATE	ITEMS	POST	CREDIT
				June 20		1	10.00

Withdrawals — Account No. 031

DATE	ITEMS	POST	DEBIT	DATE	ITEMS	POST	CREDIT
June 30		1	1.00				

Income Account No. 41

DATE	ITEMS	POST	DEBIT	DATE	ITEMS	POST	CREDIT
				June 26		1	2.00

Miscellaneous Expense Account No. 51

DATE	ITEMS	POST	DEBIT	DATE	ITEMS	POST	CREDIT
June 28		1	5.00				

4 C

CASH JOURNAL

CASH RECEIPTS / CASH DISBURSEMENTS

DATE	ACCOUNT CREDITED	POST	AMOUNT	DATE	ACCOUNT DEBITED	POST	CK. NO.	AMOUNT
Feb 5	Income from fees	41	50.00	Feb 6	Office Suppl. Exp.	51	101	20.00
10	Income from fees	41	80.00	12	Janitorial Exp	52	102	25.00
13	Lucy	31	500.00	15	Furniture	12	103	150.00
23	Income from fees	41	95.00	18	Signs	13	104	21.00
	Total	11	725.00	25	Withdrawals	031	105	5.00
				28	Utility Exp	53	106	30.00
					Total	11		251.00
		↑				↑		

(This column was added in problem 4D)

(4) D

LEDGER

Cash — Account No. 11

DATE	ITEMS	POST	DEBIT	DATE	ITEMS	POST	CREDIT
Jan 31	Balance	✓	1000.00	Feb 28		CJ	251.00
Feb 28		CJ	725.00				
	1474.00		1725.00				

Furniture — Account No. 12

DATE	ITEMS	POST	DEBIT	DATE	ITEMS	POST	CREDIT
Jan 31	Balance	✓	600.00				
Feb 15		CJ	150.00				
			750.00				

Signs — Account No. 13

DATE	ITEMS	POST	DEBIT	DATE	ITEMS	POST	CREDIT
Feb 18		CJ	21.00				

Lucy — Account No. 31

DATE	ITEMS	POST	DEBIT	DATE	ITEMS	POST	CREDIT
				Jan 31	Balance	✓	1200.00
				Feb 13		CJ	500.00
							1700.00

4 D

Withdrawals — Account No. 031

DATE	ITEMS	POST	DEBIT	DATE	ITEMS	POST	CREDIT
Feb 25		CJ	5.00				

Income from Fees — Account No. 41

DATE	ITEMS	POST	DEBIT	DATE	ITEMS	POST	CREDIT
				Jan 31	Balance	✓	580.00
				Feb 5		CJ	50.00
				10		CJ	80.00
				23		CJ	95.00
							805.00

Office Supplies Expense — Account No. 51

DATE	ITEMS	POST	DEBIT	DATE	ITEMS	POST	CREDIT
Jan 31	Balance	✓	50.00				
Feb 6		CJ	20.00				
			70.00				

Janitorial Expense — Account No. 52

DATE	ITEMS	POST	DEBIT	DATE	ITEMS	POST	CREDIT
Jan 31	Balance	✓	50.00				
Feb 12		CJ	25.00				
			75.00				

4 D

Utility Expense Account No. 53

DATE	ITEMS	POST	DEBIT	DATE	ITEMS	POST	CREDIT
Jan 31	Balance	✓	80.00				
Feb 28		CJ	30.00				
			110.00				

4 E

CASH JOURNAL

CASH RECEIPTS				CASH DISBURSEMENTS				
DATE	ACCOUNT CREDITED	POST	AMOUNT	DATE	ACCOUNT DEBITED	POST	CK. NO.	AMOUNT
Jan 12	Income	401	30.00	Jan 5	Car	102	1	3000.00
18	Income	401	40.00	10	Advtg. Exp	501	2	50.00
25	Income	401	50.00	16	Off. Suppl. Exp	503	3	75.00
26	Tools & Equip.	30	10.00	18	Car Expense	502	4	5.00
	Total	101	130.00	27	Accts Payable	202	5	30.00
				27	Withdrawals	301	6	40.00
					Total	101		3200.00

GENERAL JOURNAL

DATE	ACCOUNT TITLE	POST	DEBIT	CREDIT
Jan 15	Tools & Equipment	103	30.00	
	Accounts Payable	202		30.00
	Beethoven's Fifth Music Co.			
18	Car Expense	503	15.00	
	Accounts Payable	202		15.00
	Bach's Garage			
			45.00	45.00

LEDGER

4E

Cash in Bank — Account No. 101

DATE	ITEMS	POST	DEBIT	DATE	ITEMS	POST	CREDIT
Jan 1	Balance	✓	5000.00	Jan 31		CJ	3200.00
31		CJ	130.00				
	1930.00		5130.00				

Car — Account No. 102

DATE	ITEMS	POST	DEBIT	DATE	ITEMS	POST	CREDIT
Jan 5		CJ	3000.00				

Car Depreciation — Account No. 102

DATE	ITEMS	POST	DEBIT	DATE	ITEMS	POST	CREDIT
				Dec 31		J2	500 00

Tools & Equipment — Account No. 103

DATE	ITEMS	POST	DEBIT	DATE	ITEMS	POST	CREDIT
Jan 1	Balance	✓	500.00	Jan 26		CJ	10.00
15		CJ	30.00				
	520.00		530.00				

(4)E

Supplies — Account No. 104

DATE	ITEMS	POST	DEBIT	DATE	ITEMS	POST	CREDIT
Dec 31		J2	20.00				

Accounts Payable — Account No. 202

DATE	ITEMS	POST	DEBIT	DATE	ITEMS	POST	CREDIT
Jan 27	Beethoven's	CJ	30.00	Jan 15	Beethoven's	J1	30.00
				18	Bach's Garage	J1	15.00
					15.00		45.00

Mr. Schroeder — Account No. 301

DATE	ITEMS	POST	DEBIT	DATE	ITEMS	POST	CREDIT
				Jan 1	Balance	✓	5500.00

Withdrawals — Account No. 0301

DATE	ITEMS	POST	DEBIT	DATE	ITEMS	POST	CREDIT
Jan 27		CJ	40.00				

4E

Income — Account No. 401

DATE	ITEMS	POST	DEBIT	DATE	ITEMS	POST	CREDIT
				Jan 12		CJ	30.00
				18		CJ	40.00
				25		CJ	50.00
							120.00

Advertising Expense — Account No. 501

DATE	ITEMS	POST	DEBIT	DATE	ITEMS	POST	CREDIT
Jan 10		CJ	50.00				

Office Supplies Expense — Account No. 502

DATE	ITEMS	POST	DEBIT	DATE	ITEMS	POST	CREDIT
Jan 16	55.00	CJ	75.00	Dec 31		J2	20.00

Car Expense — Account No. 503

DATE	ITEMS	POST	DEBIT	DATE	ITEMS	POST	CREDIT
Jan 18		CJ	5.00				
18		J1	15.00				
			20.00				

4E

Depreciation Expense — Account No. 504

DATE	ITEMS	POST	DEBIT	DATE	ITEMS	POST	CREDIT
Dec 31		J2	500.00				

Schroeder's Tune Ups
Trial Balance
January 31, 1976

Account Title	No.	Debit	Credit
Cash in Bank	101	1930.00	
Car	102	3000.00	
Tools & Equipment	103	520.00	
Accounts Payable	202		15.00
Mr. Schroeder	301		5500.00
Withdrawals	0301	40.00	
Income	401		120.00
Advertising Expense	501	50.00	
Office Supplies Expense	502	75.00	
Car Expense	503	20.00	
		5635.00	5635.00

4F

GENERAL JOURNAL

page 2

DATE	ACCOUNT TITLE	POST	DEBIT	CREDIT
Dec 31	Depreciation Expense	504	500.00	
	Car Depreciation	0102		500.00
	Expected to last 6 years			
31	Supplies	104	20.00	
	Office Supplies Expense	502		20.00
	Value of Inventory			
	(This column was added in problem 4G)			

4G

Schroeder's Tune ups
Trial Balance
December 31, 1976

Account Title	No.	Debits	Credits
Cash in Bank	101	1930.00	
Car	102	3000.00	
Car Depreciation	0102		500.00
Tools & Equipment	103	520.00	
Supplies	104	20.00	
Accounts Payable	202		15.00
Mr Schroeder	301		5500.00
Withdrawals	0301	40.00	
Income	401		
Advertising Expense	501	50.00	120.00
Office Supplies Expense	502	55.00	
Car Expense	503	20.00	
Depreciation Expense	504	500.00	
		6135.00	6135.00

(4) G

Schroeder's Tune Ups
Income & Expense Statement
For Year Ending December 31, 1976

Income			$ 120.00
Expenses:			
Advertising Expense		$ 50.00	
Office Supplies Expense		55.00	
Car Expense		20.00	
Depreciation Expense		500.00	
Total Expenses			625.00
Net Loss			$ 505.00

Schroeder's Tune Ups
Balance Sheet
December 31, 1976

Assets			Liabilities		
Cash in Bank		$1930.00	Accounts Payable		$ 15.00
Car	$3000.00		Owner's Equity		
Less Depreciation	500.00		Mr Schroeder:		
Current Value		2500.00	Investment	$5500.00	
Tools & Equipment		520.00	Less Withdrawals	40.00	
Supplies		20.00	Less Net Loss	505.00	
			Equity Dec 31		4955.00
Total Assets		$4970.00	Total Liabilities & Equity		$4970.00

GENERAL JOURNAL

page 3

4H

DATE	ACCOUNT TITLE	POST	DEBIT	CREDIT
Dec 31	Income	401	120.00	
	Mr Schroeder	301		120.00
31	Mr Schroeder	301	50.00	
	Advertising Expense	501		50.00
31	Mr Schroeder	301	55.00	
	Office Supplies Expense	502		55.00
31	Mr Schroeder	301	20.00	
	Car Expense	503		20.00
31	Mr Schroeder	301	500.00	
	Depreciation Expense	504		500.00
31	Mr Schroeder	301	40.00	
	Withdrawals	0301		40.00
	Closing Entries		785.00	785.00

Schroeder's Tune Ups
Post Closing Trial Balance
December 31, 1976

Account Title	No.	Debits	Credits
Cash in Bank	101	1930.00	
Car	102	3000.00	
Car Depreciation	0102		500.00
Tools & Equipment	103	520.00	
Supplies	104	20.00	
Accounts Payable	202		15.00
Mr Schroeder	301		4955.00
		5470.00	5470.00

LEDGER

(4) H

Mr. Schroeder — Account No. 301

DATE	ITEMS	POST	DEBIT	DATE	ITEMS	POST	CREDIT
Dec 31	Advtg Exp	J3	50.00	Jan 1	Balance	✓	5500.00
31	Off. Suppl Exp	J3	55.00	Dec 31	Income	J3	120.00
31	Car Exp	J3	20.00		4955.00		5620.00
31	Deprec Exp	J3	500.00				
31	Withdrawals	J3	40.00				
			665.00				

Withdrawals — Account No. 0301

DATE	ITEMS	POST	DEBIT	DATE	ITEMS	POST	CREDIT
Jan 27		CJ	40.00	Dec 31	Closing Entry	J3	40.00

Income — Account No. 401

DATE	ITEMS	POST	DEBIT	DATE	ITEMS	POST	CREDIT
Dec 31	Closing Entry	J3	120.00	Jan 12		CJ	30.00
				18		CJ	40.00
				25		CJ	50.00
			120.00				120.00

Advertising Expense — Account No. 501

DATE	ITEMS	POST	DEBIT	DATE	ITEMS	POST	CREDIT
Jan 10		CJ	50.00	Dec 31	Closing Entry	J3	50.00

Office Supplies Expense — Account No. 502 (4)H

DATE	ITEMS	POST	DEBIT	DATE	ITEMS	POST	CREDIT
Jan 16		CJ	75.00	Dec 31		J2	20.00
				31	Closing Entry	J3	55.00
			75.00				75.00

Car Expense — Account No. 503

DATE	ITEMS	POST	DEBIT	DATE	ITEMS	POST	CREDIT
Jan 18		CJ	5.00	Dec 31	Closing Entry	J3	20.00
19		J1	15.00				
			20.00				20.00

Depreciation Expense — Account No. 504

DATE	ITEMS	POST	DEBIT	DATE	ITEMS	POST	CREDIT
Dec 31		J2	500.00	Dec 31	Closing Entry	J3	500.00

GENERAL JOURNAL (4)I

page 4

DATE	ACCOUNT TITLE	POST	DEBIT	CREDIT
1977				
Jan 1	Office Supplies Expense	502	20.00	
	Supplies	104		20.00
	After closing entry			

(4) I

LEDGER

Supplies — Account No. 104

DATE	ITEMS	POST	DEBIT	DATE	ITEMS	POST	CREDIT
Dec 31		J2	20.00	1977 Jan 1		J4	20.00

Office Supplies Expense — Account No. 502

DATE	ITEMS	POST	DEBIT	DATE	ITEMS	POST	CREDIT
Jan 16		CJ	75.00	Dec 31		J2	20.00
				31		J3	55.00
			75.00				75.00
Jan 1, '77		J4	20.00				

Summary Problems

A. What is it?

1. closing
2. Items
3. Posted
4. ledger
5. Depreciation Expense
6. explanation
7. journal
8. journalizing
9. Account Title
10. depreciation
11. posting
12. Cash Receipts
13. Cash Disbursements
14. Supplies
15. Car Depreciation

B. Using What You Know

CASH JOURNAL

CASH RECEIPTS				CASH DISBURSEMENTS					
DATE	ACCOUNT CREDITED	POST	AMOUNT	DATE	ACCOUNT DEBITED	POST	CK. NO.	AMOUNT	
June 6	Income	41	50.00	June 2	Rent Expense	51	1	200.00	(2)
8	Income	41	30.00	5	Gas Expense	52	2	120.00	(3)
20	Income	41	35.00	15	Withdrawals	031	3	15.00	(6)
25	Income	41	80.00	18	Withdrawals	031	4	5.00	(7)
		11	195.00	22	Mortgage Payable	21	5	250.00	(9)
					Miscellaneous Exp	53		50.00	(9)
						11		640.00	(14)
		(14)				(14)			

GENERAL JOURNAL

DATE	ACCOUNT TITLE	POST	DEBIT	CREDIT	
June 1	Plane	13	16000.00		(1)
	Cash in Bank	11	500.00		
	Mortgage Payable	21		13000.00	
	Snoopy	31		3500.00	
	Original Investment				
24	Miscellaneous Expense	53	100.00		(10)
	Accounts Payable	22		100.00	
	Plane repairs-Doghouse Hanger				
30	Gas Supplies	12	50.00		(12)
	Gas Expense	52		50.00	
	Allowing for gas on hand				
30	Depreciation Expense	54	166.67		(13)
	Plane Depreciation	013		166.67	
	Plane Depreciation at				
	$2000 per year, $166.67 per mo.				
		(14)	16816.67	16816.67	(14)
30	Income	41	195.00		(16)
	Snoopy	31		195.00	
30	Snoopy	31	200.00		
	Rent Expense	51		200.00	
30	Snoopy	31	70.00		
	Gas Expense	52		70.00	
30	Snoopy	31	150.00		
	Miscellaneous Expense	53		150.00	
30	Snoopy	31	166.67		
	Depreciation Expense	54		166.67	
30	Snoopy	31	20.00		
	Withdrawals	031		20.00	
	Closing Entries		801.67	801.67	
		(16)			
July 1	Gas Expense	52	50.00		(17)
	Gas Supplies	12		50.00	
		(17)			

LEDGER

Cash in Bank — Account No. 11

DATE	ITEMS	POST	DEBIT	DATE	ITEMS	POST	CREDIT
June 1		J	500.00	June 30		CJ	640.00
30		CJ	195.00				
	55.00		695.00				

(14) (14)

Gas Supplies — Account No. 12

DATE	ITEMS	POST	DEBIT	DATE	ITEMS	POST	CREDIT
(14) June 30		J	50.00	July 1		J	50.00 (17)

Plane — Account No. 13

DATE	ITEMS	POST	DEBIT	DATE	ITEMS	POST	CREDIT
(14) June 1		J	16000.00				

Plane Depreciation — Account No. 013

DATE	ITEMS	POST	DEBIT	DATE	ITEMS	POST	CREDIT
				June 30		J	166.67 (14)

Mortgage Payable — Account No. 21

DATE	ITEMS	POST	DEBIT	DATE	ITEMS	POST	CREDIT
(14) June 22		CJ	250.00	June 1	12,750.00	J	13000.00 (14)

Accounts Payable — Account No. 22

DATE	ITEMS	POST	DEBIT	DATE	ITEMS	POST	CREDIT
				June 24		J	100.00 (14)

Snoopy — Account No. 31

DATE	ITEMS	POST	DEBIT	DATE	ITEMS	POST	CREDIT
June 30	Rent Exp	J	200.00	June 1		J	3500.00 (14)
30	Gas Exp	J	70.00	30	Income	J	195.00 (16)
(16) 30	Misc Exp	J	150.00		3088.33		3695.00
30	Deprec. Exp	J	166.67				
30	Withdrawals	J	20.00				
			606.67				

Withdrawals — Account No. 031

DATE	ITEMS	POST	DEBIT	DATE	ITEMS	POST	CREDIT
June 15		CJ	15.00	June 30	Closing Entry	J	20.00
(14) 18		CJ	5.00				(16)
			20.00				20.00

Income — Account No. 41

	DATE	ITEMS	POST	DEBIT	DATE	ITEMS	POST	CREDIT	
16	June 30	Closing Entry	J	195.00	June 6		CJ	50.00	
					8		CJ	30.00	
					20		CJ	35.00	14
					25		CJ	80.00	
16				195.00				195.00	

Rent Expense — Account No. 51

	DATE	ITEMS	POST	DEBIT	DATE	ITEMS	POST	CREDIT	
14	June 2		CJ	200.00	June 30	Closing Entry	J	200.00	16

Gas Expense — Account No. 52

	DATE	ITEMS	POST	DEBIT	DATE	ITEMS	POST	CREDIT	
14	June 5	70.00	CJ	120.00	June 30		J	50.00	14
					30	Closing Entry	J	70.00	16
14				120.00				120.00	
17	July 1		J	50.00					

Miscellaneous Expense — Account No. 53

	DATE	ITEMS	POST	DEBIT	DATE	ITEMS	POST	CREDIT	
	June 24		J	100.00	June 30	Closing Entry	J	150.00	16
14	22		CJ	50.00					
				150.00				150.00	16

Depreciation Expense Account No. 54

	DATE	ITEMS	POST	DEBIT	DATE	ITEMS	POST	CREDIT	
(14)	June 30		J	166.67	June 30	Closing Entry	J	166.67	(16)

Snoopy Squadron Flying School
Trial Balance
June 30, 1976

	Account Title	No	Debits	Credits
	Cash in Bank	11	55.00	
	Gas Supplies	12	50.00	
	Plane	13	16,000.00	
	Plane Depreciation	013		166.67
	Mortgage Payable	21		12,750.00
	Accounts Payable	22		100.00
(15)	Snoopy	31		3,500.00
	Withdrawals	031	20.00	
	Income	41		195.00
	Rent Expense	51	200.00	
	Gas Expense	52	70.00	
	Miscellaneous Expense	53	150.00	
	Depreciation Expense	54	166.67	
			16,711.67	16,711.67

(15)

Snoopy Squadron Flying School
Income & Expense Statement
For Month Ending June 30, 1976

Income			$ 195.00
Expenses:			
Rent Expense		$ 200.00	
Gas Expense		70.00	
Miscellaneous Expense		150.00	
Depreciation Expense		166.67	
Total Expenses			586.67
Net Loss			$ 391.67

(15)

Snoopy Squadron Flying School
Balance Sheet
December 31, 1976

Assets			Liabilities		
Cash in Bank		$ 55.00	Mortgage Payable		$12,750.00
Gas Supplies		50.00	Accounts Payable		100.00
Plane	$16,000.00		Total Liabilities		$12,850.00
Less Depreciation	166.67		Owner's Equity		
Current Value		15,833.33	Snoopy:		
			Investment	$3,500.00	
			Less Withdrawals	20.00	
			Less Net Loss	391.67	
			Equity 6/30		3,088.33
Total Assets		$15,938.33	Total Liabilities & Equity		$15,938.33

ANSWER KEY
FINAL SUMMARY PROBLEM

113 $150 00/00
Dec 12 1976
Shop Owner
Rent

	DOLLARS	CENTS
BAL. FOR'D	4000	00
DEPOSITS		
"		
TOTAL		
THIS CHECK	150	00
OTHER DEDUCTIONS		
BAL. FOR'D	3850	00

113

Dec 12 1976 2-52/710

PAY TO THE ORDER OF Shop Owner $150 00/00

One hundred Fifty and 00/00 DOLLARS

NATIONAL BOULEVARD BANK OF CHICAGO

SAMPLE-VOID
DELUXE CHECK PRINTERS, INC.

MEMO

Your Signature

⑆0710⑉0052⑆ ⑈123456 7⑈ 0163

DELUXE CHECK PRINTERS • RJ-1

①

③

114 $30 00/00
Dec 15 1976
Magazine
subscription

	DOLLARS	CENTS
BAL. FOR'D	3850	00
DEPOSITS		
"		
TOTAL		
THIS CHECK	30	00
OTHER DEDUCTIONS		
BAL. FOR'D	3820	00

114

Dec 15 1976 2-52/710

PAY TO THE ORDER OF Magazine $30 00/00

Thirty and 00/00 DOLLARS

NATIONAL BOULEVARD BANK OF CHICAGO

SAMPLE-VOID
DELUXE CHECK PRINTERS, INC.

MEMO

Your Signature

⑆0710⑉0052⑆ ⑈123456 7⑈ 0164

DELUXE CHECK PRINTERS • RJ-1

(8)

115 $ 90 00/00

Dec 21 19 76

TO Supplier

Shampoo & supplies

	DOLLARS	CENTS
BAL. FOR'D	3967	99
DEPOSITS		
"		
TOTAL		
THIS CHECK	90	00
OTHER DEDUCTIONS		
BAL. FOR'D	3877	99

115

Dec 21 19 76 2-52/710

PAY TO THE ORDER OF Supplier $ 90 00/00

Ninety and 00/00 DOLLARS

NATIONAL BOULEVARD BANK OF CHICAGO

SAMPLE-VOID
DELUXE CHECK PRINTERS, INC.

MEMO

Your Signature

⑆0710⑉0052⑆ ⑈123456 7⑈ 0165

DELUXE CHECK PRINTERS • RJ-1

(9)

116 $ 200 00/00

Dec 22 19 76

TO Mr Brown

withdrawal

	DOLLARS	CENTS
BAL. FOR'D	3877	99
DEPOSITS		
"		
TOTAL		
THIS CHECK	200	00
OTHER DEDUCTIONS		
BAL. FOR'D	3677	99

116

Dec 22 19 76 2-52/710

PAY TO THE ORDER OF Mr Brown $ 200 00/00

Two hundred and 00/00 DOLLARS

NATIONAL BOULEVARD BANK OF CHICAGO

SAMPLE-VOID
DELUXE CHECK PRINTERS, INC.

MEMO

Your Signature

⑆0710⑉0052⑆ ⑈123456 7⑈ 0166

DELUXE CHECK PRINTERS • RJ-1

(13)

117 $ 150 00/00

Dec 27 19 76

TO Mr Brown

withdrawal

	DOLLARS	CENTS
BAL. FOR'D	3931	86
DEPOSITS		
"		
TOTAL		
THIS CHECK	150	00
OTHER DEDUCTIONS		
BAL. FOR'D	3781	86

117

Dec 27 19 76 2-52/710

PAY TO THE ORDER OF Mr Brown $ 150 00/00

One hundred fifty and 00/00 DOLLARS

NATIONAL BOULEVARD BANK OF CHICAGO

SAMPLE-VOID
DELUXE CHECK PRINTERS, INC.

MEMO

Your Signature

⑆0710⑉0052⑆ ⑈123456 7⑈ 0167

DELUXE CHECK PRINTERS • RJ-1

(14)

118 $180 00/00
Dec 28 1976
TO Janitor services

	DOLLARS	CENTS
BAL. FOR'D	3781	86
DEPOSITS		
"		
TOTAL		
THIS CHECK	180	00
OTHER DEDUCTIONS		
BAL. FOR'D	3601	86

118

Dec 28 1976 2-52/710

PAY TO THE ORDER OF Janitor $180 00/00

One hundred eighty and 00/00 DOLLARS

NATIONAL BOULEVARD BANK OF CHICAGO

SAMPLE-VOID
DELUXE CHECK PRINTERS, INC.

MEMO

Your Signature

⑆0710⑉0052⑆ ⑈123456 7⑈ 0168

DELUXE CHECK PRINTERS • RJ-1

(15)

119 $100 00/00
Dec 29 1976
TO Dan Druff Dist on account

	DOLLARS	CENTS
BAL. FOR'D	3601	86
DEPOSITS		
"		
TOTAL		
THIS CHECK	100	00
OTHER DEDUCTIONS		
BAL. FOR'D	3501	86

119

Dec 29 1976 2-52/710

PAY TO THE ORDER OF Daniel Druff Distributors $100 00/00

One hundred and 00/00 DOLLARS

NATIONAL BOULEVARD BANK OF CHICAGO

SAMPLE-VOID
DELUXE CHECK PRINTERS, INC.

MEMO

Your Signature

⑆0710⑉0052⑆ ⑈123456 7⑈ 0169

DELUXE CHECK PRINTERS • RJ-1

(18)

120 $21 00/00
Dec 31 1976
TO Petty Cash
$11-Misc, $10-Suppl

	DOLLARS	CENTS
BAL. FOR'D	3774	36
DEPOSITS		
"		
TOTAL		
THIS CHECK	21	00
OTHER DEDUCTIONS		
BAL. FOR'D	3753	36

120

Dec 31 1976 2-52/710

PAY TO THE ORDER OF Petty Cash $21 00/00

Twenty-one and 00/00 DOLLARS

NATIONAL BOULEVARD BANK OF CHICAGO

SAMPLE-VOID
DELUXE CHECK PRINTERS, INC.

MEMO

Your Signature

⑆0710⑉0052⑆ ⑈123456 7⑈ 0170

DELUXE CHECK PRINTERS • RJ-1

121 $2 10/00
Dec 31 1976
TO State Internal Revenue - sales tax

	DOLLARS	CENTS
BAL. FOR'D	3753	36
DEPOSITS		
"		
TOTAL		
THIS CHECK	2	10
OTHER DEDUCTIONS		
BAL. FOR'D	3751	26

121

Dec 31 1976 2-52/710

PAY TO THE ORDER OF State Internal Revenue Service $2 10/00

Two and 10/00 DOLLARS

NATIONAL BOULEVARD BANK OF CHICAGO

SAMPLE-VOID
DELUXE CHECK PRINTERS, INC.

MEMO Dec sales tax Your Signature

⑆0710⑉0052⑆ ⑈123456 7⑈ 0171

DELUXE CHECK PRINTERS • RJ-1

(19)

(21)

122 $341 92/00
Dec 31 1976
TO Nat'l Boulevard
FICA - $138.12
Fed w/h - 203.80

	DOLLARS	CENTS
BAL. FOR'D	3751	26
DEPOSITS		
"		
TOTAL		
THIS CHECK	341	92
OTHER DEDUCTIONS SC		85
BAL. FOR'D	3408	49

122

Dec 31 1976 2-52/710

PAY TO THE ORDER OF National Boulevard Bank $341 92/00

Three hundred forty-one and 92/00 DOLLARS

NATIONAL BOULEVARD BANK OF CHICAGO

SAMPLE-VOID
DELUXE CHECK PRINTERS, INC.

MEMO Dec FICA + Fed w/h Your Signature

⑆0710⑉0052⑆ ⑈123456 7⑈ 0172

DELUXE CHECK PRINTERS • RJ-1

No. 1 $ 3 00/00

RECEIVED OF PETTY CASH

DATE Dec 16 19 76

FOR Newspaper ⑤

CHARGE TO Miscellaneous Expense
ACCOUNT

APPROVED BY

RECEIVED BY Y J

TOPS FORM 3008

No. 2 $ 8 00/00

RECEIVED OF PETTY CASH

DATE Dec 19 19 76

FOR Window washing ⑦

CHARGE TO Miscellaneous Expense
ACCOUNT

APPROVED BY

RECEIVED BY Y J

TOPS FORM 3008

No. 3 $ 10 00/00

RECEIVED OF PETTY CASH

DATE Dec 26 19 76

FOR Shampoo & Supplies ⑫

CHARGE TO Supplies Expense
ACCOUNT

APPROVED BY

RECEIVED BY Y J

TOPS FORM 3008

(4)

CHECKING ACCOUNT DEPOSIT TICKET

DATE Dec 16 1976

Brown's Barber Shop

NATIONAL BOULEVARD BANK OF CHICAGO

CASH	CURRENCY	405	00
	COIN	30	00
CHECKS			
TOTAL FROM OTHER SIDE			
TOTAL			
LESS CASH RECEIVED			
NET DEPOSIT		435	00

[redacted]

2-52/710

USE OTHER SIDE FOR ADDITIONAL LISTING

BE SURE EACH ITEM IS PROPERLY ENDORSED

SAMPLE-VOID
DELUXE CHECK PRINTERS, INC.

⑈123456 7⑈

DELUXE JD-3 CHECKS AND OTHER ITEMS ARE RECEIVED FOR DEPOSIT SUBJECT TO THE TERMS AND CONDITIONS OF THIS BANK'S COLLECTION AGREEMENT.

(10)

CHECKING ACCOUNT DEPOSIT TICKET

DATE Dec 23 1976

Brown's Barber Shop

NATIONAL BOULEVARD BANK OF CHICAGO

CASH	CURRENCY	565	00
	COIN	10	00
CHECKS			
TOTAL FROM OTHER SIDE			
TOTAL			
LESS CASH RECEIVED			
NET DEPOSIT		575	00

[redacted]

2-52/710

USE OTHER SIDE FOR ADDITIONAL LISTING

BE SURE EACH ITEM IS PROPERLY ENDORSED

SAMPLE-VOID
DELUXE CHECK PRINTERS, INC.

⑈123456 7⑈

DELUXE JD-3 CHECKS AND OTHER ITEMS ARE RECEIVED FOR DEPOSIT SUBJECT TO THE TERMS AND CONDITIONS OF THIS BANK'S COLLECTION AGREEMENT.

(16)

CHECKING ACCOUNT DEPOSIT TICKET

DATE Dec 30 1976

Brown's Barber Shop

NATIONAL BOULEVARD BANK OF CHICAGO

CASH	CURRENCY	540	00
	COIN	32	00
CHECKS			
TOTAL FROM OTHER SIDE			
TOTAL			
LESS CASH RECEIVED			
NET DEPOSIT		572	00

[redacted]

2-52/710

USE OTHER SIDE FOR ADDITIONAL LISTING

BE SURE EACH ITEM IS PROPERLY ENDORSED

SAMPLE-VOID
DELUXE CHECK PRINTERS, INC.

⑈123456 7⑈

DELUXE JD-3 CHECKS AND OTHER ITEMS ARE RECEIVED FOR DEPOSIT SUBJECT TO THE TERMS AND CONDITIONS OF THIS BANK'S COLLECTION AGREEMENT.

305

DATE Dec 16 1976

TO Red Bard

FOR

BAL. FOR'D	3820 00	TOTAL WAGES	180 00
DEP. 12/16	435 00 (4)	SOCIAL SEC. TAX	10 53
		U. S. INC. TAX	30 80
TOTAL	4255 00		
THIS CHECK	138 67	TOTAL DED.	41 33
BALANCE	4116 33	CHECK	138 67

DETACH BEFORE CASHING CHECK
STATEMENT OF EARNINGS AND DEDUCTIONS FOR EMPLOYEE'S RECORD COVERING PAY PERIOD TO AND INCLUDING DATE SHOWN BELOW

DATE Dec 16 1976

TO Red Bard

TOTAL WAGES	180 00
SOCIAL SECURITY TAX	10 53
WITHHOLDING U. S. INCOME TAX	30 80
STATE INCOME TAX	
TOTAL DEDUCTIONS	41 33
AMOUNT THIS CHECK	138 67

(6) **305**

Dec 16 1976 2-52/710

PAY TO THE ORDER OF Red Bard $138 67/00

One hundred thirty-eight and 67/00 DOLLARS

NATIONAL BOULEVARD BANK OF CHICAGO

SAMPLE-VOID
DELUXE CHECK PRINTERS, INC.

Your Signature

000335 0710 0052 123456 7

306

DATE Dec 16 1976

TO Curly Hart

FOR

BAL. FOR'D	4116 33	TOTAL WAGES	192 50
DEP.		SOCIAL SEC. TAX	11 26
		U. S. INC. TAX	32 90
		STATE INC. TAX	
TOTAL			
THIS CHECK	148 34	TOTAL DED.	44 16
BALANCE	3967 99	CHECK	148 34

DETACH BEFORE CASHING CHECK
STATEMENT OF EARNINGS AND DEDUCTIONS FOR EMPLOYEE'S RECORD COVERING PAY PERIOD TO AND INCLUDING DATE SHOWN BELOW

DATE Dec 16 1976

TO Curly Hart

TOTAL WAGES	192 50
SOCIAL SECURITY TAX	11 26
WITHHOLDING U. S. INCOME TAX	32 90
STATE INCOME TAX	
TOTAL DEDUCTIONS	44 16
AMOUNT THIS CHECK	148 34

(6) **306**

Dec 16 1976 2-52/710

PAY TO THE ORDER OF Curly Hart $ 148 34/00

One hundred forty-eight and 34/00 DOLLARS

NATIONAL BOULEVARD BANK OF CHICAGO

SAMPLE-VOID
DELUXE CHECK PRINTERS, INC.

Your Signature

000336 0710 0052 123456 7

307

DATE Dec 23 1976

TO Red Bard

FOR

BAL. FOR'D	3677 99	TOTAL WAGES	200 00
DEP. 12/23	575 00 (10)	SOCIAL SEC. TAX	11 70
		U. S. INC. TAX	35 00
TOTAL	4252 99		
THIS CHECK	153 30	TOTAL DED.	46 70
BALANCE	4099 69	CHECK	153 30

DETACH BEFORE CASHING CHECK
STATEMENT OF EARNINGS AND DEDUCTIONS FOR EMPLOYEE'S RECORD COVERING PAY PERIOD TO AND INCLUDING DATE SHOWN BELOW

DATE Dec 23 1976

TO Red Bard

TOTAL WAGES	200 00
SOCIAL SECURITY TAX	11 70
WITHHOLDING U. S. INCOME TAX	35 00
STATE INCOME TAX	
TOTAL DEDUCTIONS	46 70
AMOUNT THIS CHECK	153 30

(11) **307**

Dec 23 1976 2-52/710

PAY TO THE ORDER OF Red Bard $153 30/00

One hundred fifty-three and 30/00 DOLLARS

NATIONAL BOULEVARD BANK OF CHICAGO

SAMPLE-VOID
DELUXE CHECK PRINTERS, INC.

Your Signature

000337 0710 0052 123456 7

308

DATE Dec 23 1976

TO Curly Hart

FOR

BAL. FOR'D	4099 69	TOTAL WAGES	220 00
DEP.		SOCIAL SEC. TAX	12 87
TOTAL		U.S. INC. TAX	39 30
THIS CHECK	167 83	STATE INC. TAX	
BALANCE	3931 86	TOTAL DED.	52 17
		CHECK	167 83

DETACH BEFORE CASHING CHECK
STATEMENT OF EARNINGS AND DEDUCTIONS FOR EMPLOYEE'S RECORD COVERING PAY PERIOD TO AND INCLUDING DATE SHOWN BELOW

DATE Dec 23 1976

TO Curly Hart

TOTAL WAGES	220 00
SOCIAL SECURITY TAX	12 87
WITHHOLDING U.S. INCOME TAX	39 30
STATE INCOME TAX	
TOTAL DEDUCTIONS	52 17
AMOUNT THIS CHECK	167 83

(11) 308

Dec 23 1976 2-52/710

PAY TO THE ORDER OF Curly Hart $167 83/00

One hundred sixty-seven and 83/00 DOLLARS

NATIONAL BOULEVARD BANK OF CHICAGO

SAMPLE-VOID
DELUXE CHECK PRINTERS, INC.

Your Signature

⑈000338⑈ ⑆0710⑉0052⑆ ⑈123456 7⑈

309

DATE Dec 30 1976

TO Red Bard

FOR

BAL. FOR'D	3501 86	TOTAL WAGES	190 00
DEP. 12/30	572 00 (16)	SOCIAL SEC. TAX	11 12
TOTAL	4073 86	U.S. INC. TAX	32 90
THIS CHECK	145 98	TOTAL DED.	44 02
BALANCE	3927 88	CHECK	145 98

DETACH BEFORE CASHING CHECK
STATEMENT OF EARNINGS AND DEDUCTIONS FOR EMPLOYEE'S RECORD COVERING PAY PERIOD TO AND INCLUDING DATE SHOWN BELOW

DATE Dec 30 1976

TO Red Bard

TOTAL WAGES	190 00
SOCIAL SECURITY TAX	11 12
WITHHOLDING U.S. INCOME TAX	32 90
STATE INCOME TAX	
TOTAL DEDUCTIONS	44 02
AMOUNT THIS CHECK	145 98

(17) 309

Dec 30 1976 2-52/710

PAY TO THE ORDER OF Red Bard $145 98/00

One hundred forty-five and 98/00 DOLLARS

NATIONAL BOULEVARD BANK OF CHICAGO

SAMPLE-VOID
DELUXE CHECK PRINTERS, INC.

Your Signature

⑈000339⑈ ⑆0710⑉0052⑆ ⑈123456 7⑈

310

DATE Dec 30 1976

TO Curly Hart

FOR

BAL. FOR'D	3927 88	TOTAL WAGES	198 00
DEP.		SOCIAL SEC. TAX	11 58
TOTAL		U.S. INC. TAX	32 90
THIS CHECK	153 52	STATE INC. TAX	
BALANCE	3774 36	TOTAL DED.	44 48
		CHECK	153 52

DETACH BEFORE CASHING CHECK
STATEMENT OF EARNINGS AND DEDUCTIONS FOR EMPLOYEE'S RECORD COVERING PAY PERIOD TO AND INCLUDING DATE SHOWN BELOW

DATE Dec 30 1976

TO Curly Hart

TOTAL WAGES	198 00
SOCIAL SECURITY TAX	11 58
WITHHOLDING U.S. INCOME TAX	32 90
STATE INCOME TAX	
TOTAL DEDUCTIONS	44 48
AMOUNT THIS CHECK	153 52

(17) 310

Dec 30 1976 2-52/710

PAY TO THE ORDER OF Curly Hart $153 52/00

One hundred fifty-three and 52/00 DOLLARS

NATIONAL BOULEVARD BANK OF CHICAGO

SAMPLE-VOID
DELUXE CHECK PRINTERS, INC.

Your Signature

⑈000340⑈ ⑆0710⑉0052⑆ ⑈123456 7⑈

Total Payroll Record
Brown's Barber Shop
Payroll for week ending 12-16

(6)

Name	Reg. Hours	O.T. Hours	Reg Pay	O.T. Pay	Gross Pay	Fed Inc Tax	FICA Tax	Net Pay
Red Bard	36		180.00		180.00	30.80	10.53	138.67
Curly Hart	35		192.50		192.50	32.90	11.26	148.34
Total	71		372.50		372.50	63.70	21.79	287.01

Total Payroll Record
Brown's Barber Shop
Payroll for week ending 12-23

(11)

Name	Reg. Hours	O.T. Hours	Reg Pay	O.T. Pay	Gross Pay	Fed Inc Tax	FICA Tax	Net Pay
Red Bard	40		200.00		200.00	35.00	11.70	153.30
Curly Hart	40		220.00		220.00	39.30	12.87	167.83
Total	80		420.00		420.00	74.30	24.57	321.13

Total Payroll Record
Brown's Barber Shop
Payroll for week ending 12-30

(17)

Name	Reg. Hours	O.T. Hours	Reg Pay	O.T. Pay	Gross Pay	Fed Inc Tax	FICA Tax	Net Pay
Red Bard	38		190.00		190.00	32.90	11.12	145.98
Curly Hart	36		198.00		198.00	32.90	11.58	153.52
Total	74		388.00		388.00	65.80	22.70	299.50

Individual Employee's Earnings Record
Name Red Bard - December

	week ending	reg. pay	o.t. pay	gross pay	cumulative pay	fed inc tax	FICA tax	net pay
					8100.00			
(6)	12-16	180.00		180.00	8280.00	30.80	10.53	138.67
(11)	12-23	200.00		200.00	8480.00	35.00	11.70	153.30
(17)	12-30	190.00		190.00	8670.00	32.90	11.12	145.98
(20)	total	570.00		570.00		98.70	33.35	437.95

Individual Employee's Earnings Record
Name Curly Hart - December

	week ending	reg. pay	o.t. pay	gross pay	cumulative pay	fed inc tax	FICA tax	net pay
					7900.00			
(6)	12-16	192.50		192.50	8092.50	32.90	11.26	148.34
(11)	12-23	220.00		220.00	8312.50	39.30	12.87	167.83
(17)	12-30	198.00		198.00	8510.50	32.90	11.58	153.52
(20)	total	610.50		610.50		105.10	35.71	469.69

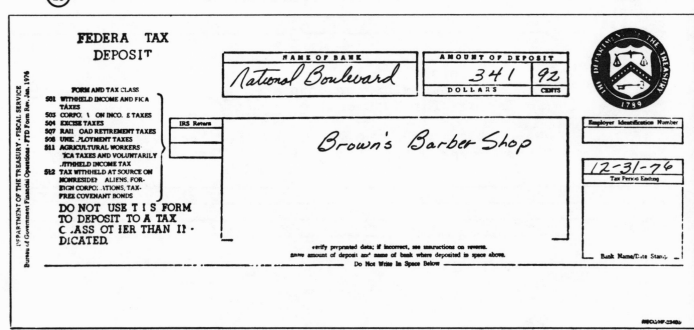

(20)

DEPARTMENT OF THE TREASURY - FISCAL SERVICE
Bureau of Government Financial Operations - FTD Form Rev. Jan. 1976

FEDERA TAX DEPOSIT

FORM AND TAX CLASS
501 WITHHELD INCOME AND FICA TAXES
503 CORPO. \ ON INCO. E TAXES
504 EXCISE TAXES
507 RAII OAD RETIREMENT TAXES
508 UNE. PLOYMENT TAXES
511 AGRICULTURAL WORKERS· 'ICA TAXES AND VOLUNTARILY .ITHHELD INCOME TAX
512 TAX WITHHELD AT SOURCE ON NONRESIDEI ALIENS, FOR-EIGN CORPO. ATIONS, TAX-FREE COVENANT BONDS

DO NOT USE T I S FORM TO DEPOSIT TO A TAX C.ASS OT IER THAN II·DICATED.

NAME OF BANK: National Boulevard

AMOUNT OF DEPOSIT: 341 DOLLARS 92 CENTS

IRS Return

Brown's Barber Shop

Employer Identification Number

12-31-76
Tax Period Ending

Bank Name/Date Stamp

erify prepnnted data; if incorrect, see instructions on reverse.
ame amount of deposit and name of bank where deposited in space above.

Do Not Write In Space Below

(21)

MONTH December 19 76

THIS FORM IS PROVIDED TO HELP YOU BALANCE YOUR BANK STATEMENT

CHECKS OUTSTANDING - NOT CHARGED TO ACCOUNT

NO.	$	
309	145	98
310	153	52
120	21	00
121	2	10
122	341	92
TOTAL	$ 664	52

BANK BALANCE SHOWN ON THIS STATEMENT $ 3501.01

ADD +

DEPOSITS NOT CREDITED IN THIS STATEMENT (IF ANY) $ 572.00

SUB-TOTAL $ 4073.01

SUBTRACT —

CHECKS OUTSTANDING $ 664.52

BALANCE $ 3408.49

SHOULD AGREE WITH CHECK BOOK BALANCE AFTER DEDUCTING SERVICE CHARGE (IF ANY) SHOWN ON THIS STATEMENT FOR PRESENT MONTH.

Each depositor insured to $40,000

FDIC

FEDERAL DEPOSIT INSURANCE CORPORATION

Petty Cash Statement
for the Month of December, 1976

(18)

Miscellaneous Expense	$11.00
Supplies Expense	10.00
Total Spent	$21.00
Amount Left	29.00
Dec 1 Total	$50.00

Journal

Date	Account Title	Post	Debit	Credit	
Dec 13	Equipment	13	300 00		(2)
	Accounts Payable	21		300 00	
	Dan Druff Distributors				
16	Salary Expense	52	180 00		(6)
	FICA Tax Payable	23		10 53	
	Fed. Income Tax Payable	22		30 80	
	Cash in Bank	11		138 67	
	Red's salary - check 103				
16	Salary Expense	52	192 50		
	FICA Tax Payable	23		11 26	
	Fed Income Tax Payable	22		32 90	
	Cash in Bank	11		148 34	
	Curly's salary - ck 104				
23	Salary Expense	52	200 00		(11)
	FICA Tax Payable	23		11 70	
	Fed. Income Tax Payable	22		35 00	
	Cash in Bank	11		153 30	
	Red's salary - ck. 107				
23	Salary Expense	52	220 00		
	FICA Tax Payable	23		12 87	
	Fed Income Tax Payable	22		39 30	
	Cash in Bank	11		167 83	
	Curly's salary - ck 108				
30	Salary Expense	52	190 00		(17)
	FICA Tax Payable	23		11 12	
	Fed Income Tax Payable	22		32 90	
	Cash in Bank	11		145 98	
	Red's salary - ck 112				
30	Salary Expense	52	198 00		
	FICA Tax Payable	23		11 58	
	Fed. Income Tax Payable	22		32 90	
	Cash in Bank	11		153 52	
	Curly's salary - ck 113				
31	Depreciation Expense	57	600 00		(22)
	Equipment Depreciation	031		600 00	
	1 year's depreciation				
31	Supplies	14	60 00		(23)
	Supplies Expense	55		60 00	
	Unused Supplies		2140 50	2140 50	
		(24)			
	Closing Entries.				
Dec 31	Income	41	20540 00		(25)
	Mr Brown	31		20540 00	
31	Sales Income	42	2104 00		
	Mr Brown	31		2104 00	
31	Mr Brown	31	1800 00		
	Rent Expense	51		1800 00	
31	Mr Brown	31	17180 50		
	Salary Expense	52		17180 50	
31	Mr Brown	31	1035 86		
	Payroll Tax Expense	53		1035 86	

(25)

Journal

Date	Account Title	Post	Debit		Credit		
Dec 31	Closing Entries:						
31	Mr Brown	31	105	20			(25)
	Sales Tax Expense	54			105	20	
31	Mr Brown	31	840	00			
	Supplies Expense	55			840	00	
31	Mr Brown	31	2056	90			
	Janitorial Expense	56			2056	90	
31	Mr Brown	31	600	00			
	Depreciation Expense	57			600	00	
31	Mr Brown	31	2041	85			
	Miscellaneous Expense	58			2041	85	
31	Mr Brown	31	1850	00			
	Withdrawals	031			1850	00	
		(25)					
Jan 1	Supplies Expense	55	60	00			(26)
	Supplies	14			60	00	
	To put supplies in expenses						
		(26)					

Cash Journal

	Cash Receipts				Cash Disbursements					
	Date	Account Credited	Posted	Amount	Date	Account Debited	Post	Check No.	Amount	
(4)	Dec 16	Income	41	425.00	Dec 12	Rent Expense	51	113	150.00	(1)
		Sales Income	42	10.00	15	Miscellaneous Ex	58	114	30.00	(3)
(10)	23	Income	41	565.00	21	Supplies Exp	55	115	90.00	(8)
		Sales Income	42	10.00	22	Withdrawals	031	116	200.00	(9)
(16)	30	Income	41	550.00	27	Withdrawals	031	117	150.00	(13)
		Sales Income	42	22.00	28	Janitorial Exp	56	118	180.00	(14)
(24)			11	1582.00	29	Accts Pay.	21	119	100.00	(15)
					31	Misc Exp.	58	120	11.00	(8)
						Supplies Exp.	55		10.00	(18)
					31	Sales Tax Exp	54	121	2.10	(19)
					31	FICA Tax Pay.	23	122	69.06	(20)
						Fed Inc Tax Pay.	22		203.80	
						Payroll Tax Exp	53		69.06	
					31	Misc. Exp-SC	58	–	.85	(21)
							11		1265.87	(24)
			(24)				(24)			

LEDGER

Cash in Bank — Account No. 11

DATE	ITEMS	POST	DEBIT	DATE	ITEMS	POST	CREDIT
Nov 30	Balance	✓	4000.00	Dec 16		J	138.67
Dec 30		CJ	1582.00	16		J	148.34
	3408.49		5582.00	23		J	153.30
				23		J	167.83
				30		J	145.98
				30		J	153.52
				30		CJ	1265.87
							2173.51

(24) (24)

Equipment — Account No. 13

DATE	ITEMS	POST	DEBIT	DATE	ITEMS	POST	CREDIT
Nov 30	Balance	✓	6000.00				
Dec 13		J	300.00				
			6300.00				

(24)

Petty Cash — Account No. 12

DATE	ITEMS	POST	DEBIT	DATE	ITEMS	POST	CREDIT
Nov 30	Balance	✓	50.00				

Equipment Depreciation — Account No. 013

DATE	ITEMS	POST	DEBIT	DATE	ITEMS	POST	CREDIT
				Nov 30	Balance	✓	500.00
				Dec 31		J	600.00
							1100.00

(24)

Supplies — Account No. 14

	DATE	ITEMS	POST	DEBIT	DATE	ITEMS	POST	CREDIT	
(24)	Dec 31		J	60.00	Jan 1		J	60.00	(26)

Accounts Payable — Account No. 21

	DATE	ITEMS	POST	DEBIT	DATE	ITEMS	POST	CREDIT	
(24)	Dec 29		CJ	100.00	Dec 13		J	300.00	(24)
						200.00			

Federal Income Tax Payable — Account No. 22

	DATE	ITEMS	POST	DEBIT	DATE	ITEMS	POST	CREDIT	
(24)	Dec 31		CJ	203.80	Dec 16		J	30.80	
					16		J	32.90	
					23		J	35.00	
					23		J	39.30	(24)
					30		J	32.90	
					30		J	32.90	
(24)				203.80				203.80	

FICA Tax Payable — Account No. 23

DATE	ITEMS	POST	DEBIT	DATE	ITEMS	POST	CREDIT
(24) Dec 31		CJ	69.06	Dec 16		J	10.53
				16		J	11.26
				23		J	11.70
				23		J	12.87 (24)
				30		J	11.12
				30		J	11.58
(24)			69.06				69.06

Mr. Brown — Account No. 31

DATE	ITEMS	POST	DEBIT	DATE	ITEMS	POST	CREDIT
Dec 31	Rent Exp	J	1800.00	Nov 30	Balance	✓	13384.80
31	Salary Exp	J	17180.50	Dec 31	Income	J	20540.00
31	Payroll Tax Exp	J	1035.86	31	Sales Inc	J	2104.00 (25)
31	Sales Tax Exp	J	105.20		8518.49		36028.80
(25) 31	Supplies Exp	J	840.00				
31	Janitorial Exp	J	2056.90				
31	Deprec. Exp	J	600.00				
31	Misc Exp	J	2041.85				
31	Withdrawals	J	1850.00				
			27510.31				

Withdrawals — Account No. 031

DATE	ITEMS	POST	DEBIT	DATE	ITEMS	POST	CREDIT
Nov 30	Balance	✓	1500.00	Dec 31	Closing Entry	J	1850.00 (25)
(24) Dec 22		CJ	200.00				
27		CJ	150.00				
			1850.00				1850.00 (25)

Income — Account No. 41

	DATE	ITEMS	POST	DEBIT	DATE	ITEMS	POST	CREDIT	
(25)	Dec 31	Closing Entry	J	20540.00	Nov 30	Balance	✓	19000.00	
					Dec 16		CJ	425.00	
					23		CJ	565.00	(24)
					30		CJ	550.00	
(25)				20540.00				20540.00	

Sales Income — Account No. 42

	DATE	ITEMS	POST	DEBIT	DATE	ITEMS	POST	CREDIT	
(25)	Dec 31	Closing Entry	J	2104.00	Nov 30	Balance	✓	2062.00	
					Dec 16		CJ	10.00	
					23		CJ	10.00	(24)
					30		CJ	22.00	
(25)				2104.00				2104.00	

Rent Expense — Account No. 51

	DATE	ITEMS	POST	DEBIT	DATE	ITEMS	POST	CREDIT	
	Nov 30	Balance	✓	1650.00	Dec 31	Closing Entry	J	1800.00	(25)
(24)	Dec 12		CJ	150.00					
				1800.00				1800.00	(25)

Salary Expense — Account No. 52

	DATE	ITEMS	POST	DEBIT	DATE	ITEMS	POST	CREDIT	
	Nov 30	Balance	✓	16000.00	Dec 31	Closing Entry	J	17180.50	(25)
(24)	Dec 16		J	180.00					
	16		J	192.50					
	23		J	200.00					
	23		J	220.00					
	30		J	190.00					
	30		J	198.00					
				17180.50				17180.50	(25)

Payroll Tax Expense — Account No. 53

	DATE	ITEMS	POST	DEBIT	DATE	ITEMS	POST	CREDIT	
	Nov 30	Balance	✓	966.80	Dec 31	Closing Entry	J	1035.86	(25)
(24)	Dec 31		CJ	69.06					
				1035.86				1035.86	(25)

Sales Tax Expense — Account No. 54

	DATE	ITEMS	POST	DEBIT	DATE	ITEMS	POST	CREDIT	
	Nov 30	Balance	✓	103.10	Dec 31	Closing Entry	J	105.20	(25)
(24)	Dec 31		CJ	2.10					
				105.20				105.20	(25)

Supplies Expense — Account No. 55

	DATE	ITEMS	POST	DEBIT	DATE	ITEMS	POST	CREDIT	
	Nov 30	Balance	✓	800.00	Dec 31		J	60.00	24
	Dec 21		CJ	90.00	31	Closing Entry	J	840.00	25
24	31		CJ	10.00					
				900.00				900.00	25
26	Jan 1		J	60.00					

Janitorial Expense — Account No. 56

	DATE	ITEMS	POST	DEBIT	DATE	ITEMS	POST	CREDIT	
	Nov 30	Balance	✓	1876.90	Dec 31	Closing Entry	J	2056.90	25
24	Dec 28		CJ	180.00					
				2056.90				2056.90	25

Depreciation Expense — Account No. 57

	DATE	ITEMS	POST	DEBIT	DATE	ITEMS	POST	CREDIT	
24	Dec 31		J	600.00	Dec 31	Closing Entry	J	600.00	25

Miscellaneous Expense — Account No. 58

	DATE	ITEMS	POST	DEBIT	DATE	ITEMS	POST	CREDIT	
	Nov 30	Balance	✓	2000.00	Dec 31	Closing Entry	J	2041.85	25
	Dec 15		CJ	30.00					
24	31		CJ	11.00					
	31	Bank Serv. Chg	CJ	.85					
				2041.85				2041.85	25

Brown's Barber Shop
Trial Balance
December 31, 1976

(24)

Account Title	No	Debit	Credit
Cash in Bank	11	3408.49	
Petty Cash	12	50.00	
Equipment	13	6300.00	
Equipment Depreciation	013		1100.00
Supplies	14	60.00	
Accounts Payable	21		200.00
Mr Brown	31		13384.80
Withdrawals	031	1850.00	
Income	41		20540.00
Sales Income	42		2104.00
Rent Expense	51	1800.00	
Salary Expense	52	17180.50	
Payroll Tax Expense	53	1035.86	
Sales Tax Expense	54	105.20	
Supplies Expense	55	840.00	
Janitorial Expense	56	2056.90	
Depreciation Expense	57	600.00	
Miscellaneous Expense	58	2041.85	
		37328.80	37328.80

Brown's Barber Shop
Post-Closing Trial Balance
December 31, 1976

(25)

Account Title	No.	Debit	Credit
Cash in Bank	11	3408.49	
Petty Cash	12	50.00	
Equipment	13	6300.00	
Equipment Depreciation	013		1100.00
Supplies	14	60.00	
Accounts Payable	21		200.00
Mr Brown	31		8518.49
		9818.49	9818.49

(24)

Brown's Barber Shop
Income & Expense Statement
For Year Ending December 31, 1976

Income:			
Income		$20,540.00	
Sales Income		2,104.00	$22,644.00
Expenses:			
Rent Expense		$ 1,800.00	
Salary Expense		17,180.50	
Payroll Tax Expense		1,035.86	
Sales Tax Expense		105.20	
Supplies Expense		840.00	
Janitorial Expense		2,056.90	
Depreciation Expense		600.00	
Miscellaneous Expense		2,041.85	25,660.31
Net Loss			$ 3,016.31

(24)

Brown's Barber Shop
Balance Sheet
December 31, 1976

Assets			Liabilities		
Cash in Bank		$ 3408.49	Accounts Payable		$ 200.00
Petty Cash		50.00			
Equipment	$ 6300.00		Owner's Equity		
Depreciation	- 1100.00	5200.00	Mr. Brown:		
Supplies		60.00	Investment	$ 13,384.80	
			Less Net Loss	3,016.31	
			Less Withdrawal	1,850.00	
			Equity 12/31		8,518.49
Total Assets		$ 8718.49	Total Liabilities & Equity		$ 8,718.49

ANSWER KEY
Chapter 5

Date	Account Title	Post	Debit	Credit
Nov 8	Purchases		300.00	
	Accounts Payable			300.00
	Bow Shirt Co. Inv. 125			
12	Purchases		1000.00	
	Accounts Payable			1000.00
	Johnny Cavett Suits, Inv. 103			
15	Accounts Payable		200.00	
	Purchases			200.00
	Johnny Cavett Suits, CM 54			
19	Purchases		100.00	
	Accounts Payable			100.00
	Count Dracula Ties, Inv 519			
20	Accounts Payable		50.00	
	Purchases			50.00
	Bow Shirt Co, CM 12			
			1650.00	1650.00

5A

Cash Journal

Cash Disbursements

Date	Account Debited	Post	Ck. No.	Debit Accts Pay	Debit Other	Credit Cash
Nov 30	Bow Shirt Co.		501	250.00		250.00
30	Johnny Cavett Suits		502	800.00		800.00
				1050.00		1050.00

5B

(5)C

Journal

Date	Account Title	Post	Debit Purchases	Debit Other	Credit Accts Pay	Credit Other
Dec 1	Sock Slack Co-inv. 201		850.00		850.00	
5	Penguin Shoe Co-inv. 305		400.00		400.00	
12	Accounts Payable-Penguin Shoe	20		40.00		
	Purchases-CM 26	50				40.00
14	Haggard Slacks-inv 503		120.00		120.00	
14	Trusty Truck Lines-inv 35		20.00		20.00	
20	Haggard Slacks-inv. 549		55.00		55.00	
26	Penguin Shoes-inv. 395		660.00		660.00	
28	Trusty Truck Lines-inv. 23		50.00		50.00	
			2155.00	40.00	2155.00	40.00
			P-50		P-20	

Debits $2195 = Credits $2195

Cash Disbursements

Date	Account Debited	Post	Ck. No.	Debit Accts Pay	Debit Other	Credit Cash	Credit Disc Inc
Dec. 8	Purchases-Still Dogs	50	106		95.00	95.00	
10	Sock Slack Co.		107	850.00		833.00	17.00
14	Penguin Shoe Co.		108	360.00		356.40	3.60
23	Trusty Truck Lines		109	20.00		20.00	
25	Haggard Slack Co.		110	175.00		173.90	1.10
				1405.00	95.00	1478.30	21.70
				P-20		P-10	P-41

Debits $1500 = Credits $1500

Ledger

5C

Cash — Account No. 10

Date	Items	Post	Debit	Date	Items	Post	Credit
				Dec 30		CJ	1478.30

Accounts Payable — Account No. 20

Date	Items	Post	Debit	Date	Items	Post	Credit
Dec 30		CJ	1405.00	Dec 30	710.00	J	2155.00
12		J	40.00				
			1445.00				

Discount Income — Account No. 41

Date	Items	Post	Debit	Date	Items	Post	Credit
				Dec 30		CJ	21.70

Purchases — Account No. 50

Date	Items	Post	Debit	Date	Items	Post	Credit
Dec 8		CJ	95.00	Dec 12		J	40.00
30		J	2155.00				
	2210.00		2250.00				

Accounts Payable Book

Haggard Slacks
100 Well Fair Road

Date	Number	Charges	Payments	Balance
Dec 14	Invoice 503	120.00		120.00
20	Inv. 549	55.00		175.00
25	Paid - check 110		173.90	
	Less 2% discount on inv. 549		1.10	—

Penguin Shoe Co.
22 Gnaw Bone Bend

Date	Number	Charges	Payments	Balance
Dec 5	Inv. 305	400.00		400.00
12	Returned - CM 26		40.00	360.00
14	Paid - ck. 108		356.40	
	Less 1% discount		3.60	—
26	Inv. 395	660.00		660.00

Sack Slack Co.
59 Petunia Point

Date	Number	Charges	Payments	Balance
Dec 1	Inv. 201	850.00		850.00
10	Paid - ck 107		833.00	
	Less 2% discount		17.00	—

Trusty Truck Lines
66 Spooky Hollow

Date	Number	Charges	Payments	Balance
Dec 14	Inv. 35	20.00		
23	Paid - ck. 109		20.00	—
28	Inv. 23	50.00		50.00

5C

List of Accounts Payable
Dec. 31

Penguin Shoe Co.	$660.00
Trusty Truck Lines	50.00
	$710.00

5D

Journal

Date	Account Title	Post	Debit Purc	Debit Acc Rec	Debit Other	Credit Acc Pay	Credit Sales	Credit S. Tax	Credit Other
Nov 10	I M Rich - SS 104			525.00			500.00	25.00	
10	B. Good - SS 105			26.25			25.00	1.25	
11	Mr Brown - SS 106			26.25			25.00	1.25	
11	Sales - CM 14				10.00				
	Sales Tax Payable				.50				
	Accts Rec - B. Good								10.50
12	B. Good - SS 107			105.00			100.00	5.00	
12	Sales - CM 15				25.00				
	Sales Tax Payable				1.25				
	Accts Rec - Brown								26.25
				682.50	36.75		650.00	32.50	36.75

Debits $719.25 = Credits $719.25

Cash Book

Cash Receipts

Date	Account Credited	Post	Debit Cash	Credit Sales	Credit S. Tax	Credit Other
Nov 10	Cash Sales		315.00	300.00	15.00	
11	Cash Sales		420.00	400.00	20.00	
			735.00	700.00	35.00	
			735 = 735			

Journal

(5) E

Date	Account Title	Post	Purch	Debit Acc Rec	Other	Acc Pay	Credit Sales	S. Tax	Other
Dec 25	Guy Sharp - SS 119			36.75			35.00	1.75	
25	Abe Abel - SS 120			90.30			86.00	4.30	
26	Guy Sharp - SS 121			89.25			85.00	4.25	
26	Homer Lee - SS 122			157.50			150.00	7.50	
29	Guy Sharp - SS 123			29.40			28.00	1.40	
30	Icabod Kane SS 124			262.50			250.00	12.50	
31	Homer Lee - SS 125			42.00			40.00	2.00	
				707.70			674.00	33.70	
				P-12			P-41	P-23	
					$707.70 = $707.70				

CASH BOOK

CASH RECEIPTS

DATE	ACCOUNT CREDITED	POST	DEBIT CASH	CREDIT SALES	SALES TAX	OTHER
Dec 25	Cash sales		544.95	519.00	25.95	
26	Cash sales		526.05	501.00	25.05	
29	Accts Rec-Homer Lee	12	157.50			157.50
29	Cash sales		609.00	580.00	29.00	
30	Cash sales		522.90	498.00	24.90	
30	Miscellaneous Expense	57	3.20			3.20
31	Accts Rec-Abe Abel	12	50.00			50.00
31	Cash sales		838.95	799.00	39.95	
31	Miscellaneous Expense	57	1.25			1.25
			3253.80	2897.00	144.85	211.95
			P-11	P-41	P-23	
			$3253.80 = $3253.80			

List of Accounts Receivable
December 31

Abe Abel	$ 40.30
Icabod Kane	262.50
Homer Lee	42.00
Guy Sharp	155.40
	$500.20

5E

Ledger

Cash — Account No. 11

Date	Items	Post	Debit	Date	Items	Post	Credit
Dec 31		CJ	3253.80				

Accounts Receivable — Account No. 12

Date	Items	Post	Debit	Date	Items	Post	Credit
Dec 31		J	707.70	Dec 29		CJ	157.50
	500.20			31		CJ	50.00
							207.50

Sales Tax Payable — Account No. 23

Date	Items	Post	Debit	Date	Items	Post	Credit
				Dec 31		J	33.70
				31		CJ	144.85
							178.55

Sales — Account No. 41

Date	Items	Post	Debit	Date	Items	Post	Credit
				Dec 31		J	674.00
				31		CJ	2897.00
							3571.00

Miscellaneous Expense — Account No. 57

Date	Items	Post	Debit	Date	Items	Post	Credit
				Dec 30		CJ	3.20
				31		CJ	1.25
							4.45

Accounts Receivable Book

5E

Abe Abel
88 Abner Alley

DATE	NUMBER	CHARGES	PAYMENTS	BALANCE
Dec 25	ss 120	90.30		90.30
31	payment		50.00	40.30

Icabod Kane
1313 Slippy Hollow

DATE	NUMBER	CHARGES	PAYMENTS	BALANCE
Dec 30	ss 124	262.50		262.50

Homer Lee
1 Home Town Lane

DATE	NUMBER	CHARGES	PAYMENTS	BALANCE
Dec 26	ss 123	157.50		157.50
29	payment		157.50	–
31	ss 125	42.00		42.00

Guy Sharp
22 Dead End Road

DATE	NUMBER	CHARGES	PAYMENTS	BALANCE
Dec 25	ss 119	36.75		36.75
26	ss 121	89.25		126.00
28	ss 123	29.40		155.40

5F

$ 50,000	Beginning Inventory
+ 300,000	Purchases
$350,000	Available for sale
- 70,000	Ending Inventory
$280,000	Cost of Goods sold
$500,000	Sales at retail
- 280,000	Sales at cost
$220,000	Gross Income or Mark up

5G

The Hook n Hanger
Income & Expense Statement
for Six Months Ending December 31, 1976

Sales		$124,900
Purchase Discount Income		100
Total Income		$125,000
Less Cost of Goods Sold:		
6/30 Inventory	$19,000	
+ Purchases	80,000	
Goods Available	$99,000	
Less 12/31 Inventroy	16,000	83,000
Gross Income		$ 42,000
Less Overhead:		
Rent Expense	$ 3,400	
Utilities Expense	2,100	
Salary Expense	25,000	
Miscellaneous Expense	1,200	31,700
		$ 10,300

5H

The Hook n Hanger
Balance Sheet
December 31, 1976

Assets		Liabilities		
Cash	$10,000	Accounts Payable		$18,800
Petty Cash	100	Sales Tax Payable		500
Accounts Receivable	15,000	Total Liabilities		$19,300
Inventory	16,000			
Store Equipment	7,000	Owner's Equity		
		Cap Hook:		
		Investment	$10,000	
		+ Net Income	5,150	
		- Withdrawals	1,000	
		Equity, 12/31		14,150
		Brent Hanger:		
		Investment	$10,000	
		+ Net Income	5,150	
		- Withdrawals	500	
		Equity, 12/31		14,650
Total Assets	$48,100	Total Liab + Equity		$48,100

Summary Problems

A. What is it?

1. Purchases
2. Accounts Payable
3. Sales slips
4. Collection fees
5. Bad debts
6. Credit Memos
7. Accrual Basis of Accounting
8. Cash Basis of Accounting
9. Inventory
10. Accounts Receivable Book
11. Purchases Discounts
12. Refund
13. Sales
15. Gross Income
16. Accounts Payable Book

B. Using What You Know

JOURNAL

DATE	ACCOUNT TITLE	POST	DEBIT PURCHASES	DEBIT ACCTS REC.	DEBIT OTHER	CREDIT ACCTS PAY	CREDIT SALES	CREDIT SALES TAX	CREDIT OTHER	
Dec 24	Purch-Inv 509		50.00							(1)
	Sweet Candy					50.00				
24	AR-Group Coop			105.00						(3)
	SS 101						100.00	5.00		
25	AR-Old Woman Shoe			210.00						(7)
	SS 102						200.00	10.00		
25	Spoilage Exp	61			4.00					(9)
	Purchases	50							4.00	
26	Purchases		100.00							(12)
	Mrs Leapober					100.00				
26	Group Coop			52.50						(13)
	SS 103 AP						50.00	2.50		
26	Sweet Candy Co	20			50.00					(14)
	Purchases	50							50.00	

(continued on following page)

(Journal, continued)

29	Purch-Inv 251		200.00						
	Kravitz Nuts					200.00			
29	Cash	10			60.00				
	Miscellaneous Exp	65			40.00				
	A.R.-Spill + Spot	11							100.00
29	Holiday Party			315.00					
	SS 104						300.00	15.00	
29	Group Coop			26.25					
	SS 105						25.00	1.25	
30	Sales-CM22	40			55.00				
	Sales Tax Pay.	21			2.75				
	AR-Holiday Party	11							57.75
31	Depreciation Exp	63			800.00				
	Truck Deprec.	013							800.00
31	Beginning Invent	51			3000.00				
	Inventory	12							3000.00
31	Inventory	12			5000.00				
	Ending Invent	52							5000.00
			350.00	708.75	9011.75	350.00	675.00	33.75	9011.75
		(29)	P-50	P-11		P-20	P-40	P-21	
					Debits 10070.50 = Credits 10070.50			(25)	
	Closing Entries:								
Dec 31	Haus Capital	30			1500.00				
	Feffer Capital	31			1500.00				
	Beg. Invent.	51							3000.00
31	Ending Inventory	52			5000.00				
	Haus Capital	30							2500.00
	Feffer Capital	31							2500.00
31	Haus Capital	30			8838.00				
	Feffer Capital	31			8838.00				
	Purchases	50							13306.00
	Rent Exp	60							1200.00
	Spoilage Exp	61							204.00
	Truck Exp	62							625.00
	Deprec. Exp	63							800.00
	Utility Exp	64							900.00
	Miscell. Exp	65							641.00
31	Sales	40			20300.00				
	Purch. Dis. Inc	41			212.00				
	Haus Capital	30							10256.00
	Feffer Capital	31							10256.00
31	Haus Capital	30			2400.00				
	Haus Withdrawal	030							2400.00
31	Feffer Capital	31			2500.00				
	Feffer Withdrawal	031							2500.00
					51088.00				51088.00
		(32)							

Cash Book

Cash Receipts

Date	Account Credited		Debit Cash	Credit Sales	Credit S. Tax	Credit Other	
Dec 24	Cash Sales		105.00	100.00	5.00		(4)
25	Cash Sales		157.50	150.00	7.50		(10)
26	Cash Sales		204.75	195.00	9.75		(15)
29	Cash Sales		136.50	130.00	6.50		(20)
30	Accts Rec - Holiday Party	11	757.25			757.25	(23)
30	Cash Sales		115.50	110.00	5.50		(24)
			1476.50	685.00	34.25	757.25	(29)
			P-10	P-40	P-21		
			Debits-$1476.50 = Credits $1476.50				

(29) (25)

Accounts Receivable Book

The Group Coop
300 Boling Alley

Date	Number	Charges	Payments	Balance	
Dec 23	Balance			500.00	
24	SS 101	105.00		605.00	(3)
26	SS 103	52.50		657.50	(13)
29	SS 105	26.25		683.75	(19)

The Holiday Party Service
5 Poverty Gulch

Date	Number	Charges	Payments	Balance	
Dec 23	Balance			500.00	
29	SS 104	315.00		815.00	(18)
29	CM 22		57.75	757.25	(21)
30	payment		757.25	—	(23)

The Old Woman's Shoe
12 Rimes Rd.

Date	Number	Charges	Payments	Balance	
Dec 23	Balance			900.00	
25	SS 102	210.00		1110.00	(7)

The Spill & Spot Cleaner
2 Possum Trot Trail

Date	Number	Charges	Payments	Balance	
Dec 23	Balance			100.00	
29	payment		60.00		(17)
	collection fee		40.00		

Cash Disbursements

Date	Account Debited		Ck No	Debit Accts Pay	Other	Credit Cash	Disc Inc
Dec 24	Purchases	50	501		10.00	10.00	
24	Miscellaneous Expense	65			1.00	1.00	
25	Knutz Nuts		502	600.00		588.00	12.00
25	Sales	40	503		5.00	5.25	
	Sales Tax Payable	21			.25		
26	Truck Expense	62	504		25.00	25.00	
30	Mrs Leapober		505	85.00		85.00	
31	Sales Tax Payable	21	506		165.00	165.00	
				685.00	206.25	879.25	12.00
				Debits $891.25 =		Credits	$891.25

(29)

Accounts Payable Book

Oscar B. Sweet Candy Co.
5 Pound Pl.

Date	Number	Charges	Payments	Balance	
Dec 23	Balance			500.00	
24	Inv. 509	50.00		550.00	(1)
26	CM 55		50.00	500.00	(14)

Knurtz Nuts
33 Tree Pt.

Date	Number	Charges	Payments	Balance	
Dec 23	Balance			600.00	
25	Ck. 502		588.00		(6)
	Cash Discount		12.00	—	(6)
29	Inv. 251	200.00		200.00	(16)

Appelohnia Leapober
102 Frog Pond Blvd.

Date	Number	Charges	Payments	Balance	
Dec 23	Balance			100.00	
26	No inv.	100.00		200.00	(12)
30	Ck. 505		85.00	115.00	(22)

Accounts Receivable List

The Group Coop	$ 683.75
The Old Womans Shoe	1110.00
	$1793.75

Accounts Payable List

Oscar B. Sweet Candy Co.	$ 500.00
Knurtz Nuts	200.00
Appelohnia Leapober	115.00
	$ 815.00

(26)

Ledger

Cash — Account No. 10

Date	Items	Post	Debit		Date	Items	Post	Credit	
Dec 23	Balance		14100	00	Dec 31		CJ	879	25
29		J	60	00					
31		CJ	1476	50					
	14757.25		15636	50					

(29)

Accounts Receivable — Account No. 11

Date	Items	Post	Debit		Date	Items	Post	Credit	
Dec 23	Balance		2000	00	Dec 29		J	100	00
31		J	708	75	30		J	57	75
	1739.75		2708	75	30		CJ	757	25
								915	00

(29)

Inventory — Account No. 12

Date	Items	Post	Debit		Date	Items	Post	Credit	
Dec 23	Balance		3000	00	Dec 31		J	3000	00
31		J	5000	00					
	5000.00		8000	00					

(29)

Truck — Account No. 13

Date	Items	Post	Debit		Date	Items	Post	Credit	
Dec 23	Balance		8400	00					

Truck Depreciation — Account No. 013

	Date	Items	Post	Debit	Date	Items	Post	Credit	
					Dec 23	Balance		800 00	
					31		J	800 00	(29)
								1600 00	

Accounts Payable — Account No. 20

	Date	Balance	Post	Debit	Date	Items	Post	Credit	
(29)	Dec 26		J	50 00	Dec 23	Balance		1200 00	
(29)	31		CJ	685 00	31		J	350 00	(29)
				735 00		815.00		1550 00	

Sales Tax Payable — Account No. 21

	Date	Items	Post	Debit	Date	Items	Post	Credit	
(25)	Dec 30		J	2 75	Dec 23	Balance		100 00	
(25)	25		CJ	25	31		J	33 75	(25)
(29)	31		CJ	165 00	31		CJ	34 25	(25)
				168 00				168 00	

Haus, Capital — Account No. 30

	Date	Items		Debit	Date	Items		Credit	
(32)	Dec 31	Beginning Inventory	J	1500 00	Dec 23	Balance		13800 00	
(32)	31	Expenses	J	8838 00	31	Ending Inventory	J	2500 00	(32)
(32)	31	Withdrawals	J	2400 00	31	Incomes	J	10256 00	(32)
				12,738 00		13,818.00		26,556 00	

Haus, Withdrawals — Account No. 030

Date	Items		Debit	Date	Items		Credit	
Dec 23	Balance		2400 00	Dec 31	Closing Entry	J	2400 00	(32)

Feffer, Capital — Account No. 31

	Date	Items		Debit	Date	Items		Credit	
(32)	Dec 31	Beginning Invent	J	1500 00	Dec 23	Balance		13800 00	
(32)	31	Expenses	J	8838 00	31	Ending Inventory	J	2500 00	(32)
(32)	31	Withdrawals	J	2500 00	31	Incomes	J	10256 00	(32)
				12,838 00		13,718.00		26,556 00	

Feffer, Withdrawals — Account No. 031

Date	Items		Debit	Date	Items		Credit	
Dec 23	Balance		2500 00	Dec 31	Closing Entry	J	2500 00	(32)

Sales — Account No. 40

	Date	Items		Debit		Date	Items		Credit		
(29)	Dec 30		J	55	00	Dec 23	Balance		19000	00	
(29)	25		CJ	5	00	31		J	675	00	(29)
(29)				60	00	31		CJ	685	00	(29)
(32)	31	Closing Entry	J	20300	00		20300.00		20360	00	
(32)				20360	00						

Purchase Discount Income — Account No. 41

	Date	Items		Debit		Date	Items		Credit		
(32)	Dec31	Closing Entry	J	212	00	Dec 23	Balance		200	00	
						31		CJ	12	00	(29)
									212	00	(29)

Purchases — Account No. 50

	Date	Items		Debit		Date	Items		Credit		
	Dec 23	Balance		13000	00	Dec 26		J	50	00	(29)
(29)	31		J	350	00	25		J	4	00	(29)
(29)	24		CJ	10	00				54	00	(29)
(29)		13306.00		13360	00	31	Closing Entry	J	13306	00	(32)
									13360	00	(32)

Beginning Inventory — Account No. 51

	Date	Items		Debit		Date	Items		Credit		
(29)	Dec31		J	3000	00	Dec31	Closing Entry	J	3000	00	(32)

Ending Inventory — Account No. 52

	Date	Items		Debit		Date	Items		Credit		
(32)	Dec31	Closing Entry	J	5000	00	Dec31		J	5000	00	(29)

Rent Expense — Account No. 60

	Date	Items		Debit		Date	Items		Credit		
	Dec 23	Balance		1200	00	Dec31	Closing Entry	J	1200	00	(32)

Spoilage Expense — Account No. 61

	Date	Items		Debit		Date	Items		Credit		
	Dec 23	Balance		200	00	Dec31	Closing Entry	J	204	00	(32)
(29)	25		J	4	00						
				204.00							

Truck Expense — Account No. 62

	Date	Items		Debit	Date	Items		Credit	
	Dec 23	Balance		600 00	Dec 31	Closing Entry	J	625 00	(32)
(29)	26		CJ	25 00					
				625 00					

Depreciation Expense — Account No. 63

	Date	Items		Debit	Date	Items		Credit	
(29)	Dec 31		J	800 00	Dec 31	Closing Entry	J	800 00	(32)

Utility Expense — Account No. 64

Date	Items		Debit	Date	Items		Credit	
Dec 23	Balance		900 00	Dec 31	Closing Entry	J	900 00	(32)

Miscellaneous Expense — Account No. 65

	Date	Items		Debit	Date	Items		Credit	
	Dec 23	Balance		600 00	Dec 31	Closing Entry	J	641 00	(32)
(29)	29		J	40 00					
	24		CJ	1 00					
				641 00					

(26)

Statement

The Haus and Feffer Cookie House

Send To: The Group Coop
300 Boling Alley
City

Date: Dec 31, 1976

Terms: 30 days net

Date	Description	Charges	Payments	Balance
Dec 23	Balance			$500.00
24	Sales Slip 101	$105.00		605.00
26	Sales Slip 103	52.50		657.50
29	Sales Slip 105	26.25		683.75

(30)

Haus & Feffer Cookie House
Trial Balance
December 31, 1976

Cash	10	14757.25	
Accounts Receivable	11	1793.75	
Inventory	12	5000.00	
Truck	13	8400.00	
Truck Depreciation	013		1600.00
Accounts Payable	20		815.00
Sales Tax Payable	21		
Haus Capital	30		13800.00
Haus Withdrawals	030	2400.00	
Feffer Capital	31		13800.00
Feffer Withdrawals	031	2500.00	
Sales	40		20300.00
Purchase Discount Income	41		212.00
Purchases	50	13306.00	
Beginning Inventory	51	3000.00	
Ending Inventory	52		5000.00
Rent Expense	60	1200.00	
Spoilage Expense	61	204.00	
Truck Expense	62	625.00	
Depreciation Expense	63	800.00	
Utility Expense	64	900.00	
Miscellaneous Expense	65	641.00	
		55527.00	55527.00

(26)

Statement

The Haus and Feffer Cookie House

Send To: The Old Womans Shoe
12 Rimes Road
City

Date: Dec 31, 1976

Terms: 30 days net

Date	Description	Charges	Payments	Balance
Dec 23	Balance			900.00
25	Sales Slip 102	210.00		1110.00

(31)

Haus and Feffer Cookie House
Income & Expense Statement
For the Six Months Ending Dec. 31, 1976

Sales......................		$20,300.00
Purchases Discount Income..		212.00
Total Income.............		$20,512.00
Less Cost of Goods Sold:		
Inventory 6/30...........	$3000.00	
Plus Purchases...........	13306.00	
Available for Sale.....	$16,306.00	
Less Inventory 12/31.....	5000.00	11,306.00
Gross Income...............		$ 9,206.00
Less Overhead Expenses:		
Rent Expense.............	$ 1200.00	
Spoilage Expense.........	204.00	
Truck Expense............	625.00	
Depreciation Expense.....	800.00	
Utility Expense..........	900.00	
Miscellaneous Expense....	641.00	4,370.00
Net Income.................		$ 4,836.00

Haus and Feffer Cookie House
Balance Sheet
December 31, 1976

(31)

Assets			Liabilities		
Cash.................,		$14,757.25	Accounts Payable.		$ 815.00
Accounts Receivable...		1,793.75			
Inventory.............		5,000.00	Owner's Equity		
Truck.................	$8400.00		Haus, Capital....	$13,800.00	
Less Depreciation...	1,600.00	6,800.00	+ Net Income....	2418.00	
			- Withdrawals...	2400.00	13,818.00
			Feffer, Capital..	$13,800.00	
			+ Net Income....	2418.00	
			- Withdrawals...	2500.00	13,718.00
Total Assets		$28,351.00	Total Liab. + O.E.		$28,351.00